AFRICA–ARCTIC FLYWAY: PHYSIOCRATIC STATES

Edited by Elisa R. Linn and Lennart Wolff

Sternberg Press

SURAH YA-SIN AYAT (36:33–36 QUR'AN)

A Sign for them is the earth that is dead; We do give it life, and produce grain therefrom, of which ye do eat. And We produce therein orchard with date-palms and Vines, and We cause springs to gush forth therein. That they may enjoy the fruits of this (artistry): It was not their hands that made this: will they not then give thanks? Glory to Allah, Who created in pairs all things that the earth produces, as well as their own kind and other things of which they have no knowledge.

PRECEDENTS, ANTECEDENTS, AND THE FUTURE NOTES ON THE BEGINNING

Imagine there's no heaven
It's easy if you try
No hell below us
Above us, only sky
Imagine all the people
Living for today

Imagine there's no countries
It isn't hard to do
Nothing to kill or die for
And no religion too
Imagine all the people
Living life in peace

John Lennon & Yoko Ono, 1971

We could say it all started in 1976 with a romance about the frontier, a yearning for a territory that was just beyond the known. Not exactly terra incognita, but a place that pushed the boundaries of the familiar into the exciting. We took as our hero the first human to travel into space, Russian cosmonaut Yuri Gagarin: he had ventured where no one had gone before. Then there were the Mercury and Apollo space missions on television that followed.

Perhaps it started as a lark, a young woman driving cross country with her head out the window, attempting to fathom the endlessness of the universe. As a young child, witnessing Sputnik moving among the stars created an awareness that something had irrevocably changed. Outer space was no longer beyond our reach. Not only could we gaze from Earth, we could visit. The logic of physics grounded us in reality but also opened us up to infinite possibilities.

For two years, we devoted ourselves to articulating our vision. Right away we succeeded in scheduling two large exhibition spaces in Providence, Rhode Island, at Brown University and Rhode Island School of Design with a proposal to bring together space artifacts with artists' works to show the influence of space exploration on contemporary culture. We chose the name "Space Window*" for its significance as the time frame during which a launch can take place and synchronize its trajectory with orbiting bodies.

Eve took a planetary geology course at Brown University, taught by Jim Head, who was simultaneously teaching the astronauts lunar geology, to better select moon rocks. His colleague Tim Mutch was developing the Viking lander, which carried the very first digital camera, which he invented, to Mars. Through their accounts, as well as the astronauts and NASA personnel we spoke with, and studying astronomy, it became clear that those who delved into these fields had expanded their consciousness in deep and subtle ways.

Through our subject, the profound relationship that bound art and science as means of seeking the truth and knowing the world appeared undeniable, yet the culture at large was not ready for alternative modes of thought as a viable means to knowledge. The dominance of an "objective" scientific view had not yet been relativized and this, in some sense, was our point of resistance. We transformed it into our vehicle. In our search for images, artists, writers, and scientists, our selections navigated inner world travel and the moon missions, the search for extraterrestrial intelligence, and the synchronicity celebrated by Jung and in the *Tao of Physics*, which linked quantum physics and Eastern religions. We read Aldous Huxley and Immanuel Velikovsky, sought out star charts from cultures, both contemporary and ancient, and autographed images of astronauts in their space suits and materials from NASA.

NASA was still a confirmed public access institution in the late '70s and had a staff dedicated to sharing their work. They also loaned us films and photographs and granted access to materials scientists had used for their own research. We found they responded with generosity to our enthusiasm about the effects of their work on American culture and sent all of the artists in our exhibition the images and information from various space missions and telescopes. Peter Fend was among those who came in contact with the materials NASA was sending.

One day an enormous yellow wooden crate came creaking up our old freight elevator. Inside we found a spacesuit that had walked on the moon and other priceless treasures: a stainless-steel suitcase hermetically sealed to carry moon rocks back, space survival supplies, and other tools used on space missions for exhibit at Brown University. Jim Head and Tim Mutch loaned us a series of large black-and-white glossy photos taken on the moon, and a huge digital mural of Mars, one of the earliest images made up of pixels. We displayed the space artifacts as if they were beyond the reach of gravity, suspending them to simulate floating through the soaring space of the gallery. The moon photos we spliced together into vast dynamic murals which fanned out across the huge walls of the Bell Gallery.

When the artifacts were installed, Jim Head and Tim Mutch came to have a look. Our presentation of the most stunning visual material being produced at the time in the "Space Window*" exhibition was revelatory to the scientists who had helped produce it. They had not thought visually beyond verisimilitude, and so it was a stellar moment for us when they were able to see their own images in a new light. It helped to open the door for an entirely new kind of conversation between artists and scientists, one that Billy Klüver had initiated from a scientific perspective with his work from Bell Labs with the first Happenings in the '60s.

One of our trips down to Washington, D.C. yielded a stack of 16mm NASA films. There were fascinating studies of impact craters and astronauts dressed up in costumes made by their wives for the first anti-gravity experiment. While some revealed how information achieved new forms of visualization through emerging technology, several films challenged Warhol in their demand for durational viewing. One film especially made a lasting impression on Peter Fend when we showed some of this material in New York. Taken from a geostationary satellite positioned over North and South America, Europe, and Africa, it was comprised of one frame per hour for a year and ran for approximately thirty minutes. It was unforgettable: a funnel cloud whirling out of the Amazon never cleared. This was the only place in the frame where the earth was not visible during the year. The film showed how the moisture generated there would build up and then drift to other parts of the world, primarily towards North Africa but also to Europe. It needed an artist's eye to interpolate what was being seen and realize the implications.

After meeting Peter Fend and Taro Suzuki, we joined forces with artists who had similar interests and began working as a group: Space Force. Our first project at the Kitchen in New York in 1982 presented satellite data facilitated through our NASA contacts. We are grateful that Peter has always candidly acknowledged the groundwork we laid for what became his lifelong career; taking up some of the ideas we introduced, he made of them something altogether different than we ever dreamed of and reversed the focus from outer space back to planet Earth.

2/22/22
Eve Vaterlaus and Joan Waltemath

WHAT THE EDITORS SAY

What if art holds solutions to the ecological crises of our time? Since the late 1970s, in proximity to the United Nations and its missions in New York, and in various other places on the planet, Peter Fend has been combining artistic with scientific ideas to effect what he calls "viable habitat" following Leon Battista Alberti's demands for clean air, water, and circulation. Fend argues while these actions are based on what is normally assigned to art, they constitute "an extension of art into inhabited space, occupied through time in what is called Architecture."

Fend, who is not an artist nor architect by training, but studied history and English, has predominantly worked collaboratively, in ventures such as The Offices, Ocean Earth, Space Force, Global Feed, or RAPID RESPONSE. For him, joining forces with artists such as Coleen Fitzgibbon, Eve Vaterlaus, and Joan Waltemath in self-organized structures, enacting their constitutional rights, and making use of legal frameworks and entities such as the corporation, has the potential to break through the confines of what he sees as a slow and stifling "gallery-museum system." This system, which continues to rely on false notions of novelty and singular authorship, in conjunction with science's disciplinary boundaries and (in)direct state censorship is what Fend argues prevents real change and forces art into inutility. He claims that if art was taken seriously for its ability to move beyond critique, for instance, Michael Heizer's earthworks could guide ecological restoration and Carolee Schneemann's performances could inform the way we harvest and dwell. In his view, art's ideas ought not only to influence and advance concrete fields such as energy supply, urban development, and governance, but also become "industrialized solutions." What could be read as Fend's unfailing belief in the notions of the avant-garde and the grandiose potential in the ideas, structural concepts, and materials of movements like Earth Art, Conceptual art, and performance art constitute the tension at the core of his practice. This tension becomes evident in his unforgiving acknowledgment that in this regard, all radical art practices—Fend's own included—so far failed, yet should still spark action. In his re-reading of (art) history Fend pits what is often framed as success—canonization and inclusion in the museum—against an inability to fundamentally overhaul society's means of production, steering it away from ecological and climate breakdown towards a livable future: one in which a democratized energy supply eclipses Big Oil, nuclear energy, and dam industries. Whilst Fend revisits modernist tropes and ideas, he uses them to attack not only the institutions of the art world, but many of the technologies and modes of production and accumulation that are synonyms with extractive modernity and its nation-states, which, as Mahmood Mamdani argues, are built on imperial and colonial conquests.

This book, Fend's first major publication since 1994's *Ocean Earth*, edited by Peter Weibel, was prompted by an eponymous exhibition. "Africa–Arctic Flyway" took place at Museo Nivola in the mountain village of Orani, Sardinia, and opened in fall 2019. At the time, the island, which is a major stop-over for birds migrating from the African continent to Europe and the Arctic, was seeing the large-scale infrastructural project of changing the main energy supply to imported fossil fuels: liquified natural gas (LNG) from the US and Africa. For Fend, who has worked countless times in Europe and the Mediterranean region developing highly specific projects for ecological development and post-fossil fuel scenarios, the conditions of the locale in the context of the larger circulatory systems of water and animal migration routes, is what he calls an "architecture for a planet." Hence Fend's claim echoed in the exhibition's and book's title—both the continents of Africa and Europe are one ecological space through their connection by bird and insect flyways, a scientific fact that demands action. As he notes: "The disaster at Chernobyl affects birds on the Nile, all the way down to Lake Nyasa."

Accordingly, the second part of this book is dedicated to four specific flyways and projects located along them, ranging from the development of an algae industry for zero-emissions biofuel in Ukraine and the United Arab Emirates to the deconstruction of dams and the re-naturalization of rivers in Italy. Some of these projects were recently updated and discussed at events such as "AFRICA THINKS, OTHERS FOLLOW" with Moroccan diplomats to the UN in New York. Others date back to the early 1980s. Against the notion of Europe as a smooth economic space afforded by the EU's trade and legal agreements and the reality of its deadly border parting the Mediterranean Sea, Fend employs a quasi-inversion of the political map by basing constitution not by land, but by water.

For instance, against the logic of (neo)colonial extraction and (under) development—most prominently described by Walter Rodney—the Mediterranean seawater basin is recognized as a shared ecological and economic space. Following Fend, saltwater basins, instead of nation-states defined along colonial and ethnic borders, should become the new paradigm for reorganizing the African and European continents into political units that make ecological administration possible.

Prior to the exhibition in Sardinia, in winter 2018, Fend and editor Lennart Wolff traveled to Paris to meet the architect and artist Yona Friedman in his apartment. Here the conversation revolved around the economic theory of physiocracy, a subject of study both of Fend and Friedman. This book provided an occasion for Fend to further develop his updated notion of this concept, prompting its subtitle, Physiocratic States. Fend envisions a satellite-aided eco-tax that can realize the physiocratic ideal of an economic foundation based on the health of ecosystems and human-animal cohabitation. In the first part of the book, new detailed writing by Fend explores the political systems in which to live and draws up an alternative to the present-day UN, which is organized around sovereign states and nuclear weapons: a "Congress of Basins" centered around the world's seas and oceans.

When working with Fend on an exhibition or book, his collaborators, especially curators, are brought into an uneasy position. As what one is working on is never meant to be limited to the space of the gallery and every project is a failure if unsuccessful in altering the course of the worsening climate and ecological crisis. Nevertheless, against lingering notions of an End of History and the fact that Fend's and Ocean Earth's projects are unrealized to date, he tirelessly insists: "ART CAN PRODUCE HISTORY."

The structure and ways in which images, scanned documents, letters, and texts—both pre-existing and new—are assembled in this book are meant to reflect Fend's understanding of art history as a history not of artworks, but of documents.

Elisa R. Linn and Lennart Wolff

WHAT THEY SAID

"You should be saving the Adriatic Sea. That's your job." Jenny Holzer, minutes after she received the top prize at the Venice Biennale in 1990, from the Premier of Italy, within a meter.

"Should not be expelled from the European Union, since what he's publishing is… we checked… factually true." A French official to a delegation from another EU-member state demanding his expulsion. 2002.

"May never again be allowed any visa in Australia," on departure from that country in 1995, after having developed a project based on scientific documents borrowed from the Library of New South Wales, Sydney; on the grounds that such documents, if acted on, would jeopardize the sale of coal to Japan; there were two other "violations."

"Now you're going to be a Communist?" after announcing a base for operations in Belgrade, in 1987 the capital of Yugoslavia.

"Warmonger" ["Kriegstreiber,"] in the same high-court legal process with an accusation that he foolishly tries to win a Nobel Prize in Peace.

"Il fait l'overselling," CEO of French earth-observation satellite, Spot Image, quoted in a French magazine, all copies of which were denied entry into the USA at JFK, 1980s.

"Il fait la pornographie politique," Paul Virilio, on French TV 1.

"The Lawrence of Arabia of the art world," Richard Prince, in view of the Iran-Iraq War exploits, plus exploits in Libya, Chad, Lebanon.

"The Ezra Pound of Colab, a pioneering art group," Tom Otterness, due to work for ecological administration of the Mediterranean Sea and its basin.

"Neoliberal," for working through a business corporation rather than a commune or a Soviet, most recently with Yugoslavia city planners.

"Global architect." Jonathan Crary, 1980, Village Voice Arts Annual, but canceled with him fired, forcing him to become a professor.

"Trading in secrets," and thus almost turned back at Auckland Airport, New Zealand, but for a promise to never publicly discuss what was learned with civil observation satellites of war zones, or Chernobyl.

"Bowled over" by documents of what happened as of 1990, Vincent Scully, architecture historian at Yale University, analyst of military architecture and its relation to nation-states.

Was asked, as a visual artist knowledgeable about motion-detection and tracking, to work for the US Defense Intelligence Agency, and for a UK defense firm. He said No to the first request but said Yes to the second.

Veteran of three trials, two UN press conferences (one hosted by both US and Russian press agencies; one hosted by Turkish press corps), a commissioned report and testimony for US Congress, with classified hearing and reports that no one may "cite, quote or publish," and one year's hiding (1981) to avoid a demand, by US District Attorney Rudy Giuliani, to be a protected witness (with microphones on body) exposing one hundred and twenty arrestees. He appears twice on the cover of publications (one, France's "Liberation," as killed. But even after three chase scenes, he's still alive. He ran track in college, so he outran his enemies, and he gives money to his college, Carleton College, in gratitude. He has spoken at many graduate schools and think tanks, but never enrolled in one. When asked, in a UK university, "What are your sources?", he answered, "My life."

THIS BOOK IS A FORM OF AUTOBIOGRAPHY OF A GROUP OF ARTISTS ON THE INTERNATIONAL STAGE, RESPONSIBLE—SOMETIMES WITHOUT INTENTION—FOR THE OUTCOMES OF THE FALKLANDS WAR, IRAN-IRAQ WAR (and subsequent invasion of Kuwait), COLLAPSE OF THE GERMAN NUCLEAR INDUSTRY, AND—we work on now—A SOLUTION TO THE RUSSIA-UKRAINE CRISIS. Over fifty percent of work product and databases have been destroyed or confiscated for reasons of "national security." One of the three trials, in US Federal Court, was dropped on "national security grounds." What we said may not be in any record.

As this book will show, Peter Fend does want to win a Nobel Prize… not in Peace, for sure, but, with his colleagues in Ocean Earth Development Corporation and TVGOV, in Economics.

He has to hurry: he's seventy-two. But his nickname, for years, has been "Beep beep, Roadrunner."

Peter Fend

TABLE OF CONTENTS

5 PRECEDENTS, ANTECEDENTS, AND THE FUTURE NOTES ON THE BEGINNING
Eve Vaterlaus and Joan Waltemath

8 WHAT THE EDITORS SAY
Elisa R. Linn and Lennart Wolff

11 WHAT THEY SAID
Peter Fend

I PHYSIOCRATIC STATES
- 19 PLANET POLICY
- 39 CONGRESS OF BASINS
- 51 POLITICAL SYSTEMS IN WHICH TO LIVE
- 71 ART AND THE MEANS OF PRODUCTION

II AFRICA–ARCTIC FLYWAY
- 91 BIRDS REIGN
- 107 POST-WAR AFRICA

III FLYWAY PROJECT SITES
- 133 FLYWAY 3: NIGERIA TO NORTH CAPE
  PROJECT SITE: BALTIC SEA BASIN; NORTH SEA BASIN
- 153 FLYWAY 4: DONAU/ODER CORRIDOR
  PROJECT SITE: ADRIATIC BASINS;
  WEST MEDITERRANEAN BASIN
- 177 FLYWAY 6: NILE–MOSCOW CORRIDOR
  PROJECT SITE: GULF OF ODESA; CRIMEAN COAST ON BLACK SEA; SEA OF AZOV
- 195 FLYWAY 8: EASTERN GULF CORRIDOR
  PROJECT SITE: BASIN OF THE GULF

223 WHAT IF ART HAD ITS WAY

229 CHRONOLOGY OF OCEAN EARTH

I PHYSIOCRATIC STATES

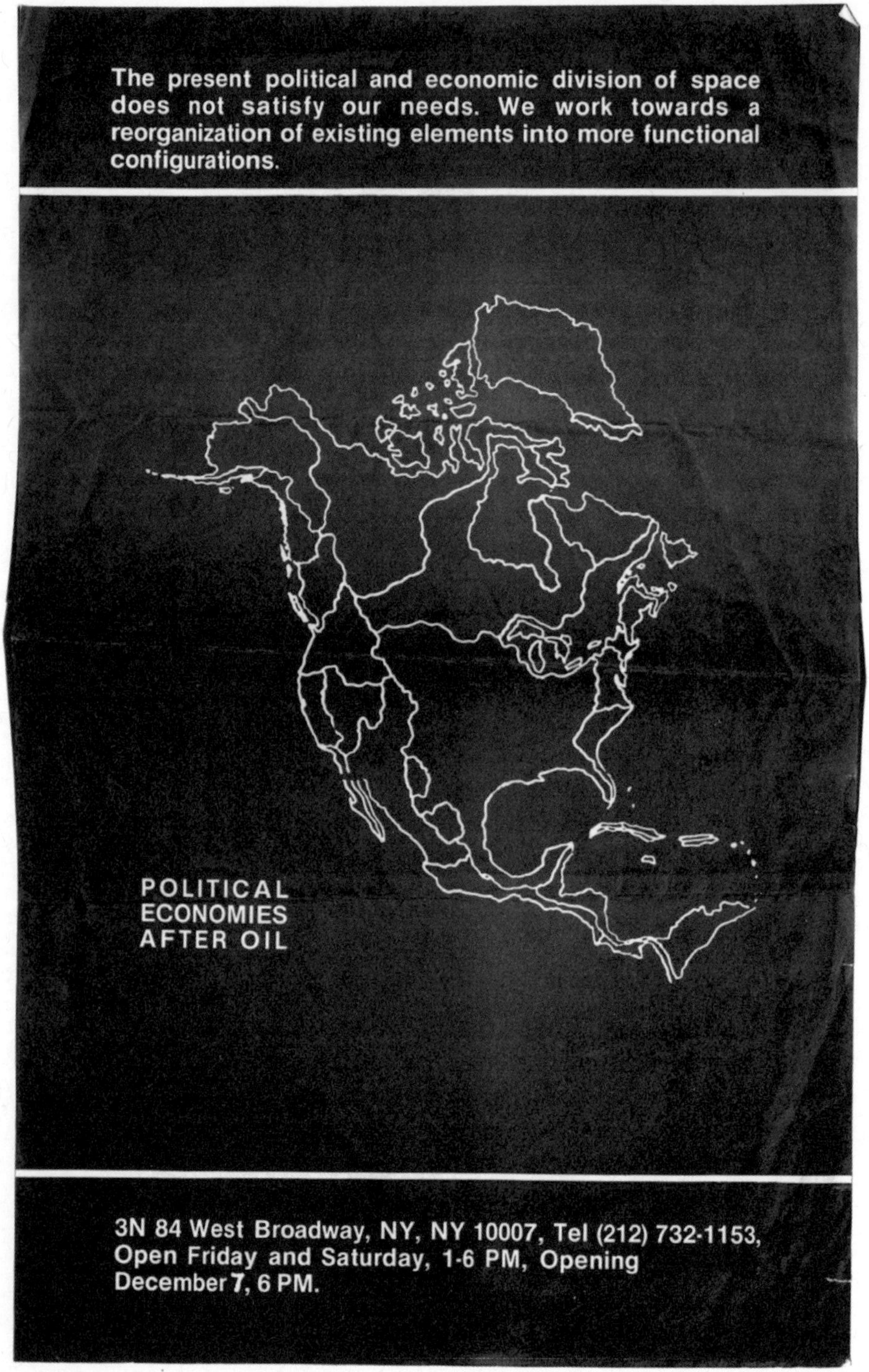

This poster was made for an exhibition at Peter Nadin Gallery in New York in late 1979, showing North America in its water basin demarcations. Jenny Holzer wrote the poster's caption. The exhibition, titled "World Space: Political Economies After Oil," also included East Asia and Europe in its basins. It was the first time that Peter Fend displayed watersheds determining a frontier.

Fend

ARCHITECTURE PROPOSITIONS

PUBLIC POLICY

The function of architecture is to organize habitat.

Habitat now is, of course, scarcely organized.

Most of the organization of habitat has been left to industrialists. Consider the automobile. Or refineries and pipelines.

The architects have confined themselves to the design of buildings.

But the city, the place where humans live, remains the premier architectural question.

To speak of city planning or regional planning as somehow separate from the planning, or design, of a personal space, is to suppose that aesthetic principles or logics somehow fade out or need transliteration at larger scales.

The architects simply have not had the nerve to do architecture on large scale — with the atmosphere, the waters, the productive hinterland, the entire technical and physical apparatus by which a city lives and breathes.

They can think on large scale, with the entire space, but they do not allow themselves to practice that way.

They fear to be denounced as megalomaniacs by the parties now determining the character of our environment.

Yet the political question, the question of establishing a territory and arranging the material conditions in that territory for well-being, remains unresolved.

The political question is an aesthetic question and an architectural question.

How else might we organize habitat, the space in which we co-exist with the species, but by the use of senses acutely trained?

If the society is to succeed in its com-petition with the species, if the society is to co-evolve rather than collapse, architects — in joint venture with artists — assume political leadership.

Peter Fend

This text was written for an exhibition at an artist-run space that included work by Carolee Schneemann, Gordon Matta-Clark, and Peter Fend, among others. It opened shortly before the more-famous "Times Square Show" in 1980. While Schneemann criticized the term "leadership" in the text, architect Diane Lewis liked Fend's approach to architecture.

CONTRACTED

Peter Fend

CONSTRUCTION OF FLYWAYS OVER KASSEL FROM AFRICA TO SCANDINAVIA

To build a flyway over a city, particularly a city with lots of ponds and marshes, like Kassel, you need more birds. To get more birds, you need more fish. To get more fish, you need less pollution, less domesticated agriculture, more wilderness. That requires less acid rain. So you need not just less but an outright replacement for fossil fuels. We act accordingly, building on relations established in these Kassel-linked sites.

PAID

1. Limfjord, Denmark. Major migratory bird hub, in a large inland sea previously freshwater, with brackish interfaces. Test site for: Clean Air Rig (CAR), to yield brown algae and displace harmful green or blue-green genera; feather tests; curved dike or ramp structures to accelerate inflow of ocean waters; systematic satellite imaging, with Danish Hydrologic Institute. Projects shifted to Oresund (Superflex), for Copenhagen Atopic Site. Last stop before long flight across water to Norway; scatter studies.

HAS BEEN PAID

2. Langenesee, Vorarlberg. File complete technical proposal with Vorarlberg government for marsh construction scheme at dammed-up lake now accumulating too much silt. Building a stepped, banked alternative to normal wall dams, 1 km long, with crane and cable-bucket system in mud-stone accumulation, use ski-lift experience. Highest part of watershed draining to Holland, which studies it.

PAID

3. Genova, Liguria. Resume residency at architecture foundation, build up satellite monitoring project with University of Genova, collaborate with artists specializing in bird and fish migration. Feather and estuarine structure tests slated for Finale Marina Liguria, or Arenzano, as clean river-ocean impact sites. First landfall in Europe after flight from Africa. In winter, test CAR.

SEEK ACCESS

4. Algeria. Grand Erg Oriental, with flow out to the Gulf of Djerba, could be eased into savannah with channels diverting waters past the now-lifeless salt lakes. US-UK oil companies have replaced French, making new projects possible. Dry wells and coastal spirals, follow Vienna models, discussed with Embassy.

PAID

5. Swiss ornithological radar team, develop digital radar display of bird-flight-clusters to form indicator of ecological health.

At end, organize a show, like "Mapping: A Response to MOMA," in anticipation of the site problem for Documenta, with pre-existing art works or art practices being found out along the flight corridors. Mel Chin is in Corsica, Marc Dion in Zurich. Dennis Oppenheim already has outdoor project in Milan. Elle-Mie Hansen builds beaches in Denmark. Dan Peterman issues stock. Build a string of sites, a stellar line-up that activates Eurafrica.

AND BERN

"Contracted" referred, in 1995, to the agreement with architecture graduate Susan Jennings to design the pavilion for the Orangerie in Kassel for display of site projects by artists on a flyway through Kassel. The notes reflect the progress noticed. Curator Kasper Koenig told Fend that the proposal was seen as an "attempt to take over documenta 1997," compelling rejection. Since then, bird and insect numbers have declined dramatically. A new contract is signed with Jennings. Are curators in the way of our survival on Earth?

J U S T I F Y I N G
T H E   C I T I Z N
A S   S (H E) ’ S
S T R U G G L I N G
W I T H   C O N T -
R A D I C T I O N S
I N   S O C I E T Y

I   J U S T   D O
W H A T   T H E Y
T E A C H   Y O U
I N   S C H O O L

I N   T H E   U S

D I F F E R E N T
F R O M   M O S T
P L A C E S   O N
T H E   E A R T H

N O   N A T I O N

B U T   A   F E W
L A W S   O N L Y

W H I C H   A L L
M U S T   O B E Y

A   C I T I Z E N
O F   T H E   U S

W I T H O U T   A
L E A D E R   O R
F O L L O W E R S

C O N T R A C T S
A N D   T R U S T
B E I N G   A L L
T H A T   W I L L
B E   P U T   T O
U S E   D A I L Y

TECHNOLOGY ASSESSMENT BOARD
TED STEVENS, ALASKA, CHAIRMAN
MORRIS K. UDALL, ARIZONA, VICE CHAIRMAN

IN G. HATCH, UTAH	GEORGE E. BROWN, JR., CALIFORNIA
RLES McC. MATHIAS, JR., MARYLAND	JOHN D. DINGELL, MICHIGAN
VARD M. KENNEDY, MASSACHUSETTS	CLARENCE E. MILLER, OHIO
EST F. HOLLINGS, SOUTH CAROLINA	COOPER EVANS, IOWA
IBORNE PELL, RHODE ISLAND	DON SUNDQUIST, TENNESSEE

JOHN H. GIBBONS

JOHN H. GIBBONS
DIRECTOR

Congress of the United States
OFFICE OF TECHNOLOGY ASSESSMENT
WASHINGTON, DC 20510-8025

December 8, 1986

MEMORANDUM

TO: Workshop Participants

FROM: Peter Sharfman, Program Manager, International Security & Commerce

SUBJECT: Background Papers for "Commercial Newsgathering From Space" Workshop

Attached are five background papers to help focus the discussion during our December 18 workshop:

- "Commercial Newsgathering from Space: Remote Sensing Technology;" Matthew Willard, EOSAT, and Stillman Chase, Hughes Santa Barbara Research.
- "News Gathering from Space: Commercial Remote Sensing and the Press;" Mark E. Brender, ABC News.
- "The Way It's Been: Mediasat and the Value-Added Industry;" Peter Fend, Ocean Earth Construction and Development Corporation.
- "Some National Security and Foreign Policy Aspects of Commercial Newsgathering from Space;" Peter D. Zimmerman, Carnegie Foundation.
- "Legal and Constitutional Issues Involved in Mediasat Activities:" Rita Ann Reimer, Congressional Research Service.

These papers are meant to encourage discussion and to stimulate new ideas; they do not necessarily represent the considered judgments of their authors, much less that of OTA. All the authors were asked to meet unreasonable deadlines and therefore have written papers that they might otherwise have regarded as early drafts.

These papers are for your information only. THEY MUST NOT BE QUOTED, CITED, REPRODUCED, OR CIRCULATED TO INDIVIDUALS NOT PLANNING TO ATTEND THE WORKSHOP. It is our hope and expectation that the discussion at the workshop will lead many participants, including perhaps the authors of these papers, to modify their views, and we do not wish to inhibit discussion by attempting to "hold" our authors or anybody else to the views expressed in these papers.

I look forward to seeing you on December 18, 1986, at 9 AM, at 600 Pennsylvania Avenue SE. Please do not hesitate to call me or Richard DalBello at 226-2026 if you have any questions.

Cover of the compilation for the December 8, 1986, US Congress Office of Technology Assessment Workshop, held on Capitol Hill, with commissioned reports by four persons. The surprise then, upon arrival and reading this cover, was the rule forbidding to quote, cite, or reproduce the papers. We reported our groundbreaking experience, which has disappeared from US history by covert maneuver. No copy of our report is now in hand.

THE STATE
HATES ART

THE STATE
FEARS ART

THE STATE
BELIEVES
ART SHALL
BE JESTER

AND NEVER
PRACTICAL

HOW COME?

TREASON
CREATES
HISTORY

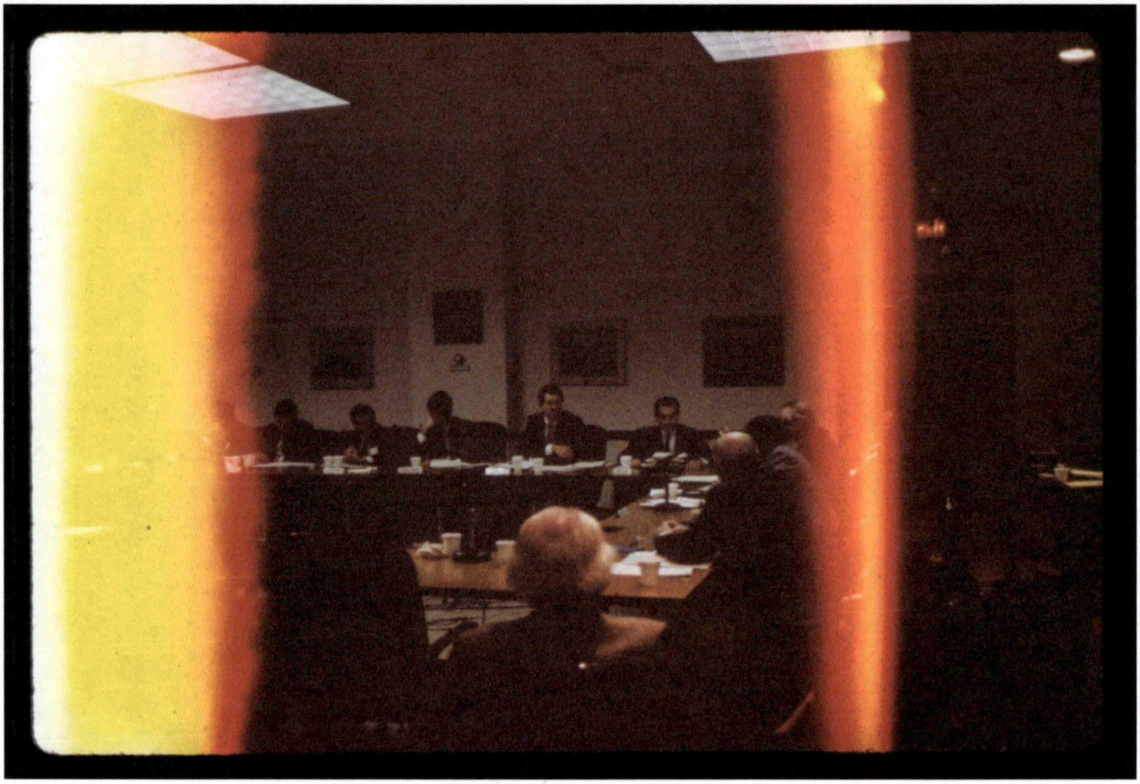

Photograph of the “workshop” of the Office of Technology Assessment taken by Wolfgang Staehle in 1986.

The only publicly-available photo document of a "Workshop" of the Office of Technology Assessment of the US Congress in December 1986 on the subject of "Commercial News-gathering from Space."
Four participants in the "Workshop" produced reports on paid commission. One of them was Peter Fend, of the US company then named Ocean Earth Construction and Development Corporation.
At the "workshop," it became clear to participants that all proceedings and papers were secret. There were printed rules that nothing be "cited, quoted or reproduced." Four people associated with Ocean Earth were present. Two were founding shareholders Wolfgang Staehle and Coleen Fitzgibbon. One was an occasional associate (e.g., Chernobyl) with Ocean Earth, also publishing about the firm: Washington-based Robert Horvitz. One was a chronicler of the company, as well as social colleague of many of its participants: writer Alan Jones. As is normal for artists attending notable events, Wolfgang Staehle took photos. To his surprise, he was told by a security agent that photographs are forbidden, and that he must take out the exposed roll from his camera. He obeyed the order. However, a small portion of the film still remained rolled up in the camera.
This image is from that portion of the film that was not destroyed. Unless advised otherwise, Ocean Earth and its founding shareholder Wolfgang Staehle will believe that the photograph, which is clearly truncated and imperfect, is acceptable in history as evidence of the "Workshop," including participation there of Peter Fend.

The photo only proves that the event occurred. It does not in any way violate any rule of secrecy about what was said or written. Therefore, we enter the photo into the history of art, and of the United States.

SOLUTIONS TO THE PROBLEMS

Ideas and techniques from art can be converted into viable means of production, or means by which we, the human animals, survive.

But a change in the means of production is often not welcome. It intrudes on the stakeholders in existing means of production.

Replace fossil hydrocarbons with biologically sourced hydrocarbons derived from this year's solar inflow.

Replace high dams and hydroelectric turbines, chosen in 1905 by the American Society of Civil Engineers, with the technology then rejected, undershot waterwheels.

Replace farms and grazing lands with wild animal tracts.

Replace highways with railroads to sharply reduce animal loss.

Finance high-speed commuter rail to save wildlife.

Replace suburbs with clusters of towers and straddling bridges to minimize impact on watershed.

Replace income tax with taxation on what we cannot afford to lose: the soil and the ecological systems.

Replace pressure for income with pressure for physiological vigor: everyone has a basic 6.5 m × 5.5 m dry, water-supplied space.

Remove any solar-energy scheme that covers green land or harms wildlife, e.g., solar panels over land (already forbidden in Italy) and solar-thermal plants.

Pyrolyze urban wastes to yield a hydrocarbon stream, upon which yeasts or other single-cell organisms can grow, which can then be keratinized for return to the food chain. Hydrocarbon engineering extended.

Keratins, both artificial and natural, much cultured, put to use in building materials, especially on roads, bridges, and foot-paths.

Concentrate architectural attention on th physiology of the inhabitant. If people are not healthy, that can be attributed to bad design. This is our approach to the mechanized spaces for intensified sleep. This is also the approach to all urban (inhabited) structures. All technologies are directed at (1) clean air, (2) living waters, (3) circulatory space (efficient moving around), (4) defense against threats to the inhabitants and their territory. This is Alberti's expectation of architecture. It's achieved with what Alberti called the highest form of painting: history painting.

Our imagery from observation satellites, or our analysis of basins and human contests, are… history paintings. These are verified historical-fact documents.

PLANET POLICY

The earth is one place. It's covered mostly by ocean, and it's going through biochemical changes now at an unprecedented rate. We humans made this happen, and we humans——for many reasons, not just survival——must correct it.

I am a citizen of the United States, and as such impact the planet. The country is the most powerful, and polluting, nation on earth. Any policy it adopts can and should be a Planet Policy.

The Earth has two poles, normally covered in ice. From these poles, cold ocean waters flow away. Five huge currents flow north from Antarctica, past South America, past Africa, past Australasia, and two huge currents flow south from the Arctic, from

Greenland to Cape Hatteras, and from the Bering Sea to just by Tokyo. The Antarctica-spinoff currents all extend to the Equator, and in the Indian Ocean beyond, while the Arctic spinoff currents meet warm waters bearing east and north, the Gulfstream and Kuroshio respectively, to dive deep and over millennia return to Antarctica. These currents have enormous biological wealth, and these currents—most notably the Antarctica spinoffs—drive the Earth's weather. The currents must be dealt with directly if one is to prevent climate catastrophe.

We must organize what we do around the ice caps.

This can be done today. This can be done this year.

This can be done in cooperation, or at least communication, with large economic powers like China and India.

ARCHITECTURE FOR A PLANET

I. PLANET

POLES
-ARCTIC TURNAROUND OF OCEAN CIRCULATION
-ANTARCTIC CENTER OF OCEAN CIRCULATION

SEAM TREATY OF TORDESILLAS, 1494
-LOMONOSOV RIDGE TO GREENLAND, AMAZON MOUTH, ANTARCTICA PENINSULA AND RIDGE, SPLIT OF JAPAN FROM BLACK DRAGON RIVER (AMUR)

FLYING-ANIMAL SEASONAL MIGRATIONS
-EURAFRICA
-EAST ASIA
-AMERICAS

SWIMMING-ANIMAL BASINS
-SALTWATER BASINS (AS IN MOON'S "SEAS")
(TREATY OF PARIS, 1763)

II. REGIONS, HYDROMETRIC AREAS, PHYSIOCRATIC STATES: FOR RUNNING/WALKING ANIMALS

TRACKED TRANSPORT ROUTES (railroads, maglev, monorail)
WATER TRANSPORT ROUTES (canals, rivers, seas)
SLOPE CITIES (set into mountains)
CLUSTER CITIES (concentrated at high-rise hubs)
MOST LAND LEFT WILD (youth gangs do the hunting/foraging/fishing)

HYDROCARBONS OR HYDROGEN FROM MARINE AND AQUATIC PLANTS
HYDROPOWER WITHOUT DAMS (waterwheels, screws, temperature tubes)
SOLAR PANELS ON BUILDINGS OR NATURAL DESERT
WIND TURBINES WITH LITTLE HARM TO BIRDS
REFINERIES BECOME RECYCLING PLANTS, PRODUCING Bioliths

PUBLIC FINANCE IS ONLY ECOLOGICAL-DEPLETION TAX ON LAND AND “MOVING LAND,” ASSESSED BY SATELLITES AND INWATER METERS; CHANGE-DETECTION LEADS TO TAX CHANGE: PHYSIOCRATIC STATES AND TELEVISION GOVERNMENT

III. EMPTY LEVELS WIRING/PLUMBING FOR PLUGINS AND MODULES

INSTEAD OF “BUILDINGS,” WHICH BLOCK AIR, OPEN-AIR LOFT LEVELS MODULES MANUFACTURED BY PRESENT-DAY CAR COMPANIES (cars and trucks on wheels sharply reduced; most transport is tracked)

ENGINEERS CONTROL ALL ARRAYS, ALWAYS CHECKING LEVELS OF OXYGEN, CO2, POLLUTION, NOISE (strict bans enforced) FOR HIGH LEVELS OF WHAT ALL ARCHITECTURE IS FOR: PUBLIC HEALTH AERIAL STRUCTURES (WALKWAYS, VEGETATION, SHADING) HELD UP BY BALLOONS BREATHING IS THE SINE QUA NON

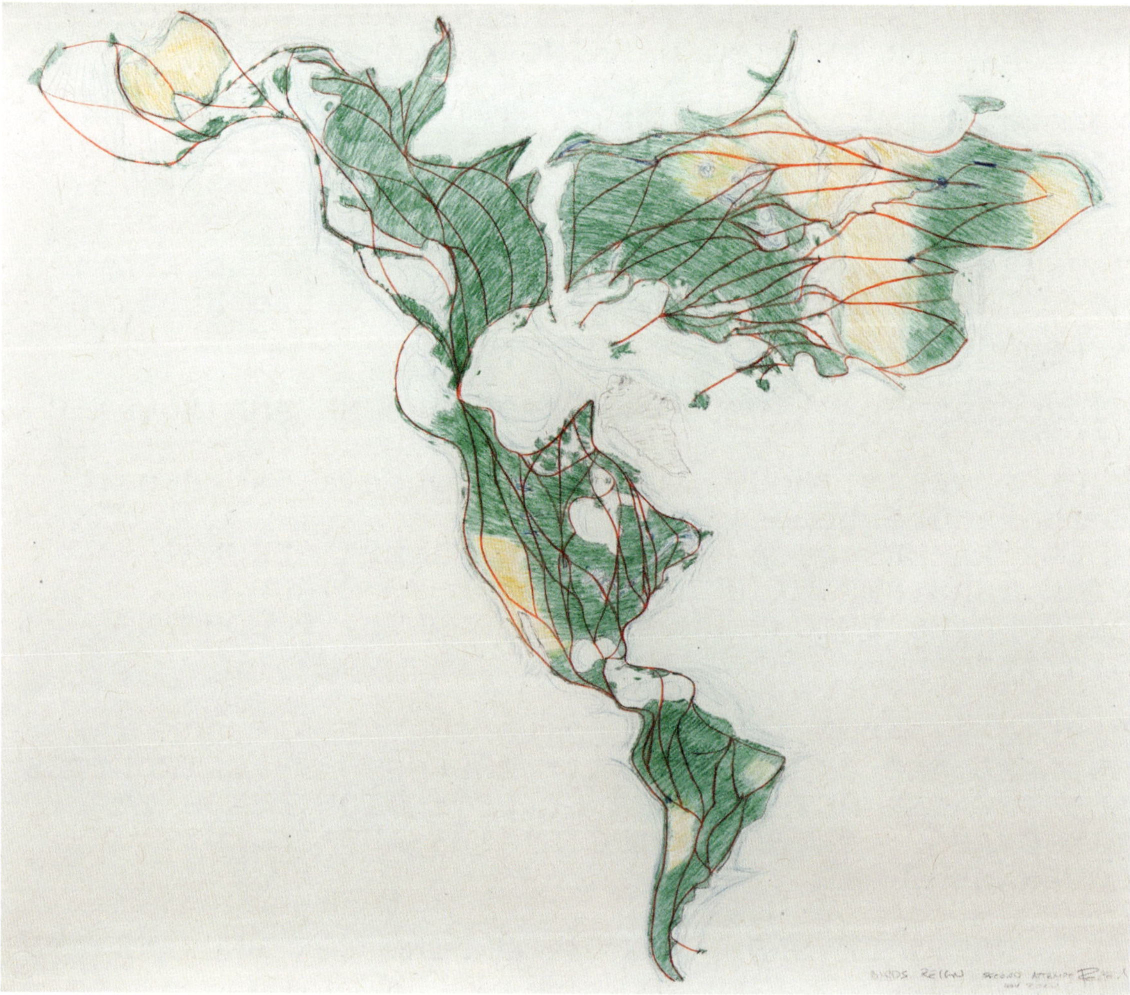

This image of bird flyways converging on the Arctic was made for an exhibition in Berlin in 2020. Emphasizing that even though we are working on Eurafrica, there is also East Asia and America.

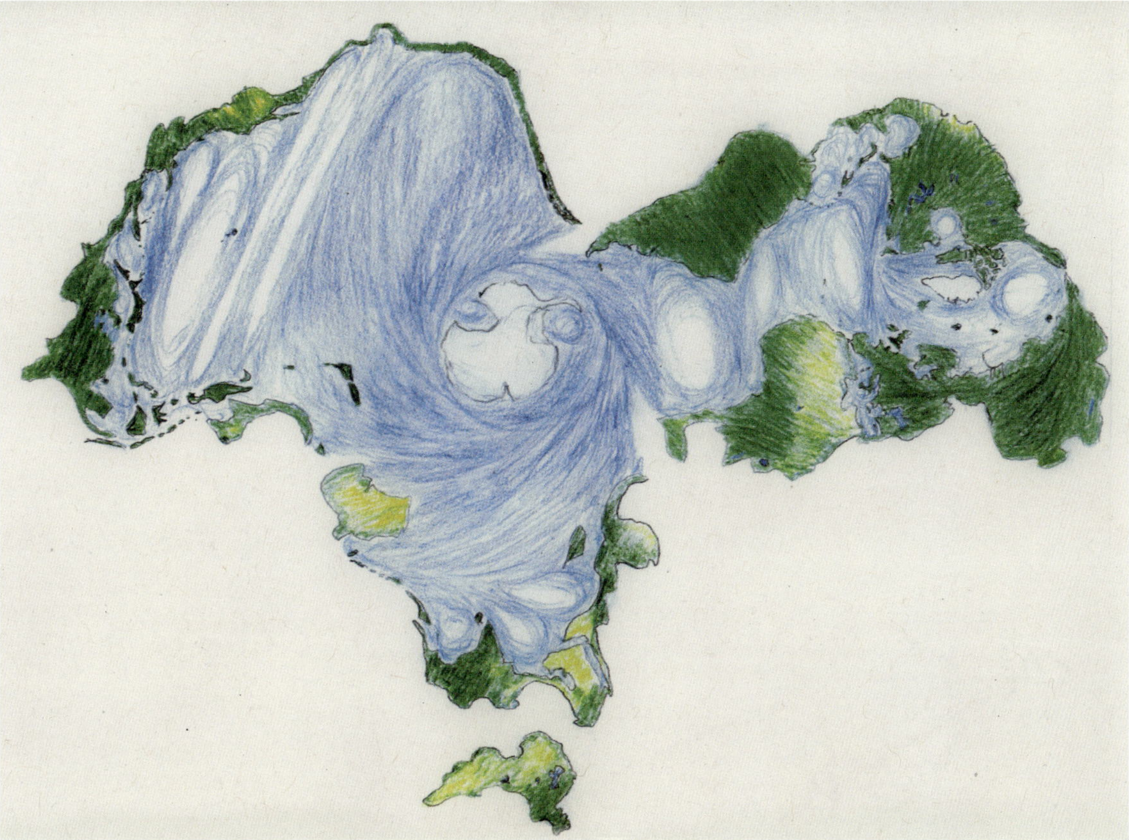

This Antarctica-centered world map, showing all the surface ocean currents, with insloping lands and rivers, from Antarctica throughout the planet, results from four meetings of this US citizen with Russian oceanographers, during 1980–1983. The citizen was already mapping ocean basins, but the Russians provided a global template: exchanges between Antarctica and the Arctic by surface currents, and between the Arctic and Antarctica by much-slower deepwater flows. US and Russian thinking, when combined, leads to comprehensive understanding. Solutions to pressing global problems, like absorbing the carbon dioxide and methane released as permafrost melts, or collecting and digesting plastics in the ocean, become evident.

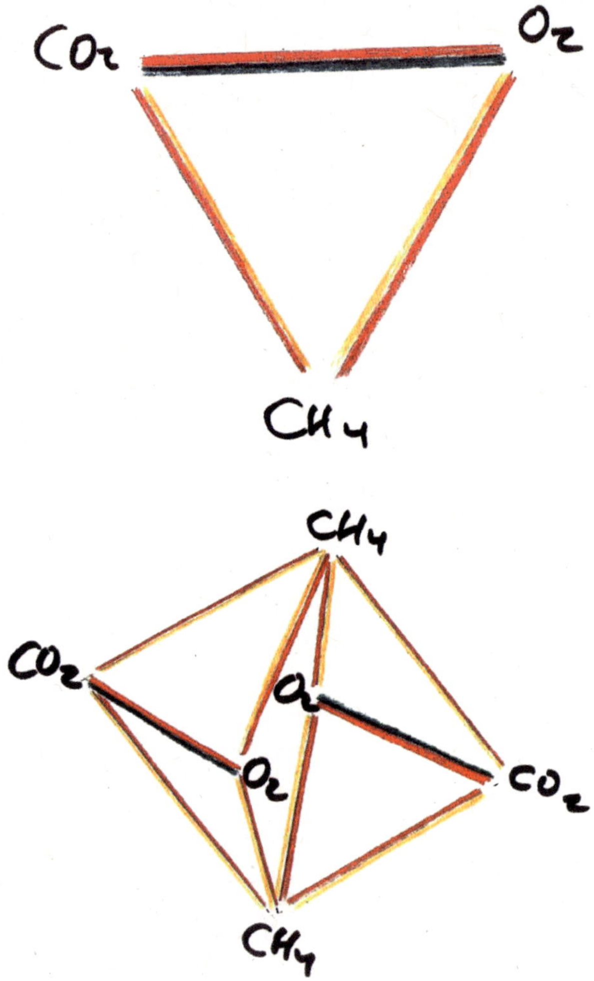

This drawing identifies the main cycles in the economy between methane, carbon dioxide, and oxygen. Biochemist Carl Woese has said everything in a living system involves the relations between these molecules by animals/plants, bacteria, and archaebacteria. Published in 1976.

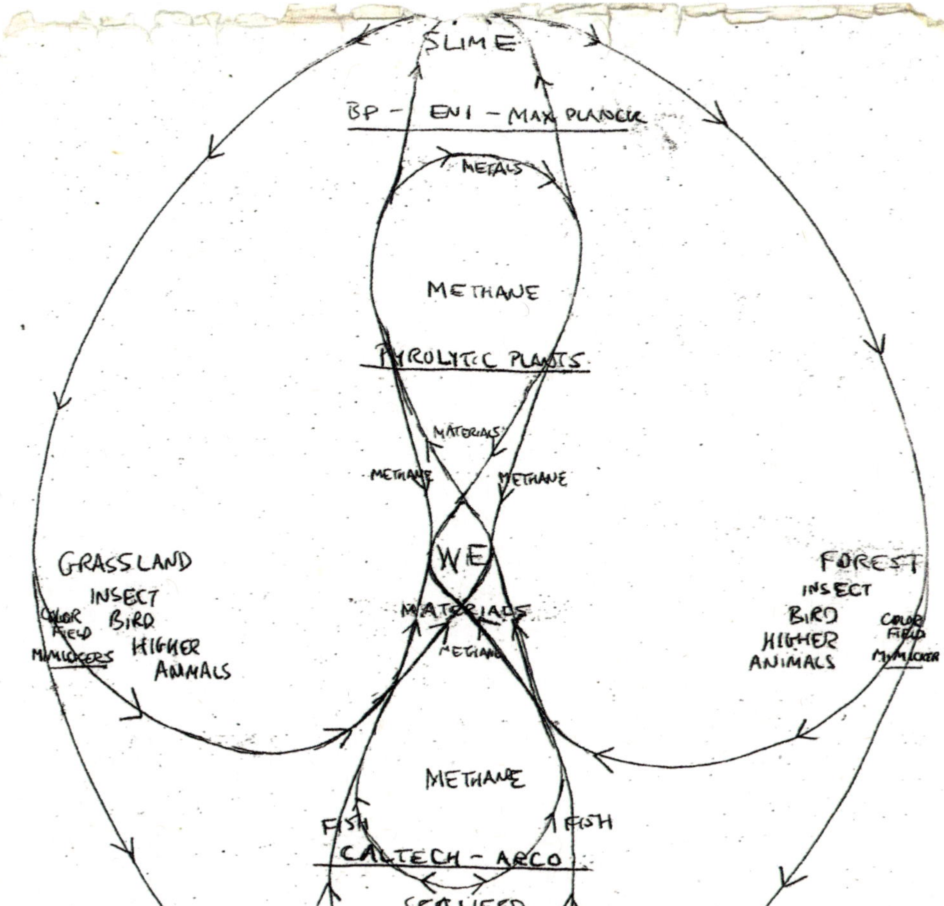

The above drawing is an attempt at applying the visual logic and methodology of Sol Lewitt to the economy. Published in 1977. The question always is how to return the materials from the "we" to the site allocated to "them," the non-human animals subject to predation. The *Fat Corner* triangle in rotation on the neighboring page is a hydrocarbon-centered version of this diagram.

EXPLICATION OF "FAT CORNER" AS BASIS FOR A WORKING SYSTEM

Joseph Beuys's "Fat Corner," analyzed, reveals the fundamental circulatory process of Life. There are three types of chemical transactions: (1) the Carbon Dioxide-Oxygen exchange in Animals and Plants; (2) Bacterial degradation of Animals and Plants; and (3) Archaebacterial, or buildup from simple hydrocarbons, like "Fat Corner," to the life processes we know in ourselves. Scientists began hypothesizing the Archaebacterial, generation of life from mere atoms, from primordial stew, in 1977. That same year, in a parallel hypothesizing about life, Beuys said, "everything must go through Fat Corner"—i.e., the methane (CH4) in a Pentane (five-fold) form. Fat Corner, made of Paraffin, is technically the simplest hydrocarbon, starting from methane (CH4), and progressing on up with the formula CnHn+2. The artist Joseph Beuys said everything must go through Fat Corner, that is, a simple methane-based series of chemical reactions. Truly, anything in this group burns clean, yielding any Carbon Dioxide and Water with some loose Carbon, if combusted.
A society with industrial combustion and materials processing that goes through Fat Corner would be ecologically efficient. It would meet the ancient requirements for Clean Air, Clean Fire, Clean Earth, Clean Water. A visual analysis of Beuys's paraffin corner, or wealth base, led to discoveries about twinpairing of essential molecules—as in a "Square Dance." It also corresponds with scientific discoveries on what appears now to be a third major branch of life, the Archaea. We already know about Animals and Plants, or Eukarya, which exchange carbon dioxide and water, and about Bacteria, which degrade these to yield methane. But with a Fat Corner analysis, we can follow the Generation of life from inorganic matter, up from methane towards Animals and Plants, towards Us in any Utopia.

WATER MUSIC
SQUARE DANCES

TAKE C, CARBON. ADD WATER.

C + H_2O

FOUR TIMES THIS YIELDS CO_2, O_2, $2(CH_4)$ + C

ADD WATER

FOUR TIMES THIS, WITH $4(H_2O)$, YIELDS $5(CO_2)$, $5(O_2)$, $10(CH_4)$ + C

IF YOU MAINTAIN A CYCLE OF FIVE, THEN IT'S $5(CH_4)$ IN THE CYCLE AND C_5H_{10} SPARE, WHICH MAKES AN ALKANE CALLED C_5H_{12} (PENTANE) IF AN EXTRA WATER MOLECULE ARRIVES AND IS BROKEN WITH THE O GOING TO THE EXTRA C.

DO THIS TWICE AND YOU HAVE THREE O'S GOING TO ONE C AND ONE C ALONE, OR

$5(CO_2) + 5(O_2) + 5(CH_4) + C_5H_{12} + CO_2 + C.$

ADD WATER

FOUR TIMES THIS YIELDS ANOTHER FOUR TIMES SET OF C + H_2O, AND THE ENTIRE PROCESS COMPOUNDS.

THE EQUATION CAN MODIFY SINCE THERE IS AN EXTRA CO_2.

THE EXCHANGE BETWEEN CO_2 AND O_2 OCCURS IN DIFFERENT DIRECTIONS IN ANIMALS AND PLANTS. THERE IS A DEGRADATION IN THESE ORGANISMS, OR AN EXCHANGE, FROM ONE OR THE OTHER TO METHANE (CH_4) THROUGH EITHER THE O_2 ROUTE (BACTERIA) OR THE CO_2 ROUTE (ARCHAEBACTERIA). THE TASK, IN ANY UTOPIA, OR EVEN ANY FUNCTIONING DYSTOPIA, IS TO KEEP THE CYCLES GOING. THE PARAFFIN SERVES AS A RESERVE, OR AS A CENTRAL CORRIDOR. WE LOOK AT PENTANE, HEXANE, HEPTANE, AND OCTANE. "GROUPS CORRESPONDING TO THE ALKALIES CAN BE CONSIDERED TO BE FORMED BY REMOVING ONE HYDROGEN TO LEAVE AN OPEN BONDING POSITION." JUST ADD WATER.

CONGRESS OF BASINS

POST-COLONIAL GLOBAL POLICY OF THE UNITED STATES

The United States, as a part of the Americas, is also a part of the world that was colonized by white European settlers within the past five hundred years.

It is not a nation with deep historical roots in one territory. Its territory, as defined by its boundaries, has no ethnic, tribal, or religious identity. It differs, therefore, from some countries in East Asia, such as Japan, Thailand, and China. And it differs from all the countries of Europe. Entities like Luxembourg or Denmark exist within an alleged European Union only because they have traditions going back thousands of years.

We continue on the planet to believe that a former colony can be a country. A former colony is just that, a former colony. There is no tradition, and no ethnic or religious identity, not even a constitutional or administrative identity, to nearly all the ex-colonies of the Americas, of South Asia, of Africa.

When some bold individuals in the North American colonies declared "independence" from Great Britain, a European colonial power, they did so with a Continental Congress, exercising their Revolution with a Continental Army and Continental Navy. Their war of independence was for all the continent of North America. As we see now, they lost. There remains a very large chunk of North America, Canada, still under the British Crown as head of state. As a United States citizen amidst the globe's ecological collapse, I aim to complete the independence from European colonialism, worldwide.

Thus we liberate Africa, South Asia, South and North America from notions of administrative space put there by European colonialists long ago.

RESCINDING THE TREATY OF BERLIN, 1885 THUS ADJUSTING THE CHARTER OF THE UN

The gap between the "developed world" and the "developing world" results chiefly from maintaining the borders decided by European colonialists.

This maintenance was codified by the Treaty of Berlin, in 1885. The host, a new imperialist on the world stage, Otto von Bismarck. He wanted to define the field of colonialist competition by defining each piece in the global competitive field as it was already decided.

With World War I, Germany lost any chance of playing the competitive game, a bitter irony.

With World War II, Italy and Japan lost any chance of playing the "game," and fifteen years later, nearly all the defined colonies were awarded "nationhood" and "independence." The award was mostly empty. How much sovereignty can a tiny entity like Benin, Ghana, Cambodia, or Burma have? Most of the colonies awarded "nationhood" and "independence" ended up permanently too small and too poor to ever be strong. Or even financially independent. The apparent generosity of 1960–1974, in having all the ex-colonies of Africa and South Asia be awarded nationhood, quickly became recognized—in many cases—as a debt trap. The colonies of a United States could unify, and then add to their number to span a continent, then proceed west, taking in a colony from Russia called Alaska, but the colonies of Africa and South Asia, or also of much of Latin America, could do no such thing. They would be permanently weak.

Yes, with nationhood came membership in the United Nations. But this status condemned most of the new "members" to permanent dependence, debt, and non-development. The Charter of the United Nations, in requiring non-aggression among member states and therefore no changes in their frontiers, or no agglomerations larger than themselves, no cohesion and expansion as occurred in the United States, became a trap.

The colonizing empires from Europe, plus their offspring the United States, plus the automatically-advantaged European-dominated Crown States of Britain (Australia, New Zealand, Canada), became the "developed" countries. They maintained their dominance through clubs like the G7 (for a while, G8) and OECD. All the former colonies were left to become debtor states, in most cases. States like Indonesia and India were somewhat different. And petroleum states like the UAE, Saudi Arabia, and Brunei were very different.

As a result, more than half the listed Member States of the United Nations are not sovereign or independent states at all. Worse, most attempts to merge or combine territories are usually interpreted as a violation of the Charter of the United Nations. They are therefore forbidden, often by "peace-keeping forces" and other exertions of force.

The world remains divided into the rich (being mainly in Europe and in its imitators like Japan, South Korea, and China) and the poor (almost all of which are former colonies, trapped by their colonial borders).

Russia differs from the other European empires in having all of its colonies, or occupied and subordinated territories, immediately next door, physically contiguous. Not one of these attached colonies, except maybe oil-rich Azerbaijan and Kazakhstan, really "maybe," can be permanently self-reliant and independent: if something goes wrong, in come the peace-keeping forces from Mother Russia.

Fighting by Russia to restore its Empire shows that the UN Charter is unenforceable.

Nearly all the member states of the UN are former colonies or bits of such, and in no sense nations of such power, economic advantage, or size as the Permanent Members of the UN Security Council, which is all empires.

Another criterion of Statehood is needed.

The UN has tolerated the admission to Statehood, and member status, to former colonies of Britain, the US, France, Germany, the Netherlands, Austria, and now—much recently, of Russia organized as a USSR. So, suddenly, one-time parts of the USSR, such as Ukraine, Belarus, and the Baltic Republics, become "sovereign states" subject to the protections of the UN Charter. That is: the break-off of parts of an Empire cannot be reversed. Really?

We of Ocean Earth call for, well, a United Basins, or more decentralized, a Congress of Basins, as opposed to a "United" "Nations." Sovereign units somehow manageable are not nations.

They are basins. The Mediterranean Basin, or Black Sea Basin, or Baltic Sea basin, or Kara and Barents Sea basins, are manageable long term. "National" or "ethnic" entities, most absurdly identified as Kosovo, or Northern Macedonia, or Donbas, are not manageable long term. The logic of "national self-determination" espoused by Woodrow Wilson after World War I, and attempted by Lenin in his reassembling of the Russian Empire under a Soviet label, does not work. It leads to war.

As various foreign policy veterans have remarked, the United Nations no longer works. 191 so-called members could vote on whether to demand that Russia leaves a former part of its empire, Ukraine. About 140 of them voted that Russia must leave. But a very significant number of ex-colonies in Africa, along with two colossal nuclear-armed states (India and China), abstained.

All the former empires need redefinition in ecological—and not national or ethnic—terms.

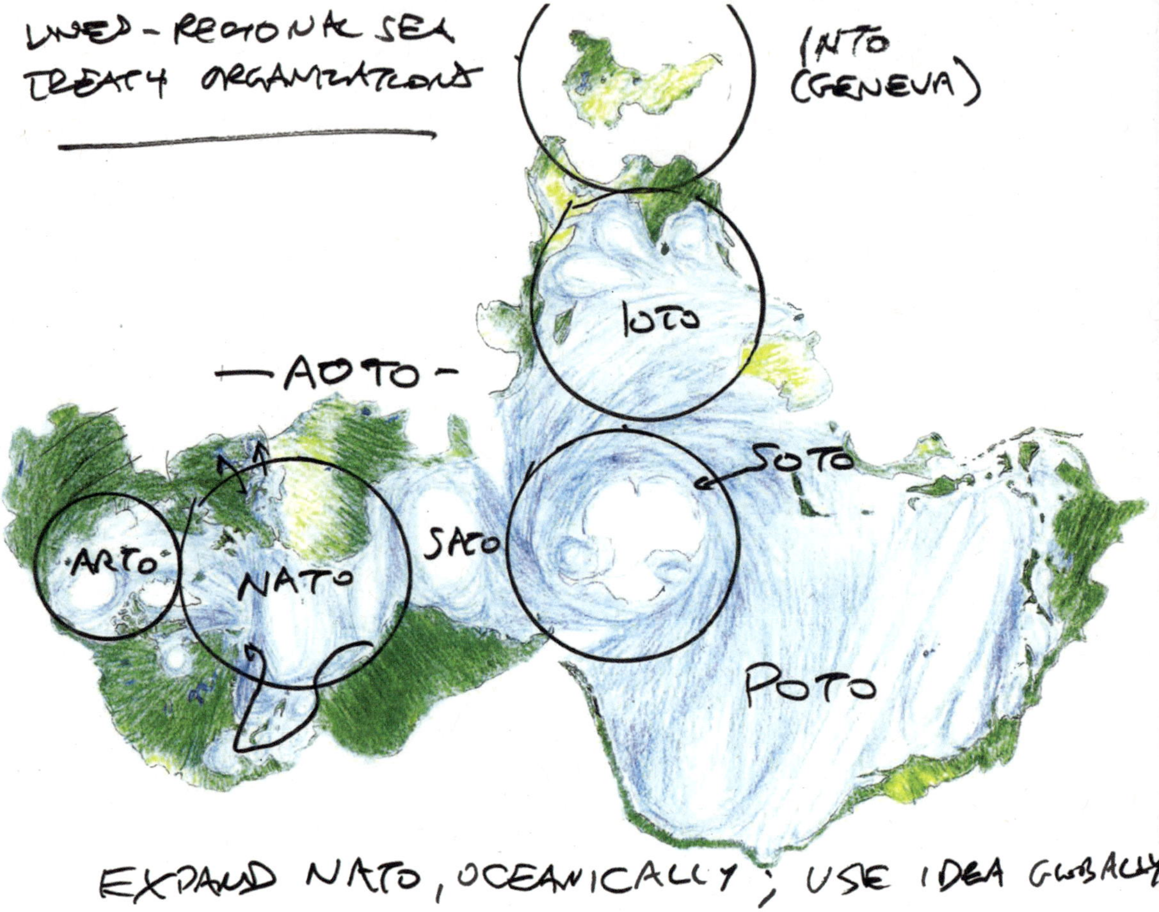

These images are sketches for an installation based on the Antarctica-centered world map of ocean circulation, first produced in 1997 and sponsored by Kenny Schachter. Much of what Fend shows now is from long ago. It's just drawn anew on photocopies. In a bid against a world divided into confronting blocks, the above shows the creation of Ocean Treaty Organizations replacing NATO: the Indian Ocean Treaty Organization (IOTO), Pacific Ocean Treaty Organization (POTO), Atlantic Ocean Treaty Organization (AOTO instead of NATO), Arctic Basin Treaty Organization (ARTO), Southern Ocean Treaty Organization (SOTO), and Inland Seas of World Treaty Organization (INTO).

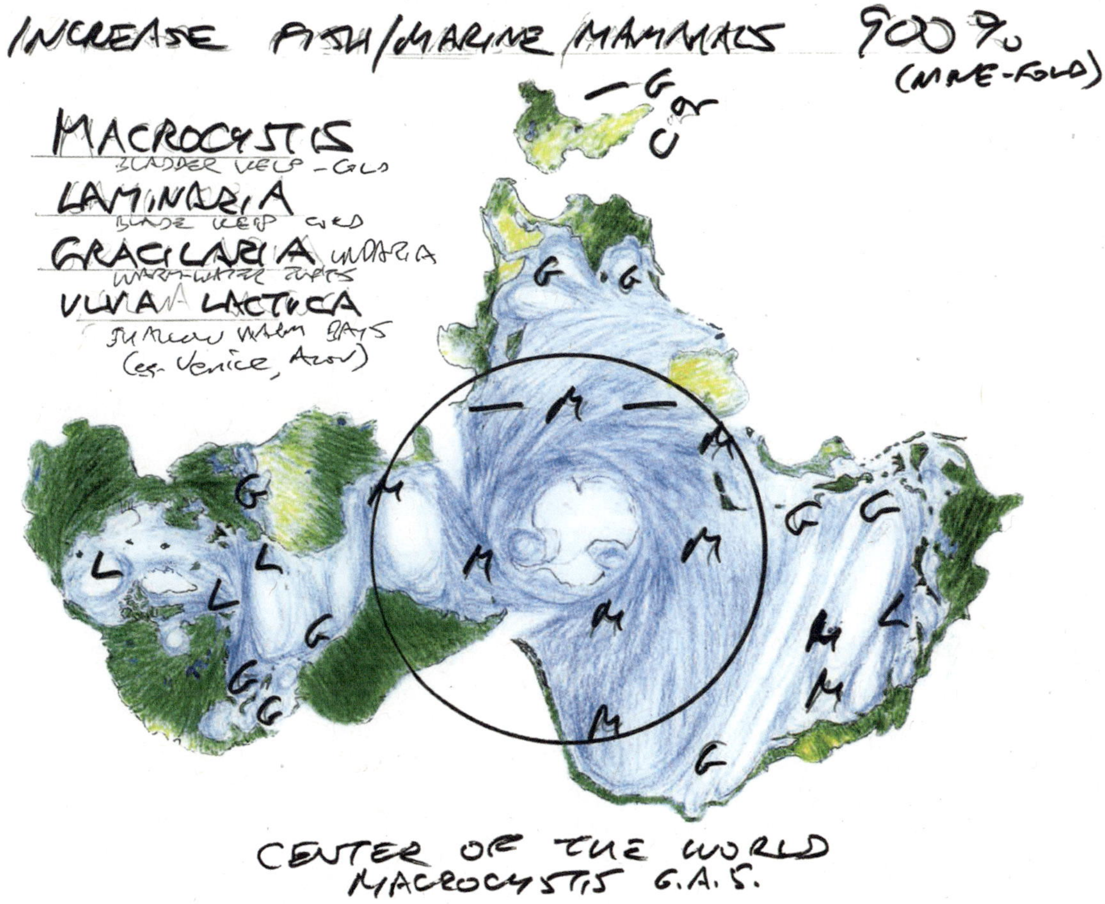

The above image reflects what was diagrammed in 1997 in a prospectus/brochure called "Giant Algae System," partly reprinted in this book. The text was about the global algae industry as a form of planet architecture, further to Alberti's prescription of architecture as an assurance of clean air and water in a habitat. A major Big Oil law firm got ahold of "Giant Algae System" in 2008, following a show with the image in the National Museum of New Zealand, and soon after erupted an affiliate of Statoil (now Equinor in Norway) with the name "Bio Architecture Lab" that used Ocean Earth's language and global plans.

UNITED NATION
ALSO THE THRE

GENERAL ASSEMBLY
NEW

OCEAN TREATY ORGANIZATIONS REPLACING THE 1947

IOTO	POTO	AOTO
INDIAN	PACIFIC	ATLANTIC
MUMBAI	TOKYO	DAKAR

WORLD E-WASTE CENTER IS AUSTRALIA, IN LAKE EYRE BASI

BIRD-INSEC

EURAFRICA

EAS

NAIROBI TO NORTH
JOHANNESBURG TO SOUTH

BEIJIN
SYDNEY/MELBOURN

OTHE

VIENNA
WASHINGTON

ROME
LONDON

Eco-tax supervision, tied to the FAO in Rome, with

ROUND OCEANS
LYWAY SWATHS

ECURITY COUNCIL
ORK

REATIONS OF NATO, CENTO AND SEATO, NOT UNDER THE UN

ARTO	SOTO	INTO
ARCTIC	ANTARCTIC	INLAND SEAS OF WORLD
OSLO	SANTIAGO	MOSCOW

esearch to be done on disassembly, or…

LYWAY SWATHS

SIA	AMERICAS
O NORTH	MEXICO CITY TO NORTH
O SOUTH	BUENOS AIRES TO SOUTH

N CITIES

NAIROBI	GENEVA
PARIS	TOKYO

emography section too, is in/near Rome.

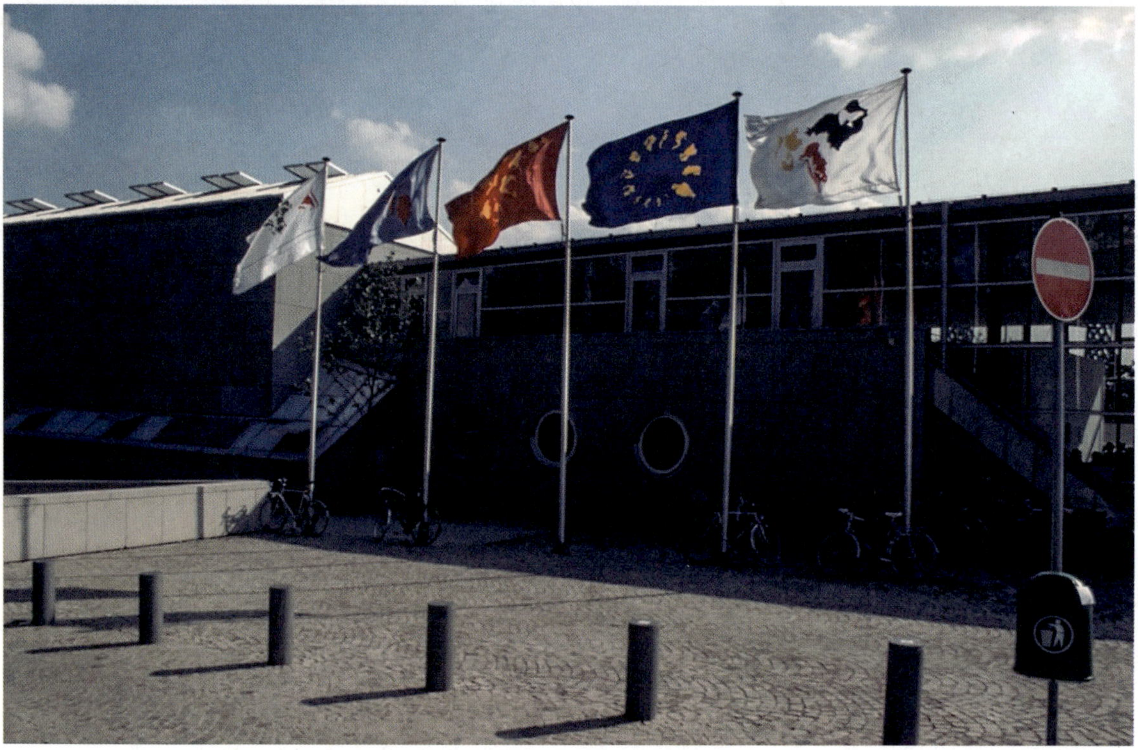

These flags for documenta IX, 1992, began with the flag for Europe from 1991 preceding from the same analysis of what elastically is called Germany in the Deutsche Historisches Museum. Based on thorough scientific research and Duchamp's urinal as antecedent and concept, the flags display new administrative spaces of water basins replacing the nation-states. Additional flags include one for Asia (red), North America, and the Southern Hemisphere.

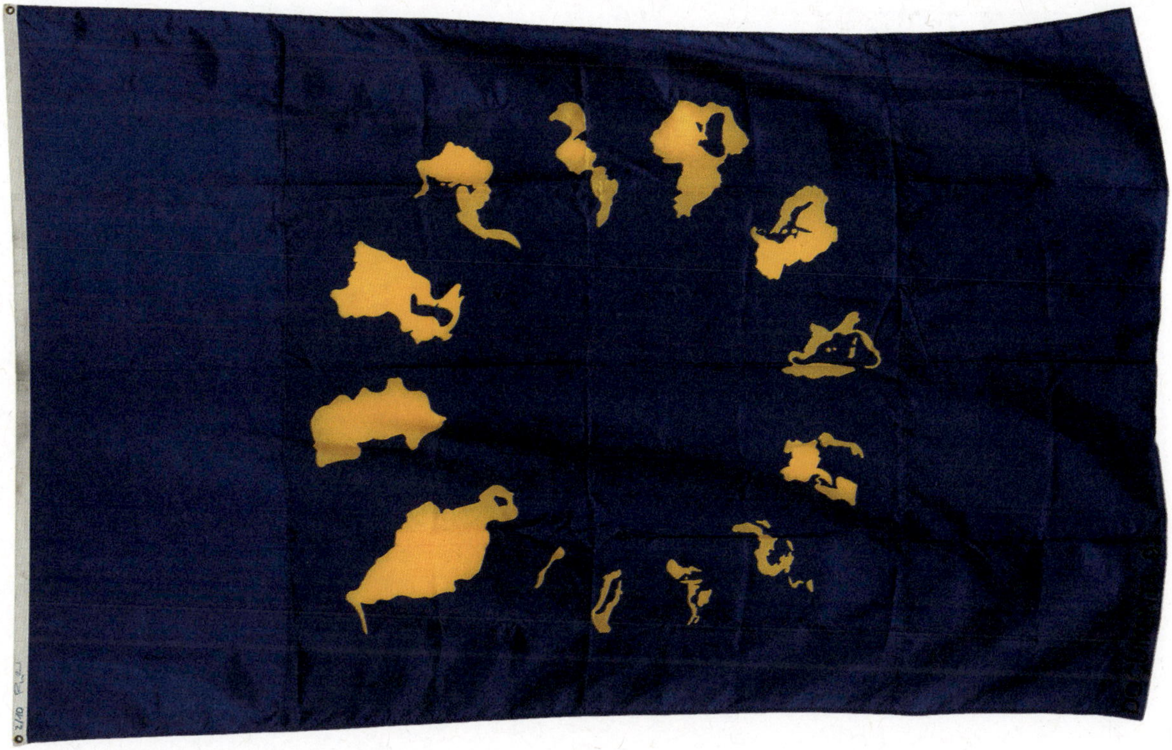

This flag displaying the water basins of Europe is prompted by Linda van Deursen making a similar chart of the existing member states of the European Union by size.

POLITICAL SYSTEMS IN WHICH TO LIVE

Democracy.
Voting is a universal right, and it determines what will be the policies of the government. Every citizen pays taxes in proportion to their ability to pay or assessed obligation to pay, but every citizen, regardless of financial or opinion power, has only one vote. In a pure democracy, the State has no voice in economic practices or status. US, France, Italy, Portugal, Switzerland. Tax avoidance or receiving benefits from the State undermine democracy.

Monarchy.
One person or family controls nearly all decisions of the State. Any business decisions of a person or family depend on the approval of the Head of State. People's Republic of China. Brunei. Russian Federation under Putin. Thailand. Any dictatorship is monarchical.

Constitutional Monarchy.
A democratic process, with voting, decides who's in the legislature and who's the chief executive, but all actions and ambitions are subordinated to the general will, and benign approval of the Crown. No one can dare to gain control of the State. Ambition is confined to different professions; the very successful will be knighted or otherwise rewarded by the Monarch, but can go no further. UK, Japan, Spain, Canada, Australia, NZ, Norway, Sweden, Denmark, Morocco. Dominance by one race or elite is assumed.

Communism.
As the symbol of Communism suggests, in hammer and sickle, the economy is run and owned by the workers and peasants. Of course, an administration is necessary, but these are elected by the workers and peasants in their councils. Any social stratification ensues from the administrators being exclusively educated. The tenure of administrators depends on the voting in councils by workers and peasants, who own the factories and fields.

Administration can easily become a dictatorship of the schooled elite. Being a capitalist or having any private business or investor-owned business is not allowed. At present, the the P.R. of China is not Communist at all. Any Communist society is primitive and rare.

Socialism.
Any society, including constitutional monarchies or democracies, in which very large adjustments to human economic and social competition are made, with massive transfers of money to the less successful, so that everyone has a safety net. The entire society receives benefits from the society's economic production, especially of essentials like energy and medicine. Many in the US would like socialism but are blocked from achieving that with extreme accumulations of wealth, hence political and political-media power, by capitalists. Many constitutional monarchies and democracies have socialist administrations and laws. Everyone enjoys a roughly equal baseline of economic and medical assurance. This usually requires a cohesive, fairly uniform society.

Fascism.
Derived from the Italian/Latin word "fasces," meaning bundle, a fascist society bundles business enterprise together with State authority and academic institutions (i.e., clergy) to form combinations of power under labels like "partnership." The partnership, or bundling, usually blocks out competitors to any of the bundled business companies. Fasces-bundling happens often in high-tech. It's common in California, and is standard business/state/university practice in the P.R. of China, the Netherlands, and small countries like New Zealand. China's state-run companies working overseas, like the Three Gorges Corporation, are fascist export ventures, with a monopoly on IP, state (tax) authority, and state-assured capital. Most of Elon Musk's "business" ventures are state-funded, blocking competition. The fasces bundling is most intense in the Netherlands, where a post-petroleum venture is fused from all the universities together with the

Royal-Dutch oil company, in "partnerships" with certain Big Oil "competitors," adopting a voice of exclusive authority, such that any challenger is told "you will not be allowed." The State dictates; everyone bows down.

Plutocracy.
Technically, rule by the rich. Most democracies are distorted by political contributions and direct propaganda mounted by the wealthy, recognized, and accepted solely or primarily due to their wealth. Zuckerberg in his campaign funding, Trump in running for President at all, the Koch Brothers in setting up think tanks and lobbies, all practice Plutocracy. Their wealth is used for political clout. They don't just relax and be philanthropists. Due to its very abusable tax code, and to Wall Street's capacity for piling up huge capitalizations on speculative business ventures, the US becomes ever more a plutocracy. Efforts at building a social safety net, or assuring equal opportunity, are afterthoughts. They're crumbs from the table. Plutocracy can be prevented with "campaign reform," but this almost never endures. The rich can always pay lawyers and accountants to find ways around the legal barriers, all for political as well as economic power.

Physiocracy.
This system of government and political economy differs from all the others, in one big way. It is not about the People. It is about the Nature, all the animals and plants on the land, in the skies, and in the seas, upon which the People depend.

Government of, by, and for the people is said to be accomplished properly by all the forms of government and political economy listed above. Xi Jinping believes he is helping the Chinese people, and even the world, as much as anyone ever did. Mark Zuckerberg believes that his plutocratic contributions to specific Congressional candidates helps the people of the United States, his country, very much. The worker-peasant committees in the Bolshevik Soviet Union thought they were achieving high industrial productivity with economic justice. But in every case, Nature—the world in which we humans have evolved, along with millions of other species is an afterthought. With Physiocracy, we have an economic program, with taxation and assessed efforts, all directed at preserving and even increasing the biological, or "physiological," wealth of the territory govern.

Physiocracy, in many versions, of course, is what we humans need now. Nearly everyone "knows" that we cannot continue living on the Planet Earth as we have. The other animals are disappearing, the oceans become empty of life, the lands dry up, the forests disappear: all that we depend on for existence is vanishing. So we become subject to plague.

As Martha Rosler correctly observed in 1985, in attacking me in front of her students as a "technocrat," yes, Physiocracy is technocratic.

That is, the Physiocratic government, like any patient of a medical doctor—such as Physiocracy's inventor, François Quesnay—requires a technocratic and scientific evaluation and management. One cannot provide medical care for a person with notions of democracy, or Communism, or socialism even. One must use the latest techniques of measurement and diagnosis, then the latest understandings on proper management, proper exercise, proper diet, plus good air and living waters.

Physiocracy allows for democracy in human affairs, but not in the assessment and management of land. By land is meant everything beneath our feet, in the waters and seas, and in the skies. There is very little doubt about what is good for our health, or the health of the plants and animals around us. The condition of the animals and plants in the seas and skies requires a Physiocratic regime. We have no choice… if we want to continue as a species.

Physiocracy was conceived in the final decades of the French Monarchy. At that time, there were very few instruments for measuring the ecological health of the land, its animals and plants. Sure, one could "see" a land well—managed or not, but one could not assign mathematical values to it. Now, and since the 1970s, we have had plenty of technology for mathematically-precise assessment. Therefore, since the 1970s, every society and community on the planet can develop a Physiocratic regime. The data for assessment can be easily obtained, at fairly low cost, by any group or even individual, so Physiocracy can be democratic. The data and any images or other proof produced from the data can be obtained and analyzed by anyone with some resources, but not a lot. So, we can have a technocratic but transparent government of territory.

Very often in human history, there's talk about "territorial integrity." This talk becomes shrill, turns into war with a crisis about borders between Ukraine and Russia. Physiocracy, in line with what we know about any physiological entity, recognizes a territory, as a site for living, and includes a body of water, with water cycles into the sky and back. So, water basins, and especially saltwater basins, are said to have "territorial integrity." A cue, even a paradigmatic icon, comes from what art historians in an international conference in 2005 said was the most influential artwork, or icon product, of the twentieth century: the Urinal, or "Fontaine," of Marcel Duchamp. Every body of land and water which has territorial integrity for Physiocratic rule is a freshwater or, better, saltwater, basin. A Physiocratic approach to the Ukraine-Russia border question is simple: identify the saltwater basins, and put them each under separate management.

By management or governance, we mean: taxation of the land, imposed on landowners or, if such are not present, on everyone, to compensate for any degradation or destruction or occupation of its Natural and biological well-being. Such degradation or destruction can be scientifically measured, with precise numbers, throughout any body of territory, in a pixel-by-pixel monitoring from satellites overhead or from measuring instruments in each stream going downhill. Since all the assessments and attendant imagery can be put on video, or the internet, in comparisons through time, we of Ocean Earth have called this TELEVISION GOVERNMENT. Taxes are imposed, and penalties are applied, according to what we see with multi-spectral and multi-sensor instruments. The seeing can be done by us, and by AI instruments. More and more people have a smartphone and a computer, so more and more people can watch their territory and its ecological integrity, and can visually see the detections and corrective actions of their televised government.

All the forms of government listed above have dangers. The fasces-bundling in the Netherlands is of course enlightened and non-violent, even if technically "fascist," in blocking competition, but it can be subordinated to a higher authority, of teledetection from space and in the waters. Even with such higher authority, a government can be democratic, or socialist, or even Communist. Probably, it cannot be as plutocratic or sharply class-divided as today, at least in the US, because the tax loopholes and indirect State subsidies that most of the rich now enjoy, including the oil companies with their US military support, oil-depletion allowances, and avoidance of payment for pollution, are no longer so easily able to accumulate lucre. They must pay, that year, for any assessed depletion due to their work. Thus we achieve ecological justice, necessary more than ever to our survival as societies on Earth.

About capitalism and the rich: with the single tax on land, hence on landowners and any communal territory around them, nothing blocks a wealthy person or group from enhancing the natural wealth, including vegetation, animals, insects, fish, and fungi of their property. If a wealthy person or group made a Paradise on earth, meaning—from the Persian—happy hunting ground of wildlife, then the tax burden would go down. That's fine. They would have spent their wealth on doing what the government must do anyway, assure the long-term ecological health of its territory. So, the rich can be with us, but they avoid tax only by doing what must be done for all of us anyway.

A controversial request, which I think is vital to keeping the people motivated, not lazy, is a very high tax also on inheritance. But every society is free to decide what to do about that. I propose a 100% tax on inheritance above $2 million, to assure as much equality of opportunity for everyone as possible. The task in society is not to make all people be equal, but to give all people an equal chance.

PHYSIO
CRATIC
STATES

SERVE THE BIRDS, AS THEY ARE ABOVE US, PHYSICALLY, AND AUTOMATICALLY SEE MORE THAN WE CAN SEE. ALIGN ALL PROJECTS NOT WITHIN STATES, BUT WITHIN FLYWAYS. THE DISASTER AT CHERNOBYL AFFECTS BIRDS ON THE NILE, ALL THE WAY DOWN TO LAKE NYASA.

For human beings to take action toward restoring pre-modern populations of birds, insects, fish, and wild mammals to pre-industrial levels. They must define economic value in what is vaguely called "Land."

By "Land" we mean the surface on which we walk.

The birds and insects can fly above the land.

The fish move beneath the deeper parts of the land, in streams, in lakes, in the sea.

We mammals tend to be on the land, or if in the water, near the surface.

To assure habitat for all the species, and so assure their proliferation, we human mammals must define value in Land, and must assess taxes or public-finance charges on that land.

For less than two centuries, people, and governments, have assumed that capital and labor have value, but land is fairly cheap. One can do with land what one wants. This assumption could prevail because of a surrogate for land, albeit coming from beneath the land, called fossil fuels. With economic activity made possible by fossil fuels, we could all forget about land as the substrate upon which we depend.

But now we know that (1) fossil fuels will be used up, and (2) fossil fuels, when consumed and burned, could destroy us. We know they are not a reliable or durable source of wealth.

Another surrogate for land, called nuclear fuels, made dangers worse.

We return to land as soil, emerged and submerged, as our source of wealth.

Today, we have technologies for evaluating land and water, both what is emerged and what is submerged. These technologies are easily accessed. They are public. They have a uniform standard anywhere in the world. The technologies are: remote-sensing satellites of civil grade; water-quality sensors, especially for suspended elements. These technologies can be systematically made use of everywhere in the world.

We can therefore start monitoring and assessing conditions on land emerged, and in waters above what's submerged, to decide what is the value of some land and waters to us all, and what therefore should be a shared cost, a tax base, for owners of land to pay.

We return to an idea from over two centuries ago that only landowners should pay tax. This re-opens the question of what is owned by no one, but maybe by the State.

Thinking thus, we introduce what some might say is a new tax. We'd say it's a replacement of the income tax, value-added tax, poll tax, state lotteries (a form of tax), and most other fees for government.

State fees are inevitable. They steer the economy. Will the economy be steered towards restoring the numbers of birds, insects, fish, and mammals of a few centuries ago?

This system of land management will be adopted where:

(1) existing jurisdictions for government align with water catchments;

(2) the people urgently want a restoration of birds, insects, fish, and wild mammals, possibly due to fright from COVID-19;

(3) civil-satellite data and water-quality sensors are widely available, already well-archived, and professionally used;

(4) the economy and reputation of the area depend on the strength of the soil and numbers, in the water, of fish.

Now, due to the worldwide fright about pandemics, which everyone can see are due ultimately to environmental degradation, the wipeout of normal numbers of birds, the insects they feed on, or fish, as well as the near disappearance of most mammal and marine-mammal populations.

Everyone "knows," if only instinctually, that humanity cannot survive such an ecological decline. But who will be persuaded to adopt a new tax? Who is ready to replace the income tax, or supplement it even, as a main state-revenue source with a price on land according to its loss of ecological vigor?

Who is ready, in sum, to set up a Physiocratic State? All this, in line with the principles for government described by the founder of Physiocracy, the first systematic economic theory. On seeing the health of the people, the physician concluded that the well-being of a nation depended on the health of the Land. The physician, writing in the early eighteenth century, did not yet know about what has become a huge delay in recognizing land's essential role: the use of mineral fuels, both fossil and nuclear.

Who is ready now to follow the physician's advice?

We present scenarios, being desired historical events, for these places.

(1) Italy, starting with Sardinia and Sicily, maybe Cortina d'Ampezzo, in 2020 suffering the highest mortality rate from COVID-19, all thoroughly mapped in its seawater catchments, all within a jurisdiction, a state territory, framed by a high mountain ridge

(2) Norway, which drains almost exclusively from high mountains to one ocean current, over a great length, with many bay and fjord basins, and rely for their national identity on great numbers of fish and marine mammals

(3) the many dam catchments, needing better long-term practices, of a fast-growing megalopolis, Moscow-Nizhny Novgorod (Upper Volga Basin); this area has pre-existing administrations for the dammed basin; could an eco-tax be acceptable to the people, to fund changes?

(4) Lake Chad Basin, with already a UN-mandated Commission du Bassin du Lac Tchad; the basin is not entirely enclosed, as it somehow drains also into a much larger and multiply-administered watershed, that of the Niger River; but a practice here, enforced with satellites and water sensors, could effect a stunning post-colonial practice in Africa

(5) Congo Basin, which has a watershed-aligned boundary for most of Zaire, all around, and is ripe for an entirely new scenario of soil and animal protection

(6) Munich, a part of a proudly-independent Bavaria with a watershed of the Isar and the Wurm river almost entirely inside Bavaria, but for a mountain fringe in like-culture Tirol; Munich is eager for world fame, and the Eres Foundation there could promote such governance

(7) Greece: we asked a Greek economist; this is possible if each island and each of the many bay catchments were identified and administered for ecological health, including fisheries; could Greece pioneer a move beyond the current obsession

with income and GNP?; we've mapped the peninsular and island nation thoroughly; foreign influence comes from a part of Bulgaria and Northern Macedonia, which might agree to "join."

One might wonder if such a list reflects global ambitions? Not really. There are no global ambitions for ourselves. We do not seek the "global governance" described for a while by Xi Jinping. We do not seek a "governance" by anyone. We agree with the view, stated by Abraham Lincoln, that a government should be of laws and not of individual persons.

The laws here applied are already well formulated. Many of the overarching laws come from the United Nations Environment Program, especially its Regional Seas Program, started in 1974. There are also laws about the mapping and management of saltwater catchments, called "hydrometric areas," that were legislated in the Republic of Ireland in 1959. We accept the notion of a United Nations, founded in the 1940s. All political entities in the world should be subordinate to such an authority, in its laws and not necessarily its persons.

A version of a Physiocratic State, being dedicated to preservation of living resources in a saltwater catchment (prior to dammed catchments), all for sustainable economic reliance on those living resources, has already existed. It was Prince Rupert's Land, being the entire catchment of the Hudson's Bay Company, functioning as an economic and public-finance unit that's also a government. It existed peaceably from 1670 to 1870. It only dissolved with the creation of a pan-continental British North America, or "Canada," after the pan-continental Union of the neighboring United States was preserved, in 1865. How controversial or "technocratic" would an updated version of a Prince Rupert's Land administration be? And, what if such a version of basin administration assured the people living there of large numbers of birds, the insects they feed on, fish, and game mammals?

A tax on ecological stresses on one's property would not be onerous; it would be part of making sure that the natural splendor thrives.

SETTING UP A PHYSIOCRATIC STATE WITH ECOLOGICAL-DEPLETION TAX ON LAND IN WATER BASINS, AND ON TRANSPORT MACHINES AND BUILDINGS BY AREA OCCUPIED AND FUEL-TYPE CONSUMED

1.
Define, in detailed topographical maps (which usually exist) a freshwater or saltwater basin to be managed as a Physiocratic State (PS). This is easy to do. Any part of the world can thus be mapped, in its basins.

2.
Overlay on these maps all indications of private property and of state property, e.g., roads, and the names of all private or state property holders.

3.
Acquire and assemble earth-observation data, from civil satellites, ideally of one or two satellite companies, for coverage of the entire mapped area. Do this for the earliest year when the satellite data became available, then much more recent years, e.g., the last calendar year, preferably during green-growth months.

4.
With experts in vegetation observation and assessment using satellite data, develop assessments of vegetation health (if any) based on each pixel, at each pixel.

5.
Prepare to receive later data, from a comparable time of year, for the same sites.

6.
Conduct "change detection" for a visual display of changes.

7.
Impose eco-tax pixel by pixel according to "vegetation vitality" readings, or simply chlorophyll readings, such that structures and pavement, as detected, have max tax, or zero vegetation, and there's a gradient upward for grass, then interspersed trees and bushes, then dense forest.

8.
An exception occurs only with covered farm fields of one-level. Imagery of soil conditions beneath the covering, made at site, leads to an adjustment. The adjustment is not proportionate to site because the overhead covering prevents access of birds, insects, and small wildlife to the soil: there's a net reduction in ecological vitality.

9.
Covered vertical-farm systems, with artificial light and water supply, are taxed highly, but not "max," because they occupy land that could otherwise be of living, microorganically active soil, contiguous with soil outside.

10.
The low end of all streams and rivers, including saltwater bays, are monitored for phytoplankton or microplankton, and are taxed to the extent that biota that would normally be present are not. Reduction in riverlife due to dams is especially noticed, and a tax is applied to the entire catchment upstream, as general basin tax borne by the territory upstream.

11.
Farmed and grazed fields have regularly changing vegetation cover, so observation and assessment should be as frequent as economically feasible throughout the year. An average figure on vegetation vitality and thickness can be reached mathematically. This average can be debated. Color, all based on the mathematically precise multi-spectral sensing, can be decisive. If mathematical sums are required with income tax assessments, hues—all having a mathematical basis in each spectral "reading" among many from

a single date flyover of an observation satellite—can lead to eco-tax assessments.

12.
While human eyes can grasp what's going on, automation and AI vision systems can handle most of what's surveyed frequently during each year. Good health of the soil and the waters is the goal. Tax assessments are made to support that goal. Procedures as in any "landscape painting," are both exact and inexact.

13.
With transport machines, notably vehicles, aircraft, and boats, taxation is assessed according to area (amount of land covered) times consumption of any polluting fuel. Owners of the machines pay the tax for each machine. This procedure can continue with any polluting fuel consumed by buildings.

14.
Tax revenue required for government is decided, or calculated, by the finance ministry. Every landowner and moving land or building owner will pay some tax simply for cost of government, but the amount of the tax differs according to the extent of ecological depletion, both at each pixel and in each catchment.

15.
Government functions to preserve the integrity, or ecological and physiological health, of the basin-defined territory. The more the landowners and moving land or building owners improve the vitality of their vegetation and wildlife, or simply gardens and forests, the less tax they will pay. Ideally, savings in the tax burden are shared with the workers at each property tract. Thus, the workers have an incentive to earn more by improving the health of the land even more.

16.
To discourage a devil-may-care attitude towards property, inheritance is heavily taxed. No individual can inherit a fortune of more than $2

million. One can be generous to one's children while one is alive, but after death, they should join the others in society in the struggle to survive. An inheritance of many millions is unkind, not just to the community but even to the legatees. They would lose the chance to keep their minds sharp and souls engaged.

17.
Because of the "import unique," or single tax on land, moving land, and fuel-consuming buildings, there is no chance for tax-deductible contributions to any charity, church, or institution.

The state does not subsidize what should be strictly-private entities. This spares society the entrenchment of interests and inability to evolve that results from what we now call "philanthropy." Of course, a wealthy individual can give money to a university or museum, etc., but that's no way in which to avoid one's tax obligation. A result of non-deductibility would be cultural, academic, and medical practices which are more responsive to our needs today. Deductibility has led to conservatism, even inaction, in culture and art. With ecological-depletion taxation, the splendor of the land and all its structures thereon become Objective Number One.

Peter Fend, presuming to practice architecture, as defined by Alberti, assuring quality of air, water, transport, and defense, in any territory inhabited by humans, among many other species

2022: ENTIRELY-NEW TAXATION

You can never escape taxes, the saying goes, although Amazon, Apple, and other Big Tech firms built businesses by doing that (they'll never die, also?), but in 2022, according to a session of the Financial Times Global Boardroom, the whole planet is going to have major tax reform.

This will be negotiated, people say with assurance: a global minimum tax for corporations, already signed on for by 137 UN member states.

In effect, for any business enterprise anywhere, there's a "floor" of tax obligation no matter what.

And this would be worked out as something like a fifteen percent rate. The OECD, a league of rich UN member states based in Paris, says that a firm "floor" can be set within the year.

Okay… and who's deciding what the profit on any business deal was?

Amazon famously avoided paying all manner of taxes when it bought Whole Foods by borrowing money for purchase, then writing off the entire enlargement as a "loss." There was no need at all to borrow any money: the debt was fake. Won't there be plenty of tricks still around?

The OECD forgot about what everyone (even pro-business groups) is now calling for: a carbon tax.

Enter OEDC: Ocean Earth Development Corporation.

A carbon tax, OEDC says (and has been saying formally through a subsidiary called TVGOV) can be elaborated into an ecological-depletion tax. The tax is on LAND, both as owned tracts and in a drainage basin, and on MOVING LAND, being things that move around and use up fuel. The tax is assessed on moving land by type of vehicle/boat/aircraft plus fuel consumption according to type of fuel (even if electric), plus land-area filled. The tax is assessed on land by "technical means of verification," chiefly observation satellites, also water-measuring equipment, air-measuring equipment, and run-off-readers at the low end. How much is a tract becoming less fertile and animal-plant rich than it was before people settled there? In many places, like big cities, the assessment is "max tax."

Many aspects of an ecological-depletion tax can be argued. The job now in history: to try it. With a concise place with known contours, and great variation in land use, some urban, some wild, develop ways of assessing the amount of degradation from raw Nature, with its abundant Oxygen in air and species all around, that should be paid for by the occupants?

All efforts are directed at making taxation unavoidable. One can pay more or less according to how one is using up and damaging the ecological resources, such as air, water, and wild-species habitat, of a place on Earth. This puts huge pressure on famous evaders like Amazon: all the trucks, airplanes, cardboard packages, and warehouse space surrounded with pavement must pay now for their burden on Nature. To demonstrate the potential of OEDC TVGOV right away, we could make eco-tax assessments on and near two giant Amazon warehouses, and surroundings, being built very nearby, in Long Island. Any such venture, and any energy-consuming business activity, must pay for its burden on our common air, water, wildlife, and soil. Eventually, such assessment and payment could be conducted throughout a global ecology treasure, the real Amazon Basin.

A new role of Art can begin. The tax is assessed chiefly with colors.

Political Power consists of the Power to Tax.

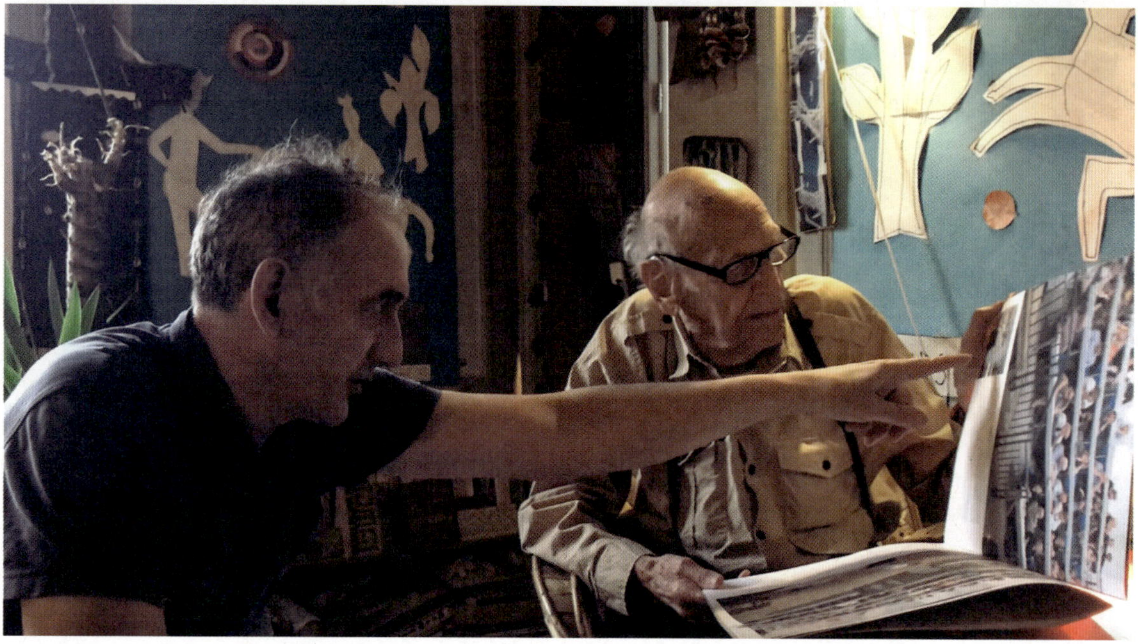

Pictured here is Peter Fend meeting architect Yona Friedman in 2018 at his apartment in Paris to discuss physiocracy.

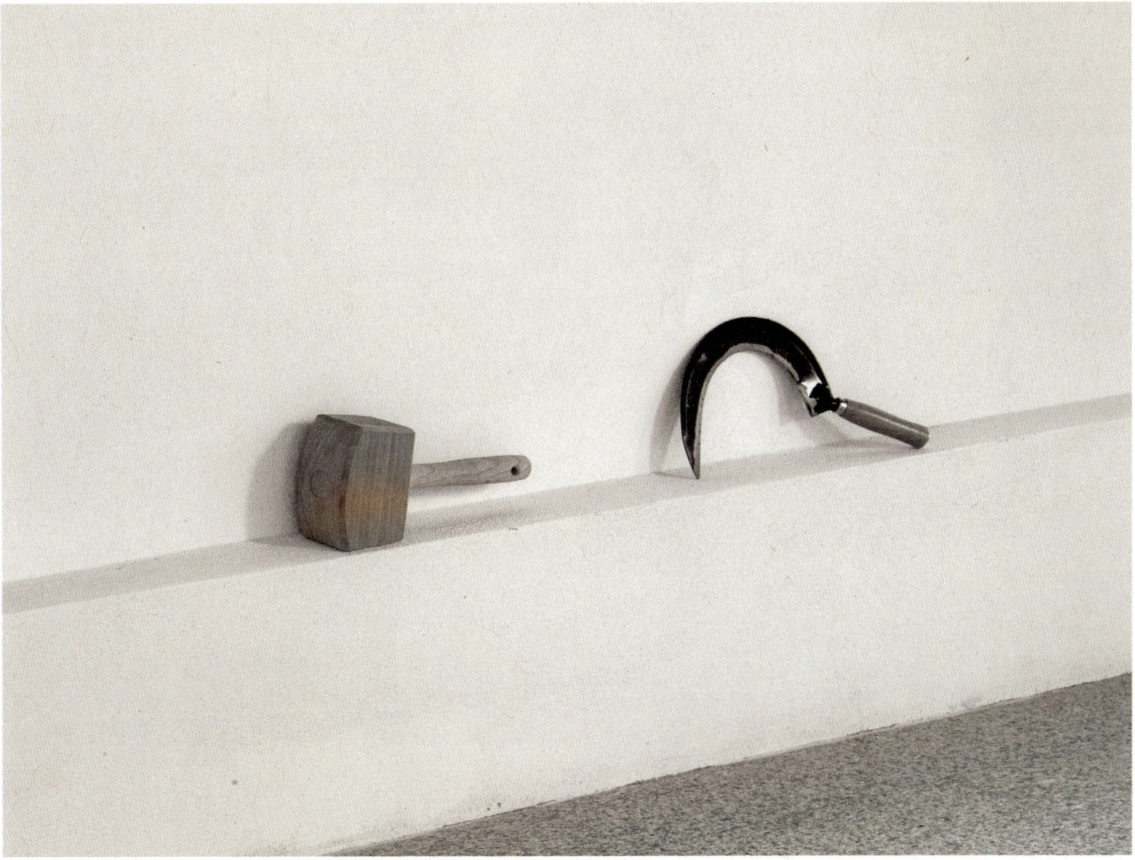

This photograph shows a hammer and sickle, the tools needed in harvesting and mashing waterplants for biodigestion to create biogas arranged in the exhibition “Africa–Arctic Flyway” at Museo Nivola in Orani in 2019.

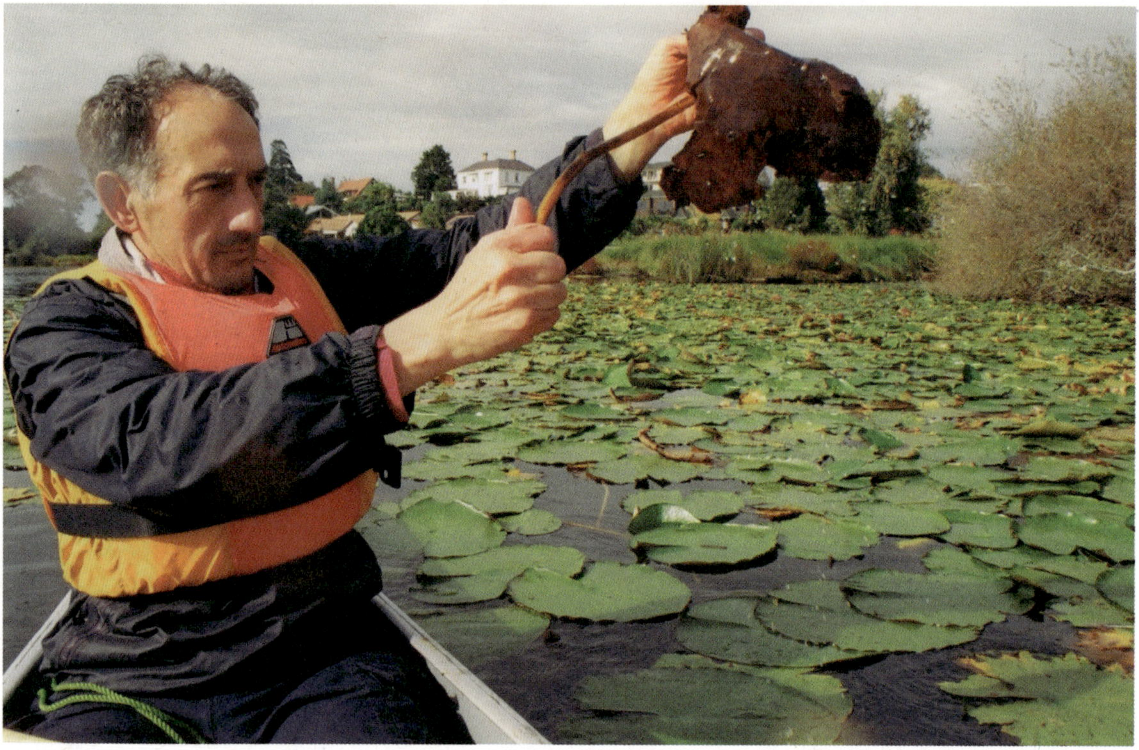

The above explains the wooden hammer and sickle that was shown at the Yinchuan Museum of Contemporary Art in China in 2018 and later at Museo Nivola in Sardinia. Hammer and sickle are needed all day for any seaweed or waterplant-harvest regime. This photograph was taken by Adrienne Livingston, an ecologist and stakeholder in Ocean Earth New Zealand, and shows Fend harvesting in a dammed reservoir in Hamilton with permission from the city government.

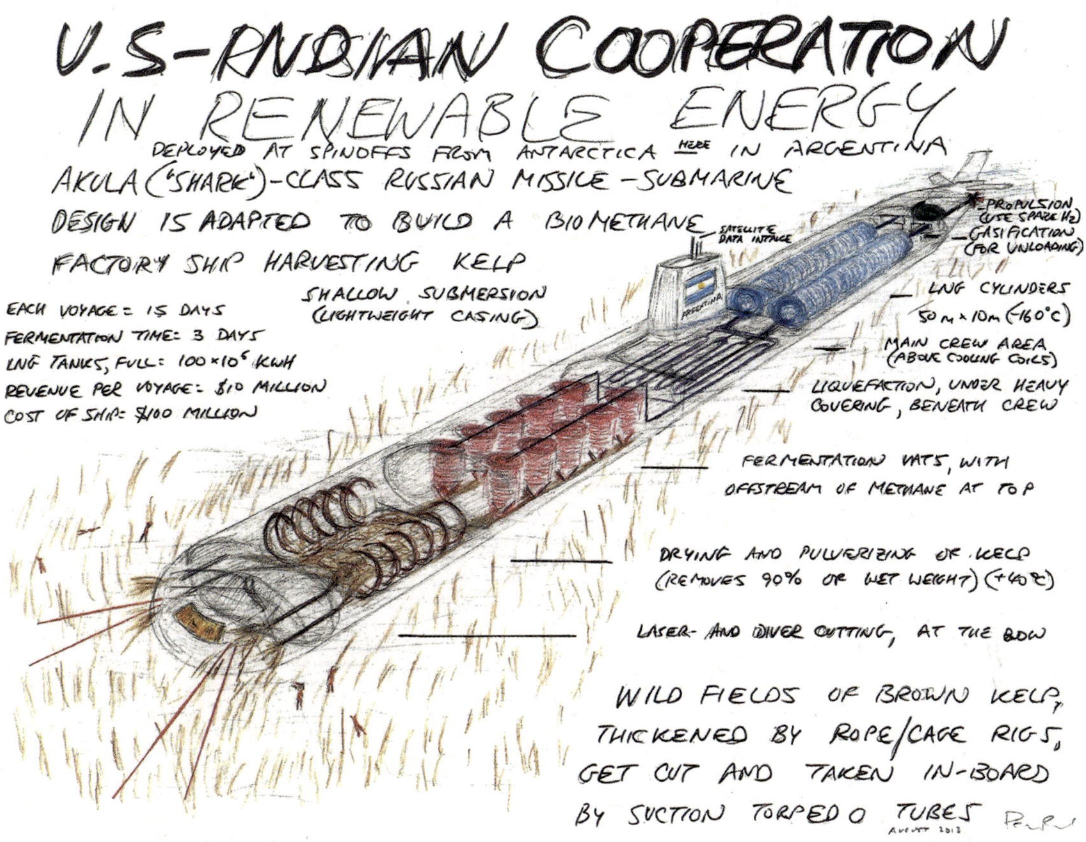

Initially, this drawing was about US–Russia cooperation in a global energy supply crisis and was first shown at White Columns in New York. In 2012, given evident shifts in friendships, this scenario for a biomethane factory ship harvesting kelp was modified into US-India cooperation, as India has a license to build the same submarine from Russia. Versions of the drawing, usually with a different national flag for a client, have been commissioned and sold a half dozen times. Also, a giant twenty-meter wall painting of the submarine has been made twice, once for ZKM in Karlsruhe.

ART AND THE "MEANS OF PRODUCTION"

If art is new, shockingly so, even to be condemned and censored, then there's a premonition of, or indication of, a new attitude towards material reality.

To achieve a desired material reality, there are what Marx called "means of production." These are means by which a society secures material well-being.

If the art is new, then it points to a new "means of production," or another manner of achieving, as defined, a material well-being.

Those who already have a material well-being, especially in the leisure mode, where they don't have to work for someone else, or be alienated from themselves, in order to enjoy the material well-being, are MORTALLY AFRAID OF NEW ART. They intuitively and instantly sense any danger to their present material well-being, with its underlying "means of production," which inevitably change the "social relations."

This explains why almost everyone who collects art, buys and sells art, or curates art, or does critiques about art, almost everyone involved in the "art world," and everyone who takes pride in having a Collection of art works, WILL DO EVERYTHING POSSIBLE TO PREVENT THE NEW ART FROM EVER FULFILLING ITS ARTISTS' OBJECTIVES. They do not want any consequent change in "social relations."

The artist who is lauded and treasured will never be allowed to fulfill any of what is intended in the work he or she produces, even if it is chokingly or significantly "new."

Any artist who is new, be that De Maria, or Matta-Clark, or Burden, or Beuys, or Oppenheim, or Schneemann, or Serra, or Cameron Rowland, must, according to those who buy, collect, laud, and appraise the work, never be allowed to make of any that work help guide the "means of production" in society, or have any practical function with the society's economy, or even ecology.

This may mean that an artist with a new material attitude, leading to a new means of production, must go work for an enemy or rival of the society from which he or she comes.

ABOUT LABOR

There's dignity in labor, in the Nature, and there's indignity in the "work," when it's just racing with robots in a warehouse, or repetitious motions on an assembly line. The quality of work is a vital question. My work in the Fulton Fish Market and elsewhere in the fishing industry was great: I saw life in exchange between species, among the elements and weather; I got plenty of exercise; I joked with the co-workers; I could think on my own. And none of it was in a gym. No doubt manual labor in the cold or heat of outdoors, and with real fish and real marine mammals making their last motions of life, has a huge impact on one's evaluation of LABOR, of ECONOMY, of BEING A HUMAN ANIMAL.

I noticed the same when cutting waterplants in the Ruhr reservoirs. I was getting as much exercise as the corporate executives who were jogging, but my exercise was more in the Nature, more healthful for the river, more real. And the art curators said that my proposal, for more people to work in the reservoirs, would not be allowed, because people who are educated may not take working-class or physical-labor jobs. Maybe that should be required.

It worries me that my daughter only gets internships with professors, so she is always cut off from our biological reality. I need to stress, more strongly, that Herman Melville didn't write "Moby Dick" by being on internships.

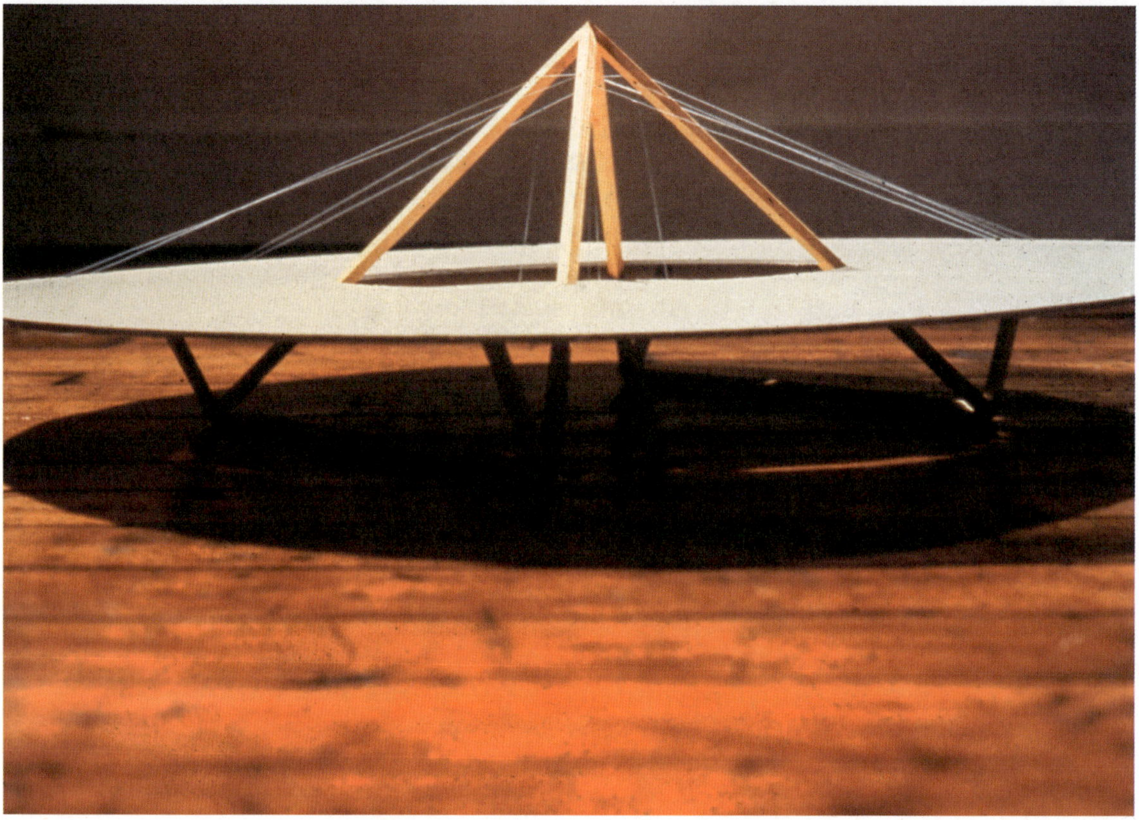

The above photograph depicts the model Peter Fend was carrying at JFK's Pan Am Terminal, which attracted the attention of some six Russian oceanographers in 1980. The model was based on work with Gordon Matta-Clark, who in turn was largely working with ideas from Russian Constructivism. Fend was combining Richard Serra's sculpture *T.W.U.* with notions of a counterweighted split building, with halves going away from an apex (*Splitting*). Serra had been told: as of that time, he was threatening to sue Fend for using his *T.W.U.*, as if everything in it were his IP; he told Fend in 2000 that he appreciated Fend's architectural use of his sculpture, so he would not sue. As for Matta-Clark, he was dead; any "authorization" to proceed with his attempts was given by his widow Jane Crawford over twenty years after he died, with Fend's chapter in an exhibition catalogue dedicated to the drawings of Gordon Matta-Clark published by Generali Foundation in 1997.

ARMORY SUPPLY

Produced in response to a request for a proposal for an exhibition at the Park Avenue Armory in 2016, not knowing that the curators were under British control.

The military question today becomes evermore occupied with ecology. The integrity of a territory, its defense against damage, becomes more about the arrival of fresh water and clean air (or even enough birds, fish, and bees) than about the arrival of foreign troops.

We see this now where wars rage: Afghanistan, Syria, Gaza Strip, Iraq, Somalia, and Ukraine, all regions with severe ecological damage and consequently struggling economies. If the drought in the US West continues, mere survival could become impossible: a state of emergency, even evacuation, could occur. Action is required. Think of it all in the context of what happened one hundred years ago: a war for control of mineral fuels. Now, address the result of that war, and its sequel: a global climate, groundwater, and air deterioration due to fossil and nuclear fuels.

As always in human evolution, cutting-edge art generates paradigms for use of materials, of land, of water, of ecology, that are applicable in its time. Art must be heeded. It must be put to use.

Mere planetary survival becomes the top concern. What tools does a country's military today need?

The tools, or technology, can come from art. Not all art, but the cutting-edge art since about a hundred years ago in Russia, the US, and Italy, dominantly. In art historical terms, these are Russian Constructivism, US Conceptual Art, Field Theory and Color Theory painting, structuralist film, Video and Digital Arts, and Italian Futurism ("fotodinamisme," territorial control by artists). There are influences from France, as in balloon-borne photography, or Germany, in ecology practices by Beuys, but the intellectual core comes from Russia and the US, chiefly, and Italy. For survival, for moving onward instead of down-and-out in history, we must put such cutting-edge art to use. The art gets converted into technology—to be developed by the military.

WORKS FOR USE BY THE MILITARY EFFECT INTEGRITY OF TERRITORY

Cycles to revive: of water, of nutrients, of wild animal migrations, of the sun, of climate, of what biochemist Carl Woese discovered, an exchange of methane-oxygen-carbon dioxide (CH4-O2-CO2) as central to life.

The structures are sourced in the US, derived from probes by artists Dennis Oppenheim, Mary Beth Edelson, Michael Heizer, Walter de Maria, Richard Serra, Gordon Matta-Clark (as he contracted and intended), Carolee Schneemann, Paul Sharits, Keith Sonnier, Robert Smithson, Marcel Duchamp (particularly during his US residence), Sol Lewitt (cycles), Vito Acconci, and—as the one person not living in the US (although met in the US and invited overseas)—Joseph Beuys. The last person's "Fat Corner" performance of 1977 leads us to a biochemical paradigm like that of Woese, also from 1977.

When the term "military" is given, recall what Napoleon said about military action: that it's a mastery of geography. Thus, his troops engineered ecological development projects, along with roadbuilding projects, wherever they occupied territory. To fight is not the aim. To improve and control land, or sea, is the aim.

TECHNOLOGIES FOR SALE TO THE MILITARY, DERIVED FROM ART

Rapid-setup footbridge, or vegetation/camouflage canopy. Russian Constructivist, Matta-Clark continues (1977–8).

Rapid-setup walls. Wide-strut connected vertical sheets of coil steel, up to three and a half meters wide wide (India). Unrolled and erected within an hour. Based on Serra; okayed by him.

Rapid-setup decks or roofs. Tripod, heavy block, and cables, when put together immediately a rigid plane as deck, or simply cover. Foundations not needed. Inspired by Serra "T.W.U." in 1979, confirmed by Acconci and Burden.

Immediate-use ultra-light waterwheel. Bicycle fork-mounted hydroelectric wide-rim wheel with Poncelet curve blades. Based on Duchamp (1914). Already, NZ troops in Afghanistan introduce micro-hydro to the people; further this.

Holdfast rigs for macro-algae, to yield biomass convertible to fuel (e.g., ethanol or methane for Navy). First tests by US Navy Undersea Warfare Center, 1970s. Continued under secret military contracts (learned in DC, 1998).

Designs by world-renowned naval architect Marc Lombard. Buoys and submergibility, with Australian Submarine Industries. A full-scale version shown in Tokyo; sea trials await.

Submarines for marine biomass harvest, conversion to gas. Our concept, but China already uses sub-marines to fish.

Moss Maritime (Norway) say they'd further develop on-board LNG storage for very small Swedish long-submersion Gotland-class submarines. Based on twin-hull design of Russia's Shark-class sub.

Sail-submarines for bulk haulage. Our concept, in response for need to not have engines that interfere with whales. Shallow, three-masts astraddle, tri-hull. Three wide-body hulls of Ohio-class (US) subs.

Rotary pentagon. Five-sided wheel set on axle across a canal or narrow river to scoop up floating vegetation. When designed for Canal Grande in Milan, awarded honor by Italian admiral. Cleans water for health and traffic.

Multi-channel canal. River flow fluctuates widely, mostly in dry regions. To prevent braiding and soil dumping, build walls for narrow channels, with one or all used, or even different directions of flow, as needs arise. Built by Iraq for diversion of Tigris/Karkheh waters into Karun, inside Iranian territory, 1985–6. Reportedly designed in Moscow. Original concept: Dennis Oppenheim.

Inter-basin channel. Easy to execute; just dig. Concept: Michael Heizer, "Double Negative." Can link sub-sealevel basins with nearby seas, expanding saltwater area and affording what a California scientist tests now near the Colorado River mouth: closed-sea biomass industry. If adopted worldwide, could reduce expected global warming sea level rise. Also yields biofuel, as US Navy tested.

Wallow constructions. Near salt flats (e.g., Nevada, Iran), install structures that absorb inflowing freshwater to become freshwater habitat, vital for migratory birds and wild land animals. Such structures, designed by Dennis Oppenheim and named "Dry Wells," "Bird Cage," "Death Hole," and "Downward Blows," were commissioned in 1977 for testing on-site in Iran, to be built by the Iranian Army. Such structures were included also in our response to a request by the Algerian Ambassador to France, who saw our satellite imagery of massive earthworks in the Iran-Iraq war zone, to then ask if such structures, and more, could be installed by the Algerian military to restore present desert to savannah. In both cases, an arid-country government sought an escape from aridity with "something like" what we know of Earth Art. Such wallow buildup is recommended by Alice Outwater in "Water: A Natural History." She says a mere startup by humans can be immensely improved by the natural wallow-building animals like buffalo and prairie dogs. Artists start the process; animals complete it, especially if they migrate.

Keratins as nutrient-supply for animal food chains. Can be produced from the urban/industrial waste stream, if a hydrocarbon mix is produced, through pyrolysis, and a single-cell protein culture absorbs it, with upgrade to keratin (e.g., feather) by membrane-mediation of cellular "information." Researched and site-tested in the UK, with proof of wild-animal uptake in ponds in Missouri. The keratins effect an "activation" of sites.

Balloon-suspended site monitors. 24/7 observation of habitat with multi-spectral sensors held in place by high-tech tethered balloons designed by QinetiQ, UK. Explored with scientists in Plymouth. Superior to drones in allowing exact change detection.

Very-rapid sequencing of spectral versions of a site often in side-by-side display, for comparisons, all mathematically registrable in 1256 gradient per band. Rapid "reading" of colors. Flickering to yield, or shake out, spectral anomalies. Best with data from different times, or sites. Color language, pioneered by Paul Sharits, approached with Global Feed with SeaWiFS and AVHRR data.

GLOBAL FEED. Oceanographic monitoring of planet with one km resolution data. Comparative currents or seas of Eastern and Western Hemisphere. Or, can compare currents at start and at end. Developed at Plymouth on world ocean-basin map centered on Antarctica, divided into four or five out splays. SeaWiFS global coverage offered for this at $100,000 per year. A world ocean-news service feasible with $1.5M.

Military history in relation to ocean-hydrological basins, e.g., Verdun, Stalingrad, Nomonhan, Dienbienphu, Saratoga, Gettysburg.

Towards an animal-behavior theory of war, from Wolfgang Wickler's untranslated (well-illustrated) "Stammesgeschichte und Ritualisierung."

Rowing equipment for marine industry, which can also be used in military operations. Catamaran-joined sculls. A revival of an ancient form of naval seamanship. It does not disturb ecosystems as motor craft do.

Immunology buildup for ecosystems, with electro-conductive rods placed equidistantly, e.g., ten m apart, to create a heightened immunogen-antigen polarity, or better ionic conditions for higher animals and plans. Evident in the Venice Lagoon, near power lines (observed 1995).

A similar project proposed by Dr. Mirella Orlandini in 2000. Discussed with conceiver and first builder, Walter De Maria, in 1977 or '78; he said that scientists had told him that such an array could improve ecological hierarchy. Artistic title: "Lightning Field."

Military history: civil satellite data processed to reveal Iraqi long-term strategy in Iran-Iraq War (with Russian help and evident use of American Earth Art designs), violations of SALT-2 at submarine bases, layout of mobile missile bases, forest clearings for jungle operations, routes of attack in the Falklands war and Israeli/Lebanon campaigns, site-engineering problems at Chernobyl, the rapidity of pan-territorial ecological collapse, e.g., North Sea. The conjunction of ecology and warfare can be seen.

TELEVISION
GOVERNMENT

THE MIRROR
SUPERSEDES
THE MASTER

The above was produced after a residency in Montenegro during the Kosovo War in 1998.

TELEVISION GOVERNMENT

TVGOV stands for "Television Government." It's a form of government, with attendant tax, border control, and defense, based on "technical means of verification," or observation satellites and on-site sensors. It results from how these instruments can record changes in soil, water, and air over time. The instruments are civil, with data easily accessed, so the means of government are democratic. Efforts toward "Television Government" started with the art firm Ocean Earth showing "Art of the State," soon afterward selling to global TV images of military positions in Lebanon and the Falklands. Such services continued for six years, but governments felt threatened—and shut things down.

With the growing capacity of digital data from civil observation satellites to be used for broadcast imagery in mass-media TV, there arises the possibility of Television Government.

The situation of the Planet can be known by everyone. We all can be informed of the conditions required for our well-being. Ever-greater capacity to solve problems, ever more frequent, will arise with new satellites in the coming few years from Germany, France, and Holland, with resolution of twenty, ten, or eight million pixels. No ecological mismanagement, no contamination of the environment, no military operation, no urban decay, no change in farming or land use, no mining, will remain undetected. Big Brother becomes known to us, and it is—via Television Government—us.

Now a new tack is tried: PHYSIOCRACY. As a governed area, every Physiocratic State is physical; any regular method of tracking physical changes can effect regular administration. A public finance system can emerge, with charges for any loss or depletion of territory resources. This is eco-tax: it's assessed in each pixel, e.g., of five m2, and in each water basin too. The eco-tax can replace income tax or value-added tax to pay for non-depletive administration. TVGOV.info, an output from Ocean Earth, can assure the durable development of where we live.

I speak here for a small group of pioneers, adjunctive to another small group of artists, which in 1979 coined the term "Television Government," being government of land and sea with observation data from space. The first group is of US citizens; the second, of mostly Latin Americans. We have studied the world, often traveling, conducting symposia, viewing data, to develop scenarios for TELEVISION GOVERNMENT, or PHYSIOCRATIC ADMINISTRATION, in these areas.

The worst enemies are within the allies. Geopolitically, Russia and China will try always to supersede the US. It's the game. The US is undermined in this by the Old Guard among its "allies." It must build new teams. Break away from Big Oil's hegemony, e.g., Holland. Nothing can be done as before. Surprise!

Coordination of OEDC and TVGOV
to establish

PHYSIOCRATIC STATES
IN WATER BASINS
ALONG BIRD FLYWAY ROUTES

II AFRICA–ARCTIC FLYWAY

B I R D S
R E I G N

N O   K I N G
E M P R E S S
E M P E R O R
&   Q U E E N
A N Y M O R E

N O W   T H E
H E A D   O F
A   S T A T E
C A N   F L Y

A N D   S E E
B E N E A T H
W H A T   W E
A T T E M P T

T H E Y ’ R E
O B E Y I N G
T H E   S U N
A N D   N O T
S O M E O N E

W E   O B E Y
T H E M   S O
T H A T   W E
S U R V I V E

O R   E L S E
P L A G U E S
K I L L   U S
Q U I C K L Y

B I R D S
R E I G N

H U M A N
S W A R M
M E E T S
T H E I R
N E E D S
T O D A Y

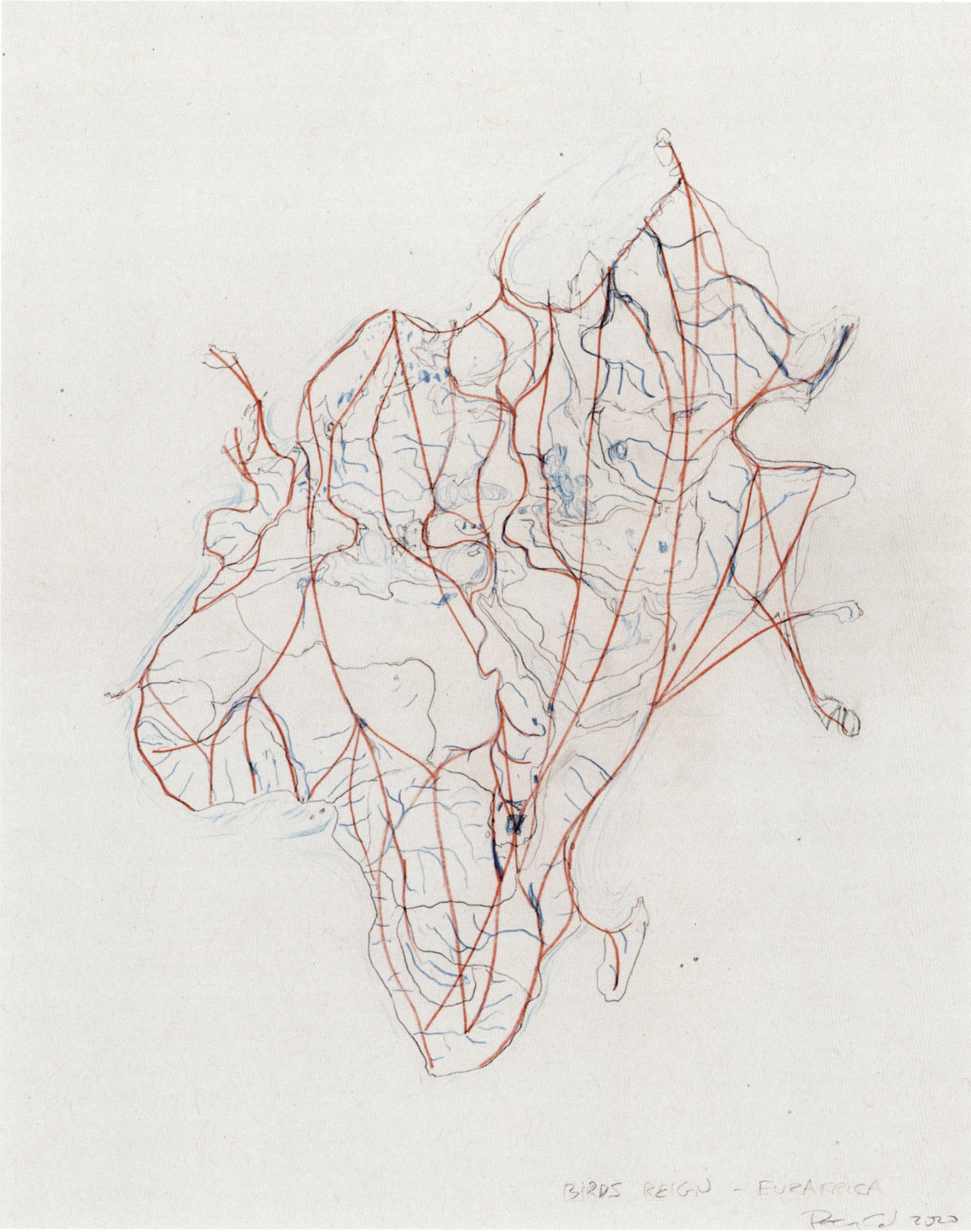

This drawing of the Africa–Arctic Flyway was produced for the Galerie Barbara Weiss for the exhibition "Birds Reign" in 2020. In the exhibition, the world is organized into three swaths: Americas, Eurafrica, and East Asia / Oceania.

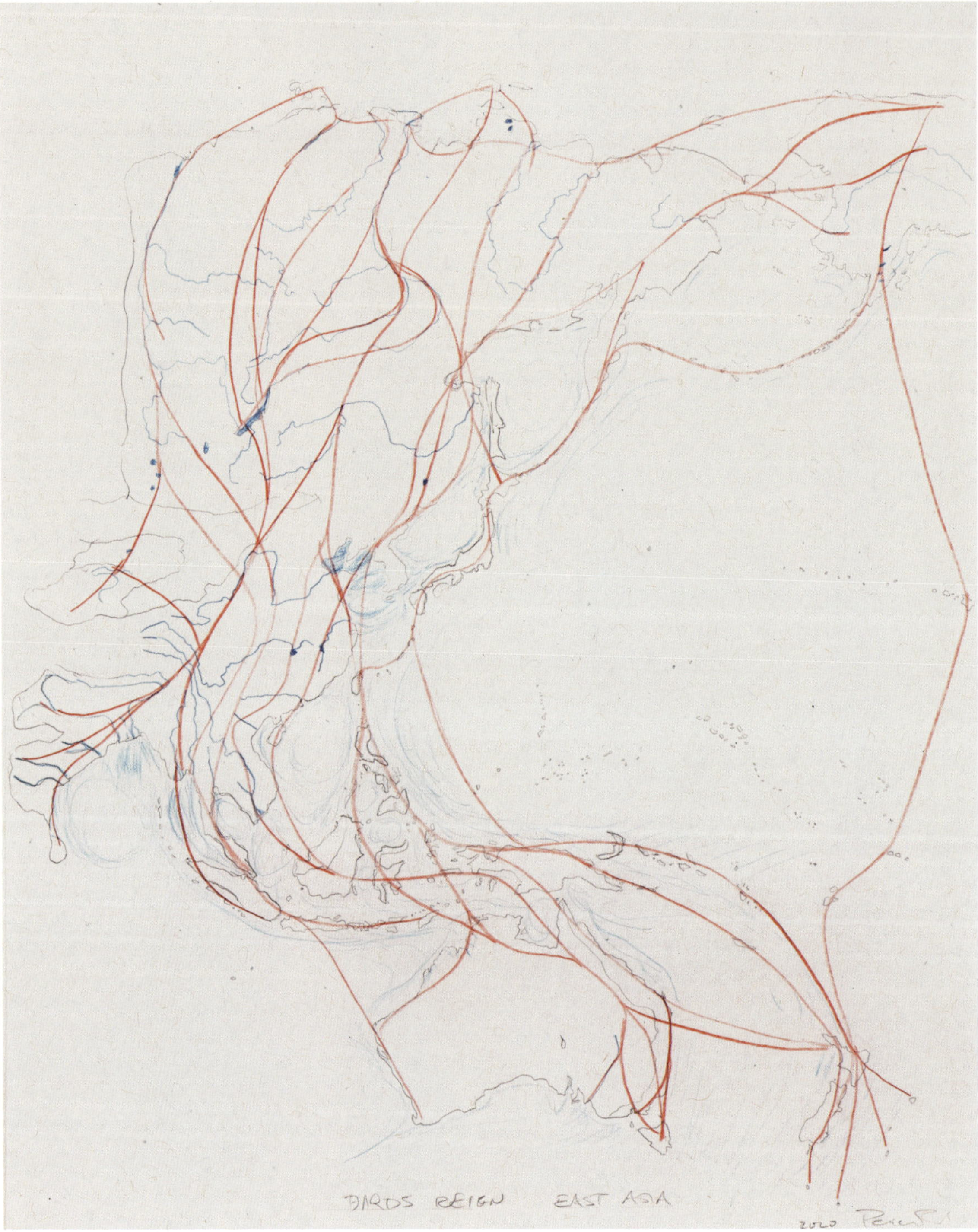

This drawing shows the East Asia / Oceania Flyways.

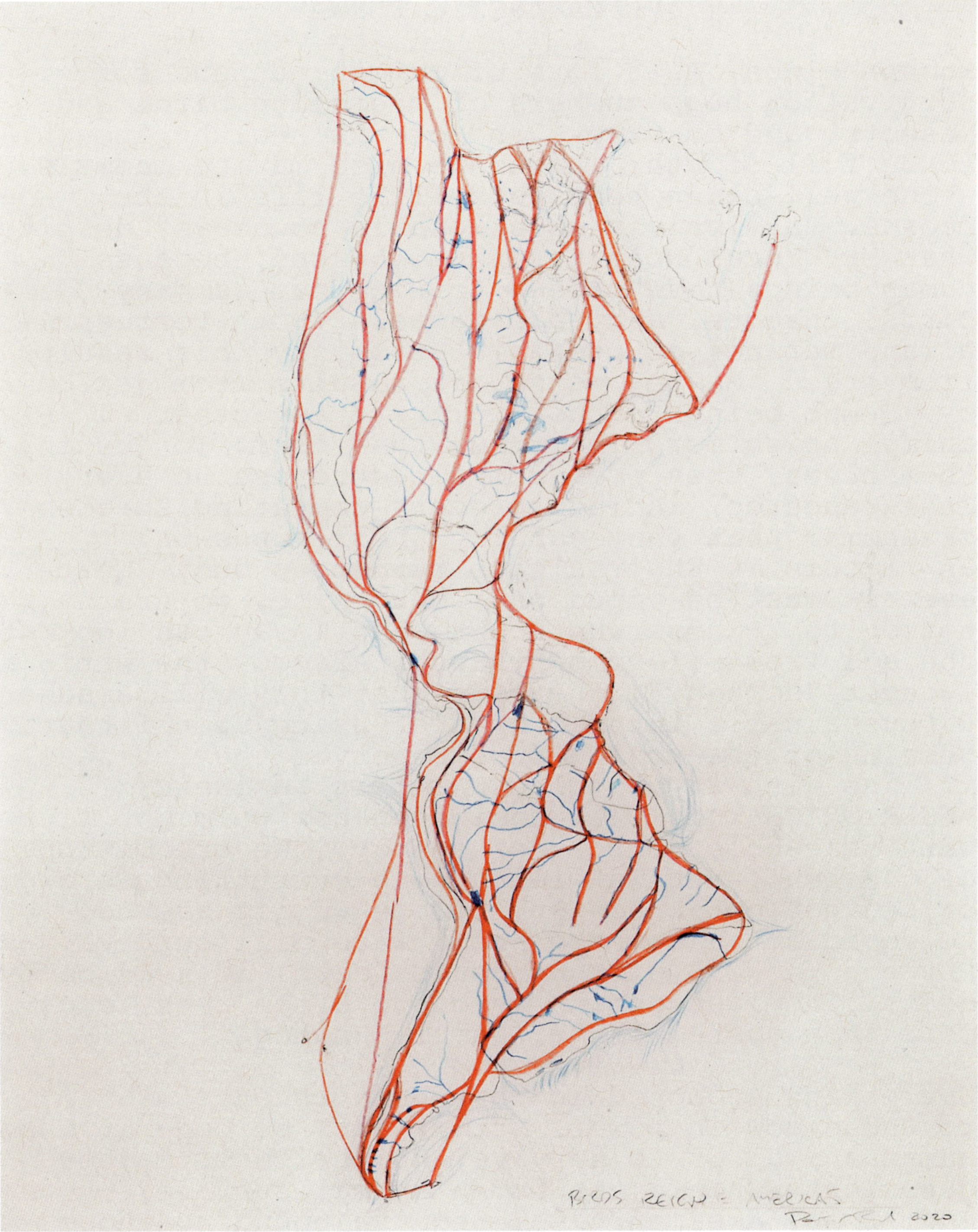

This drawing shows the Americas Flyways.

Human beings, as a form of mammal, depend for survival on huge numbers of migrating birds and insects, and on rivers and oceans healthy enough to be full of fish. There are also marine mammals, whose well-being helps stabilize life in the oceans. Survival is questionable nowadays, despite what Mr. Yuval Noah Harari might say, because human beings have chosen to wipe out as many birds, insects, fish, and mammals (both terrestrial and marine) as possible. Some say this results from greed. Maybe, worse, it results from jealousy. Human beings cannot tolerate any other animal being more important than them. To justify themselves, they feel compelled to use up every last resource, including every competing species of animal that they can lay their hands on, as if this is their always-murderous duty. Whatever is must be wiped out; otherwise, we are not on top. Those who doubt what I say can look at the ads from oil-company Saudi Aramco, the world's largest "company": they say that they will assure a "sustainable future" by first using up all that remains of the fossil-fuel reserves they possess, in line with anyone else in their business, AFTER WHICH they will decide on how we might live with renewable sources of energy. "We are on top of the heap, and we will use up everything we own, or can get our hands on, before we get around to deciding on how the human race will survive." Any challengers will be beaten down, if need be by death. The last option is quite often used, much more than just with Mr. Jamal Khashoggi.

Everything proposed in this book is onerous to those now in power, but it must be done if the human animal is to survive. Which itself raises questions. Should the human animal survive? And if so, does survival require upending those now in power?

In the proposition that humans could survive, we set about to restore migratory routes of birds and insects, all aerial animals, on the planet.

After that, we will work, on restoring what has been the huge numbers of fish roaming the rivers, lakes, and salt seas of the planet. A symbol for such urgent action could be the hero in the greatest novel of the United States: a marine mammal, a whale, named Moby Dick.

One can speak of what is above us, being the animals that fly, and what is below us, being the animals that swim. We are in between. Can we save their habitat and their ability to reproduce? Can we allow them a place in the world much bigger than ours? The skies above and the waters below?

There are three flyway zones in the world mostly for flights converging on the Arctic: Americas, Eurafrica, East Asia/Oceania. I proceed, in this book, outlining what can be done about aerial animals in their flyways and the corresponding water basins in one of three major flyway zones of the planet: the Africa–Arctic Flyway located in the Eurafrica zone.

If the Antarctic is at the center of the world's oceans, the Arctic is at the center—or final destination—of the world's aerial migrations. A few exceptions exist, for birds flying from the Equator south in Africa or South America, but these exceptions are rare. Notice, too, that the birds of Antarctica, the penguins, cannot fly at all. They join the fish and marine mammals in being swimmers.

In perhaps over-simplified terms, the Arctic is a center for the flying animals, and the Antarctic is a center for the swimming animals.

The three zones described here include flights from far, far south, in Patagonia and New Zealand, all the way to Alaska, Siberia, and Canada, on the Arctic Ocean.

The three zones are separated from each other by impassable barriers: the Himalayas and Gobi Desert, which divide East Asia from Eurafrica; the Pacific, which divides the Americas from East Asia except by the Arctic; and the Atlantic, which divides Eurafrica from the Americas, again except by the Arctic.

Recognizing such facts as birds do, then we would not indulge in the hubris of seeking a Pan-Eurasian union, or even a Belt and Road Initiative. We would concentrate instead on north–south movements of our aerial counter-parts.

Someday, maybe, we will describe the flyway routes in the Americas, which are largely sourced in the world's biggest and most valuable river basin, of the Amazon (not that delivery "company").

Someday, maybe, we will show the nutrient linkages between Australasia and Alaska via China, both Koreas, and Japan. But now, in this book, we portray the nutrient linkages, made by birds and insects, between Africa, even as far south as Lake Tanganyika, and Europe, often as far north as the Arctic Circle and Arctic Ocean.

The ten flyways are:
1. Atlantic coast
2. Rhone mouth to Rhine/Meuse mouth
3. Nigeria to North Cape
4. Donau/Oder corridor
5. Balkan Peninsula to Baltic/Kirkenes
6. Nile–Moscow corridor
7. Rift via Mesopotamia and the Caspian Sea
8. Eastern Gulf corridor
9. Indus Basin
10. West India

In this book, as the title suggests, "Africa–Arctic Flyway," we focus on the major flyway zone of Eurafrica. After looking at various sites on the African continent, we will present a series of specific site studies for the following flyways and locations:

FLYWAY 3: Nigeria to North Cape
Project Site: Baltic Sea basin; North Sea basin

FLYWAY 4: Donau/Oder corridor
Project Site: Adriatic Basins; west Mediterranean basin

FLYWAY 6: Nile–Moscow corridor
Project site: Gulf of Odesa; Crimean coast on Black Sea; Sea of Azov

FLYWAY 8: Eastern Gulf corridor
Project Site: Basin of the Gulf

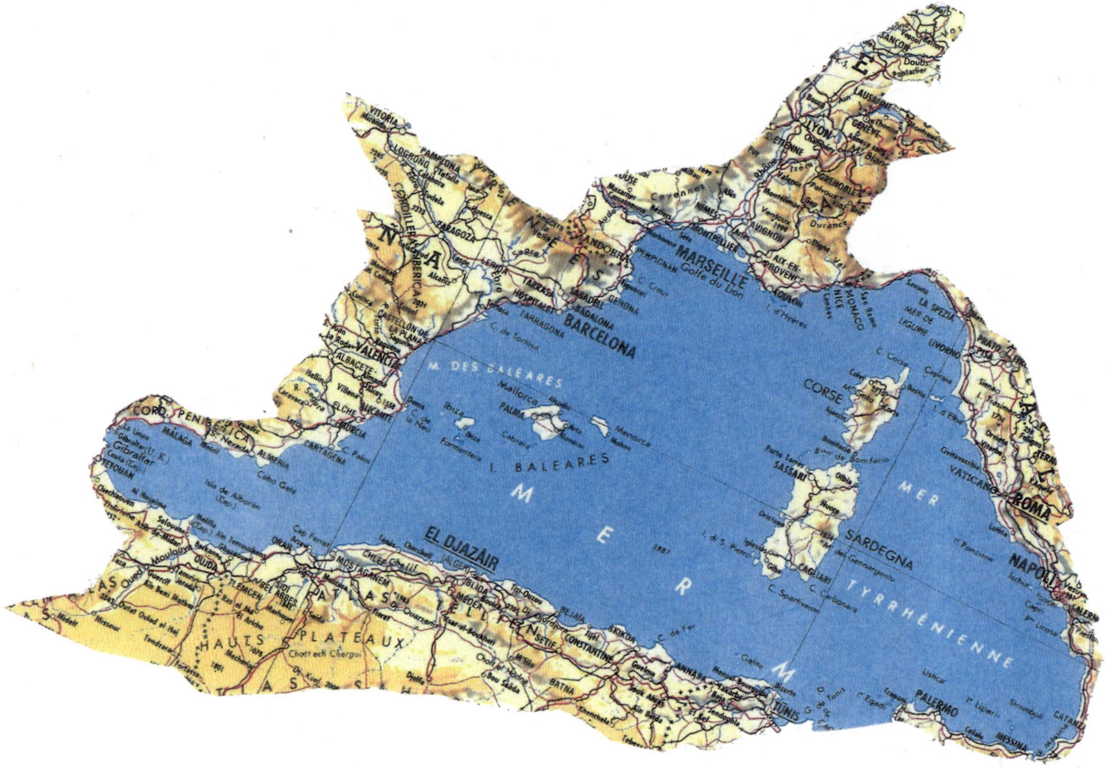

The very first seawater basin ever made by Peter Fend in 1978, in response to a request by Maja Hoffmann to Dennis Oppenheim for an ecological project on her property near Arles in Camargue. Fend wanted to identify the physical context for any such project. Many people have expressed tremendous rejection of such images as these break conventional ideas of what is an acceptable political unit, the nation-state. The central point in Vincent Scully's talk in 1977, titled "Garden and Fortress: The Shape of France," was that the nation-state is a geometric concept. There are implications from Earth Art that the nation-state can be replaced with another paradigm: the saltwater basin. The main problem of architecture is gravity. Water obeys gravity. When you deal with land, it is usually not flat; it is sloped. In doing any architectural planning, one has to work with slopes. Therefore water, as well as pollution, accumulates at the low end. Hence adding elevation has to be considered when thinking of the "Garden Fortress."

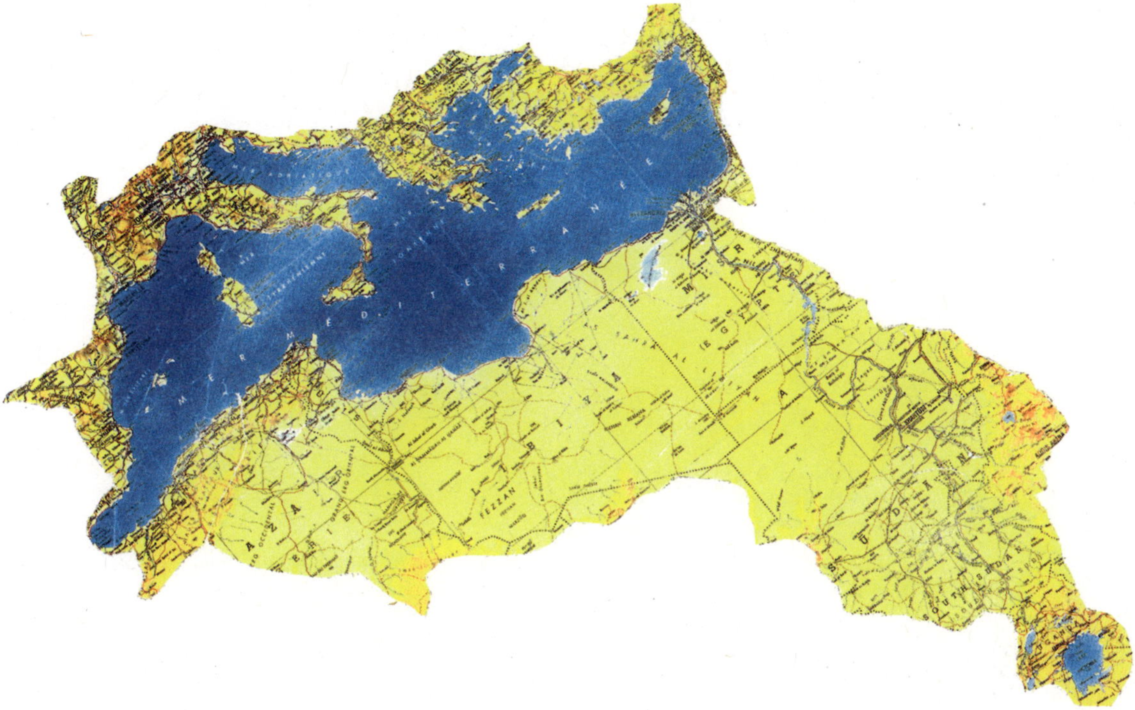

After identifying the west Mediterranean basin with its own circulation, one can very easily chart the entire Mediterranean basin. There is no artistry in this act nor any politics. This was done using arguments from Jack Burnham's *Beyond Modern Sculpture* and *Great Western Salt Works: Essays on the Meaning of Post-Formalist Art*. Only later did Fend full-on declare that each basin was a *Urinal* (after Duchamp). The first time the above was shown in 1981 to the public was in the "New York / New Wave" exhibition in the same room with David Byrne at PS1 Contemporary Art Center.

RELAY Telecast service of OECD 228 Front Street New York, NY 10038 212-732-7531 Telex 177817

Peter Fend Principal

Feb 6, 1981

Monsieur J. Ghesquiere
European Space Agency
Washington Office
955 L'Enfant Plaza
Washington, DC 20024

Dear Monsieur Ghesquiere:

In view of our scheduled meeting at the ESA Washington office this Monday, February 9, I present a brief explanation of our purpose.

I represent, as Principal, a business corporation comprised almost entirely of artists and dedicated to realizing practical applications of recent advances in art technique and theory. The corporation, Ocean Earth Construction and Development Corporation, has been organized to provide three different kinds of services: earthworks and land-engineering services (Ocean Earth); architectural and city-planning services (City Bild); and telecast-video services (Relay). A recent--and probably continuing--contract of the corporation has been the exposition and development of an infrastructure-megastructure design plan, along with a comprehensive energy plan, for the City of Duisburg in West Germany. The Relay service, meanwhile, is contracting with the National Audobon Society in the U.S. to plan a series of short television programs advocating the Audobon Society's energy plan for the U.S.

OECD has few staff-artists. It is organized with the recognition that artists have individual careers. The artists involved in any one project may well also be exhibiting work under their own name at a museum or gallery, and they may well be involved in that corporate role for only a few months. OECD functions as a conduit by which advances in visual and structural theory, as developed by individual artist-researchers, can be brought to bear upon the scientific, technical and media communities.

Through Relay, we attempt to bring advances of the past several decades in color projection with motile (film-video) media to the attention of earth-observation agencies. We organize, then, a team of the very artists who have made these advances. The lead artist on this team might be known to you: he is known throughout the world as perhaps <u>the</u> pioneer in very-rapid interjection of color frames in <u>films</u> for an intensified, but not always consciously recognized, flow of information. His name is Paul Sharits.

Letter to European Space Agency from 1981, which has yet to be acted on. The recipient responded favorably.

M. Ghesquiere, Page Two

Feb 6, 1981

But in visual research, as in scientific research, the leading pioneer at one time might not be making breakthroughs at another time: we have formed a team of independent researchers, each with a potential of developing new techniques for display and organization of earth-observation data. Colen Fitzgibbon, like Paul Sharits, has received grants from Agfa-Gaevert for innovative studies in color filming: she might well develop--alone or in collaboration with Sharits--a film or video program with multi-spectral data that especially helps scientists "read" what is happening on the earth. Glenn Steigelman, who has correlated color theory with photography since his days at Yale with Josef Albers (author of Interaction of Color), proposes ways of combining color transparencies to more clearly communicate the information scientists seek. Wolfgang Staehle translates Albers' teachings into motion pictures with rapid color sequences, often with colors in pairs at any one time; Staehle draws on centuries of German studies into the theory of color perception, and he knows, for example, that colors become meaningful best in comparison. Terry Mohre and Neil Zusman, both grant-winning artists at the New York State Experimental Television Center, have specialized in converting computer programs to video imagery, and they have then adapted that imagery to formats of computer-graphics. Their work will support the other artists, and it may lead to advances in the organization and display of earth-observation data. In a number of different ways, experienced artists stand ready to experiment with the imagery and techniques of earth observation.

Collaboration with scientists is expected. We artists intend to apply the advances of recent decades in field-theory and color-theory to realistic situations. If Renaissance picture-theory was eventually mechanized in the camera, and if the camera has since then been elaborated into multi-spectral scanners suited for video programs, we would like to apply the correspondingly-sophisticated visual theories of recent times to that advanced technology. We believe that MSS data can be organized to better-represent ground-truth conditions than it does now. We hold ourselves responsible ultimately to increasing the accuracy and speed of perception of useful ground-truth. Two scientists in the U.S. Geological Survey, Virginia Carter and Morris Deutsch, have helped us towards meeting this responsibility. One specializes in marshes as vital centers of ecological systems; the other develops image-enhanced mosaics of entire hydrological basins. We would like to continue working with such scientists.

A distinct project has formed, with a distinct geographical location. We of OECD, acting through Relay, would like to cooperate with ESA in realization of this project, which I describe now.

We would like to develop a video mosaic of the Mediterranean Basin.

The Basin, as I have mapped it, includes both the Mediterranean Sea and Black Sea, all the river basins draining into those Seas, and all the land that slopes towards those Seas but not, due to drought, now draining into them. If one conceives of the Mediterranean Sea as an enormous river debouching in the Straits of Gibralter, then one can conceive of the hydrological basin of the Mediterranean Sea. Maps are enclosed.

In effect, we want to develop--in collaboration with scientists--a comprehensive picture of an enclosed ocean. The picture would include not only the sea itself, but also all the land that now or eventually can spill waters into that sea.

We do not want to make this hydrological mosaic just in still images: we want to render the visual data in video and film formats. We believe that the many different possible spectral readings of the basin, or of sites within the basin, can be incorporated into video or film programs for more rapid comprehension. We suppose also that video manipulation of data from the multi-spectral scanner can more rapidly yield those elements of a mosaic which most inobtrusively fit. NASA scientists say that mosaics must be constructed with separate photographs; we suppose that they can be constructed with separate, rapidly-discovered video interpretations. The spectral-overlay and enhancements with photographs made, say, by Glenn Steigelman, can help maintain control, but our ultimate achievement would be in motile media.

Even though the entire Mediterranean Basin does not lie within the normal range for data acquisition of ESA Earthnet antennae, we affirm our interest in it. We have these reasons: 1) urgent need for a comprehensive view, at least of the Sea and its major river basins, given the danger of ecological collapse; 2) enclosed and therefore systemic character of the basin, suitable for study; 3) prominent role of the Mediterranean Sea Commission, part of the Regional Seas Programme of the U.N. Environment Programme, altogether setting precedents in the international management of earth resources; 4) relative absence of cloud cover; 5) urgent need for comprehensive management of the Nile River Basin; 6) ability to trace the effects of nutrient-transfer migrants such as birds and insects--all of which vitally affect Europe; 7) first comprehensive views towards that hydrological and ecological engineering which could restore the Sahara to savannah; 8) the likely public, and even political, impact of such a survey of such an historical site; 9) an invitation to present an image of the Basin, along with detailed descriptions, at an art museum in Florence. This last reason is also, in a sense, our first reason: when asked to exhibit in the Mediterranean region, we want to show the people there, with advanced techniques, where they live.

M. Ghesquiere, Page Four Feb 6, 1981

Our purpose, then, is to collaborate or otherwise engage with the European Space Agency in producing a video mosaic of the Mediterranean Basin. We expect that the task will involve a number of advances in the state of the art of earth observation--or rather, earth exposition. We believe that such advances will help make what the multi-spectral scanner senses be more accessible--both to scientists and the public. And we believe that the video character of the landscape mosaic will make regular telecasts of environmental conditions become common. Once such telecasts are common, perhaps the populace, seeing for themselves, will address more directly the ecological problems we humans have wrought on this ocean earth.

Sincerely yours,

Peter Fend

Ghesquiere was visiting from Europe. The appointment had been pre-arranged by the head of the Washington Office. Ghesquiere is Head of User Services, Earthnet, ESA.

After a two hour meeting, Ghesquiere proposed to take a substantial body of papers back to ESA and to the European Economic Community people handling the first EEC ecological project, the Adriatic Sea project. The project runs 1981-1985.

Ghesquiere proposed that we think of preparing a video mosaic, and other visual documents, of the Adriatic Sea basin.

The first site in which to test this thinking would be that heavily-invstigated Pamlico Sound-Cape Hatteras site in the United Stases.

Copies of this letter are being circulated within the US Geological Survey.

Europe—along with immediate adjuncts like the United States and Australia—has behaved towards Africa and the Middle East as reservoirs of petroleum.

This explains the fury of many people on the African Continent and the Middle East towards Europe and its immediate adjuncts. The people there do not exist, except as agents for access to petroleum. I've seen this first-hand in the UAE: there, the subjects of the Ruler, being UAE-born, can dismiss as unapproachable and somehow beneath humanity the guest-workers brought in from places like Peshawar, Pakistan. Value and identity consist of citizenship-access to all the region now has to offer the Europeans and their adjuncts: petroleum. People in the UAE from Peshawar have no access to petroleum, so they have no value.

In such a dismissal of entire populations, one can be surprised that the violence now besetting Africa, especially North Africa, and the Middle East has not become much greater.

The ongoing refugee crisis in Europe results from a century of abuse extending back to the first struggle for control of access to Africa and the Middle East: World War I.

The 1918 defeat of the Ottoman, Austrian, and German Empires created the early twenty-first century collapse of social and economic order in much of North Africa and the Middle East. The victors of World War I, especially the US, UK, and France, have imposed on much of Africa and the Middle East economic pressures directed almost entirely at extractible minerals. Now the payback happens, especially in the truncated states that remain of the Ottoman, Austrian, and German Empires.

As it happens in the evolution of cultures, Europe and its immediate adjuncts, especially the United States, have generated new technologies that make petroleum obsolete. These technologies arise from several fields of innovation. One is research science, of course, but another is Art.

In this book, we present the innovations in energy supply coming from Art, from imagination at the forefront of material culture. We present them intending to sharply adjust the relation of Europe to North Africa and the Mideast.

Everyone knows that petroleum cannot last as a basis of the economy. Even the sheikhs in Saudi Arabia know this.

But no one has been able to supplant petroleum as the basis of economy. Attempts to do so, even by entrepreneurs in the US or Australia, are met with roadblocks, red tape, even murder. I have experienced the roadblocks, and the attendant violence, many times. Given the impasse, as often witnessed, I conclude after forty years of struggle that (1) there is no "free world," so that Russia and the US/UK are equally restrictive of freedom, just in different ways, and (2) the areas most oppressed by Europe and its immediate adjuncts are those now in rebellion in Africa and the Middle East. I could have realized this before my experiences by taking John Milton's Paradise Lost, especially in Book Six, more seriously. Lucifer creates Hell on Earth by worshipping Mammon and making all the world rely on "Naphtha," i.e., petroleum. Isn't that the City of London, the aspiration of Houston and Moscow, and Wall Street in the US? No hesitation appears in the Wall Street Journal when it discusses oil or gas reserves in Iran and Saudi Arabia, or when it emphasizes the "economic gains," never mind river-water destruction, from fracking. The poisoning of water in Flint, the city in Michigan USA, is an iceberg tip of a much larger fact: the poisoning of most of the rivers in North America. Paradise, which North America had been, is surely lost.

And so Paradise has been lost in North Africa and the Middle East.

When I release such remarks, as I did for documenta in 1992, many control people from many governments will swoop down on me, to make sure that damage is not done to the credibility of the State. No one must question that we live in a free world.

But the damage gets done anyway: the derangement of climate, with attendant pollution of air and water, from the use of petroleum. Even if no social harm resulted from the dependence on petroleum, there would still be a spreading Hell on Earth through destruction of our habitat.

An entirely post-petroleum era must begin.

It can begin in many places on the Planet.

One place can be North Africa and the Middle East.

In this place, we can simply respond to what was requested of me in 1985, over thirty years ago, by the Ambassador of Algeria to France, and by an embassy official for Iran in Germany. The Ambassador had asked if the mammoth earthworks we revealed with satellite imagery of the Iran–Iraq war zone could be adapted to restore animal-rich savannah in what is now desert. The Iranian official had asked, on seeing the same mammoth earthworks revealed by satellite, if we could propose an "Islamic solution" to the war; my answer then, which remains, was "Islamic Garden."

All that I propose here comes from some on-site experiments, some review of scientific literature, but chiefly from innovations by artists in Europe and its immediate adjunct the United States. There have also been lessons from cultures and scientists in the Middle East, especially the UAE. And ancient practices of Persia, such as qanats, have been promoted for use.

Ultimately, the source of ideas and technologies will not matter. What will work, we ask each day, in replacing savannah for desert, and in replacing petroleum, or "naphtha," as the source of hydrocarbons?

Most of what we present has yet to be proven.

We have produced clean-burning biofuel from water plants, yes, but we have no systematic proof of how much fuel can be produced with how much work. No one does.

And while we have demonstrated how to cut a channel between a sub-sealevel trough, called sabkha, and the ocean, we do not yet know how to make such cutting customary, or how to build an economic base there.

Presented here are proposals in the Unknown.

They should be essayed, evaluated, and essayed again, no matter what.

Economic activity must move in such a direction.

All that is shown here is meant to be started and learned from now.

Without a scenario such as what is here, we as a species stand a good chance, along with many other "higher" species, of being wiped out.

Peter Fend, January 2016, during the one-century anniversary of what caused the present misery on earth, World War I.

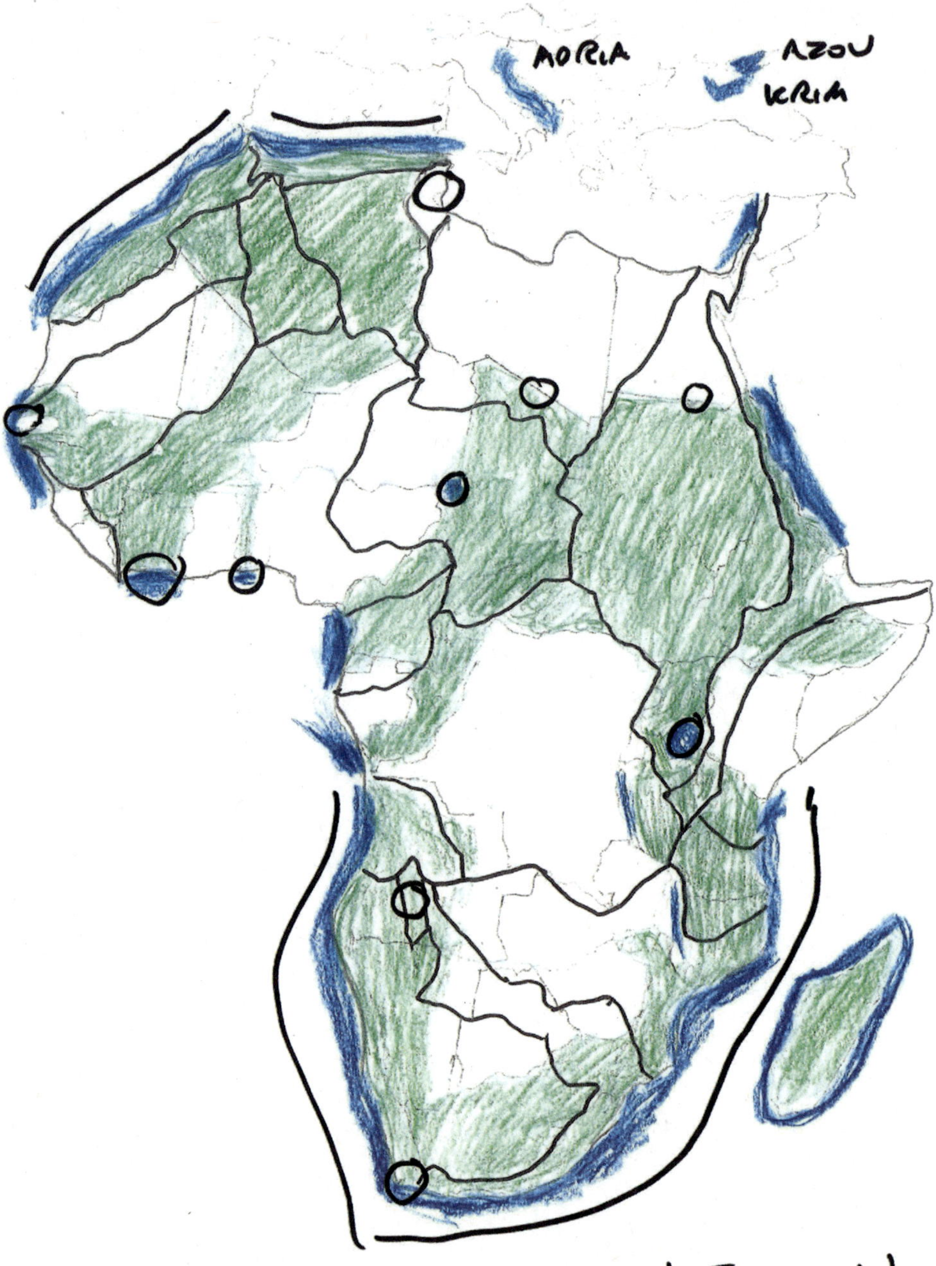

COASTAL WATERS IN POST-WAR AFRICA, FOR BIOMASS-TO-FUEL INDUSTRY

POST-WAR AFRICA

In this map of Africa on the neighboring page, green represents the counties that decided not to join a UN General Assembly resolution about a 2022 war in a bid against bloc alignment.

Black lines inside Africa show the outlines of saltwater basins. These are the shapes of Physiocratic States. Bold black lines offshore show the standout regions of complete sea-current control: notice the Benguela Current, Canary Current, Algerian Current, Agulhas Current, and Mozambique Channel.

The strong blue bodies of water fall under control, or dominant influence, of the green countries.

These countries can start NOW a post-petroleum energy industry, and even a post-dam program inland. They can lead the world in the abandonment of Big Oil, still dominant in the West, even in Russia and China.

We, Ocean Earth, think of basin work on submersible rig and submarine-serviced biomass technologies in the two shipyards in Africa where submarines are built, in South Africa in Durban and Cape Town. That same country led the movement evident in the green colors, not only in Africa but also in once-colonized South Asia and Latin America. Or… do we work in the submarine shipyards of Japan, France, or Italy…?

Several objectives are met.
(1) To escape the World Bank/IMF, and competitive Chinese, treatment of the "developing world" as permanently-defined ex-colonies.
(2) With that, to rescind the Treaty of Berlin of 1885, which continues to prevent any organization of Africa or anywhere else in the once-colonized world (e.g., Americas) by ecological (soil-water) principles rather than colonial conquest ones.
(3) To allow Africa, as a population-boom continent, to govern its future.

(4) To link Africa with its fish, in the lakes via rivers to the seas, and with its birds, which fly from the tropics both north, to the Arctic, and south, towards the Southern Ocean.
(5) To prove that ocean industry can develop in entire sea currents.
(6) To tackle problems of hydrology in three major rivers of Africa, even if some of their territory is not "green": Congo, second largest by volume in the world, with massive outflow to the green-coast areas northwards; Nile, longest in the world, with major questions on soil-water flow upstream from Egypt and its Aswan Dam (we know this with Adel Darwish); Niger, with impacts in the Gulf of Guinea, congested and very energy-rich in ex-colonies eastwards.

Given what's going on now in 2022, artists and architects should conceive and publicize all of their work as POST-WAR ART.

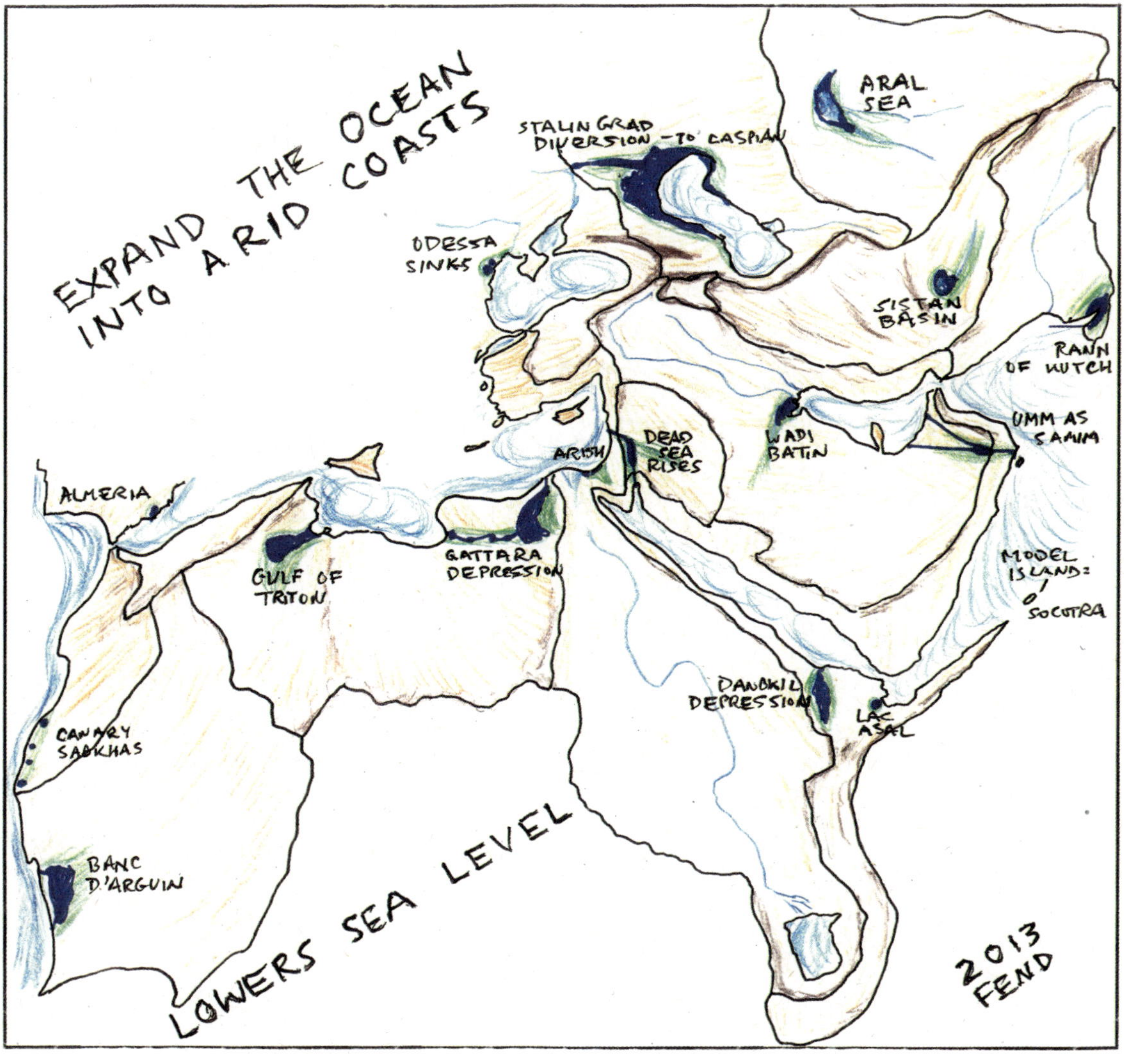

This drawing was made in 2013 for an *Artforum* ad to identify sites for action, all of which are saltwater bodies. Such thinking was further discussed at the 2018 event that the MICA Foundation hosted in New York, titled: "AFRICA THINKS, OTHERS FOLLOW—ECOLOGICAL STRUCTURES FOR AFRICAN WATER FLOW REQUIRED FOR ECONOMIC GROWTH OVER LONG TERM." Peter Fend hand-delivered invitations to all the UN missions of the African countries, and Moroccan diplomats attended the event.

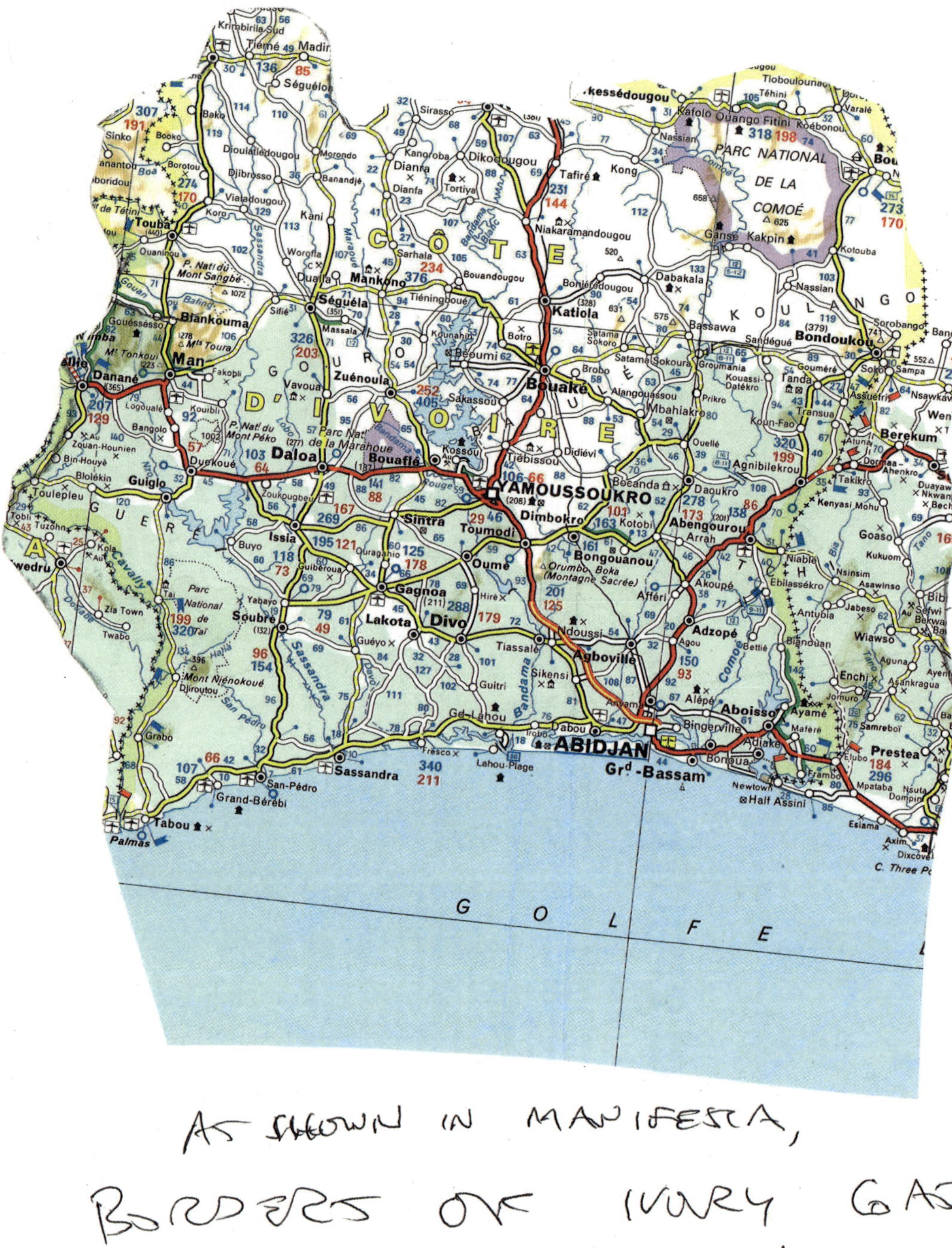

AS SHOWN IN MANIFESTA,
BORDERS OF IVORY COAST
ADJUSTED TO MAKE A
HYDROMETRIC AREA, WITH
A SINGLE OCEAN BAY

The Ivory Coast has a watershed, which includes territory north of the current borders. In effect, administration should include the entire slope.

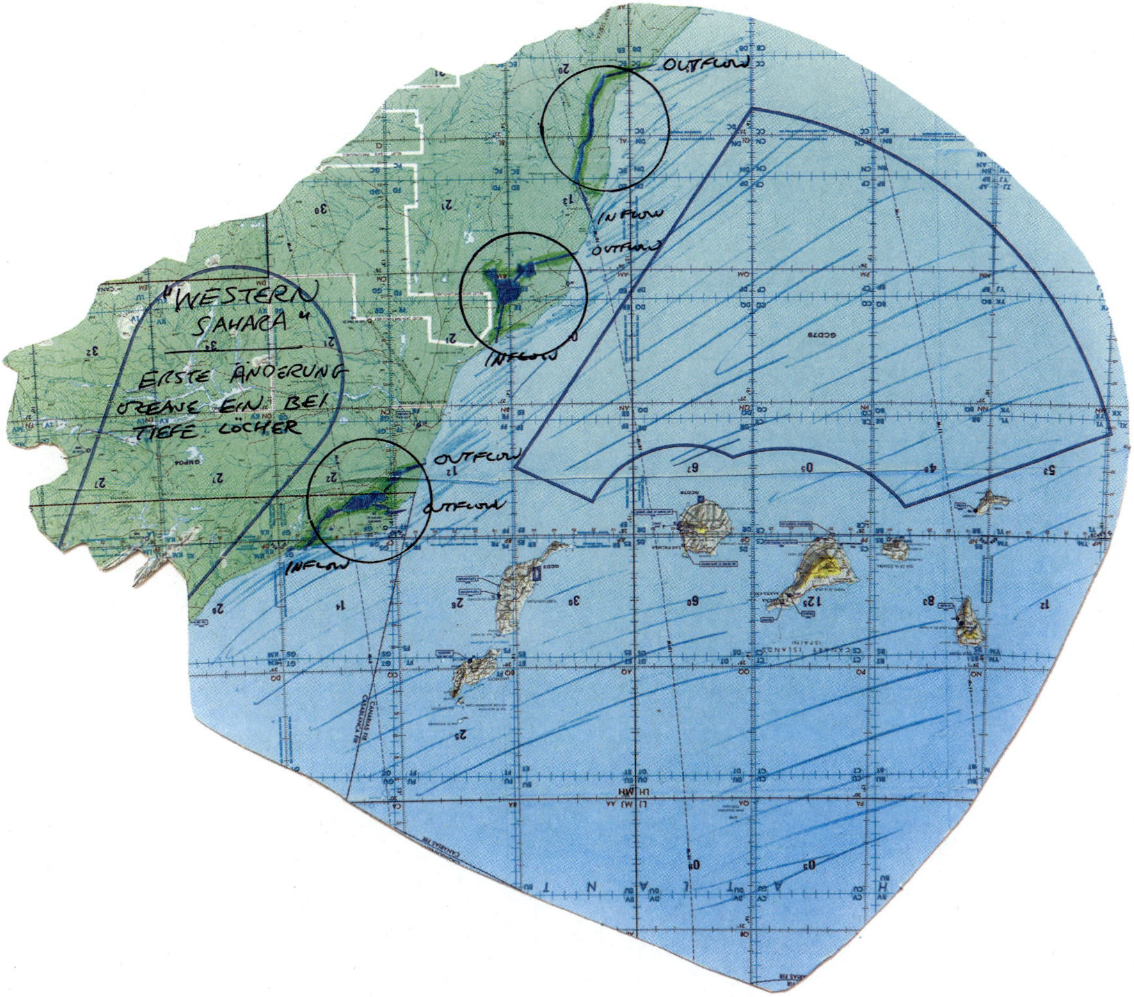

Sub-sealevel basins, or sabkhas, could be flooded from the sea with in-and-out channels for intensive bioindustry.

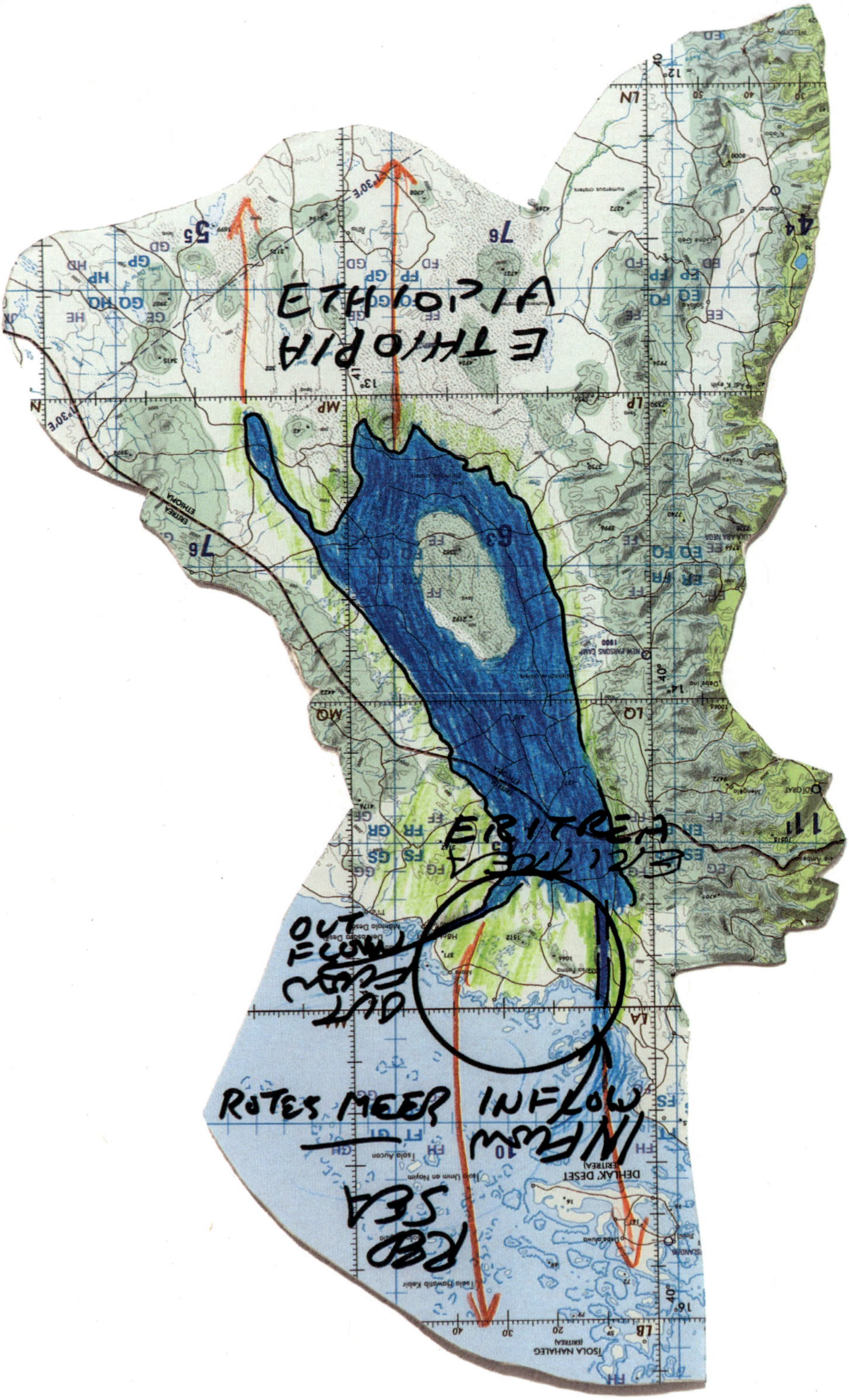

Detail of the Arabic sabkhas for a saltwater pond near the coast that could be systematically harvested for fish and algae.

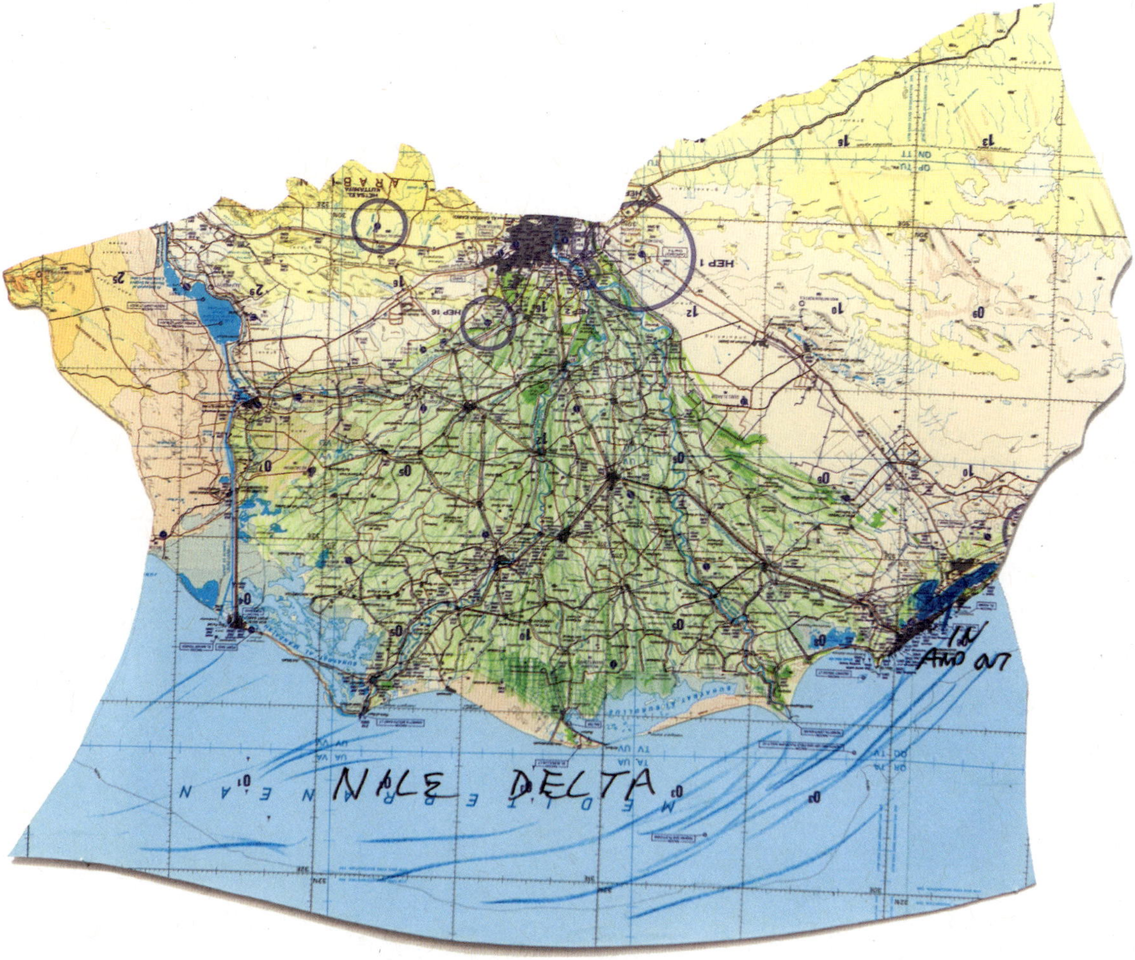

Possible areas of sabkha work in the Nile Delta. This was presented at the "AFRICA THINKS" event.

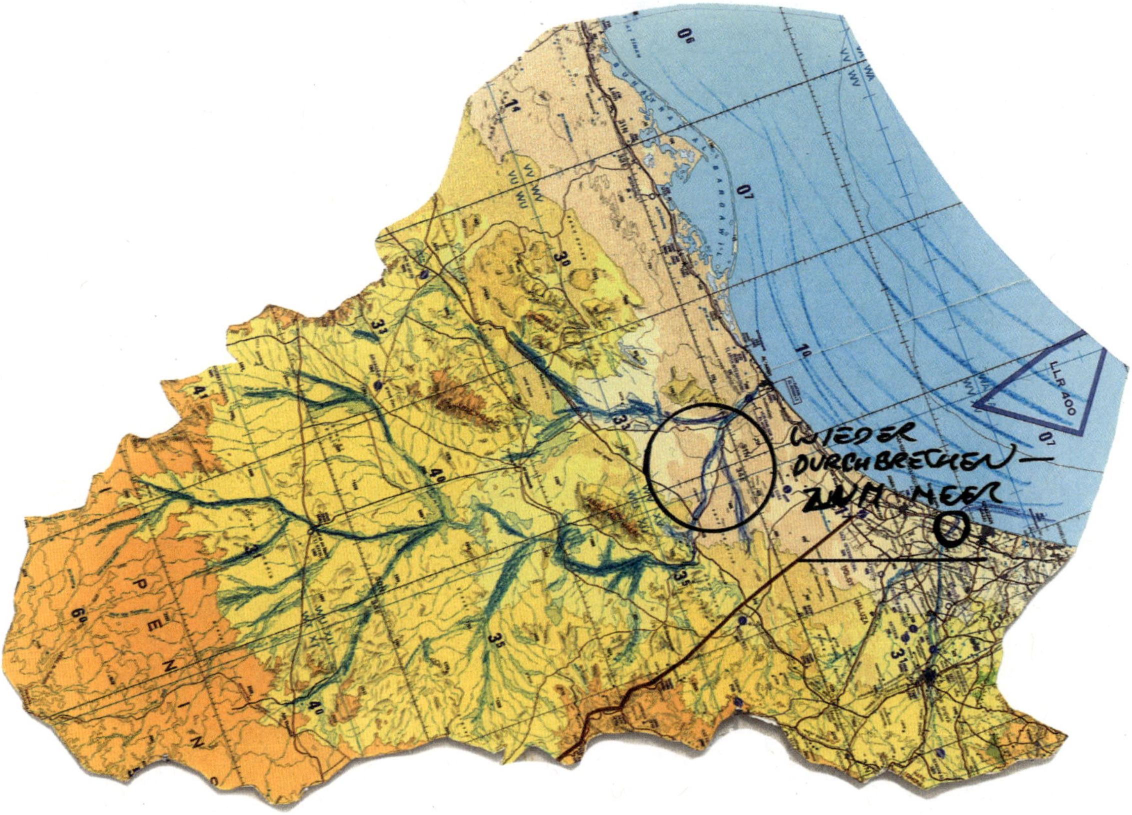

The Wadi el-Arish is a degraded river system between Mount Sinai and the sea. It could be a test zone for hydrological restoration. It is on the Nile flyway from Lake Victoria to Moscow and the Barents Sea.

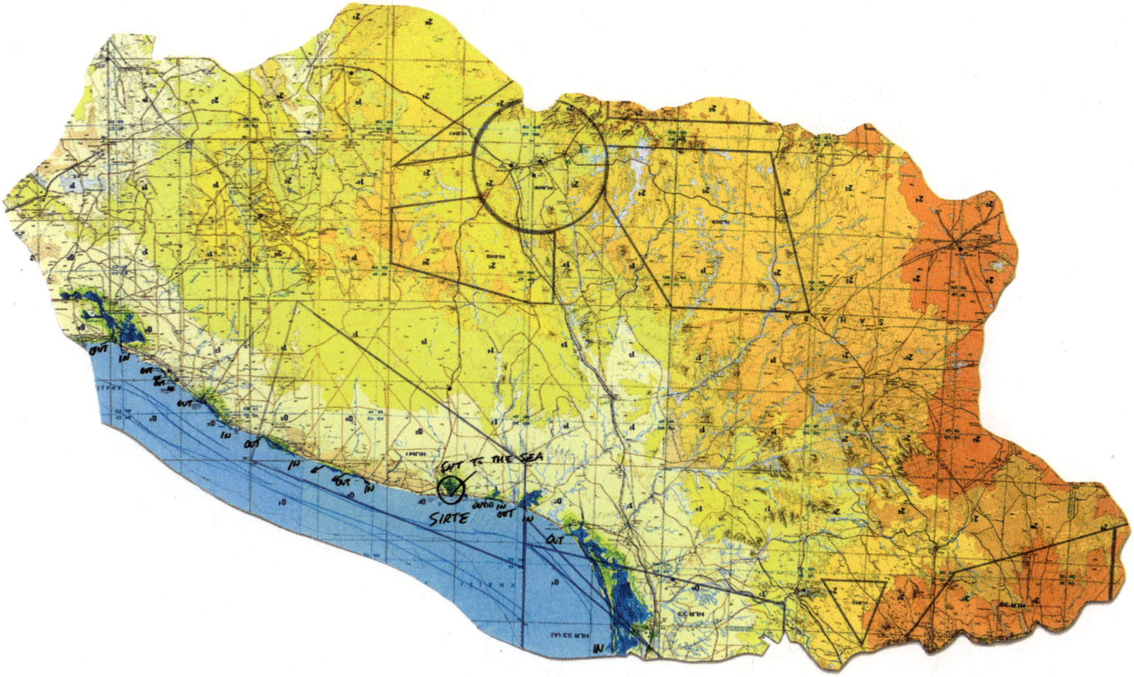

Sub-sealevel wadi on Libyan coast between Misrata and Brega. All the areas emphasized in blue and green could be bioindustry sites.

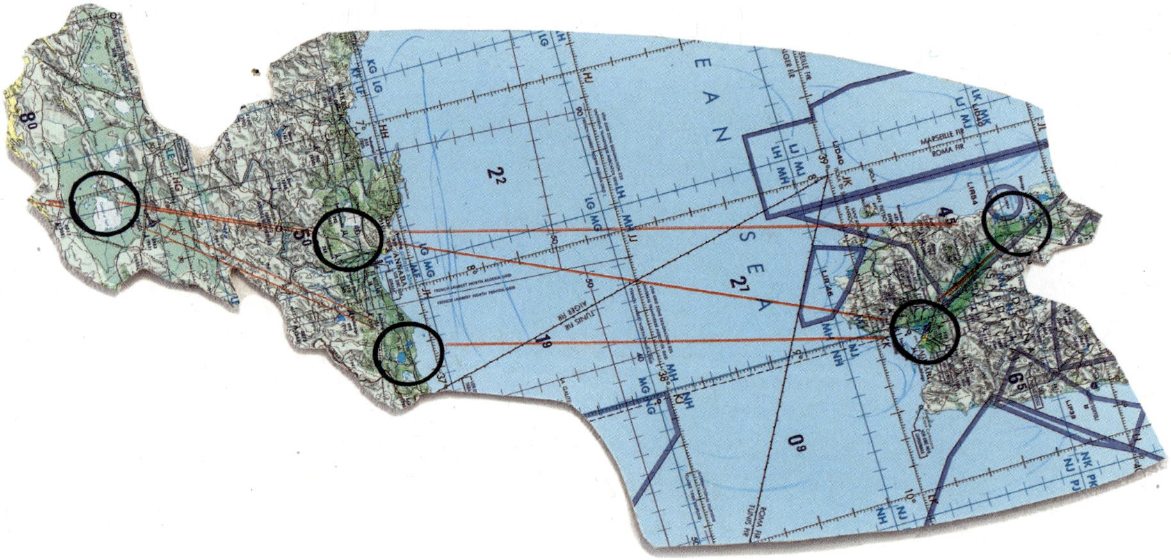

Bird flyway link between marshes in Algeria and marshes in Sardinia.

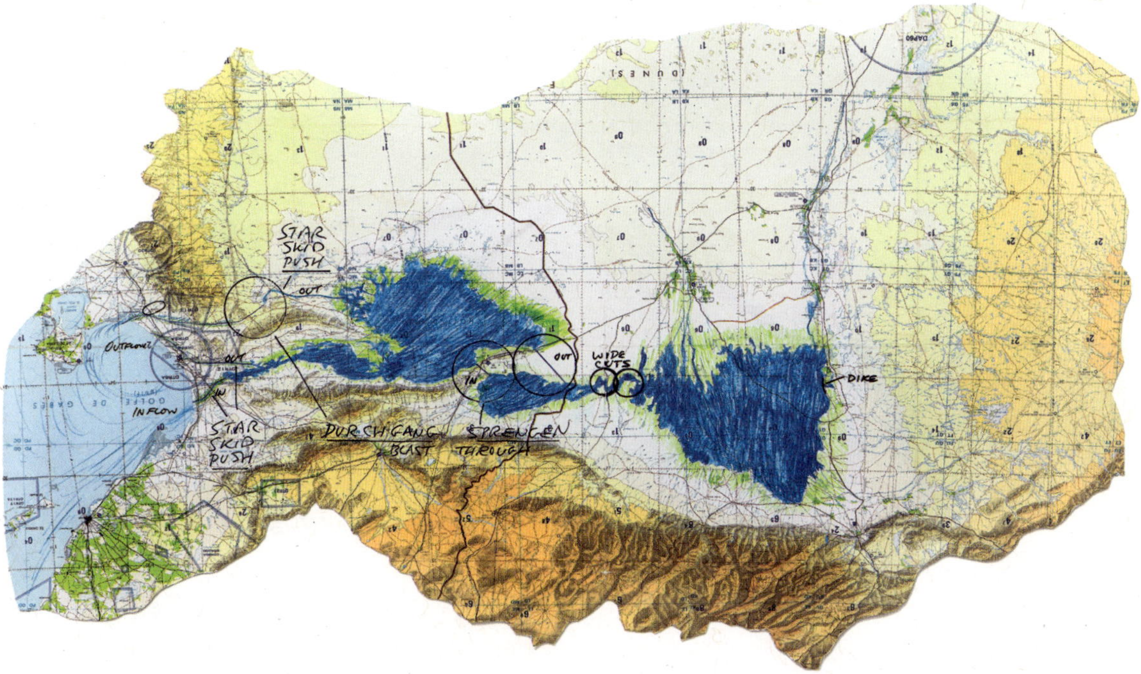

Reconstructing the Gulf of Gabes

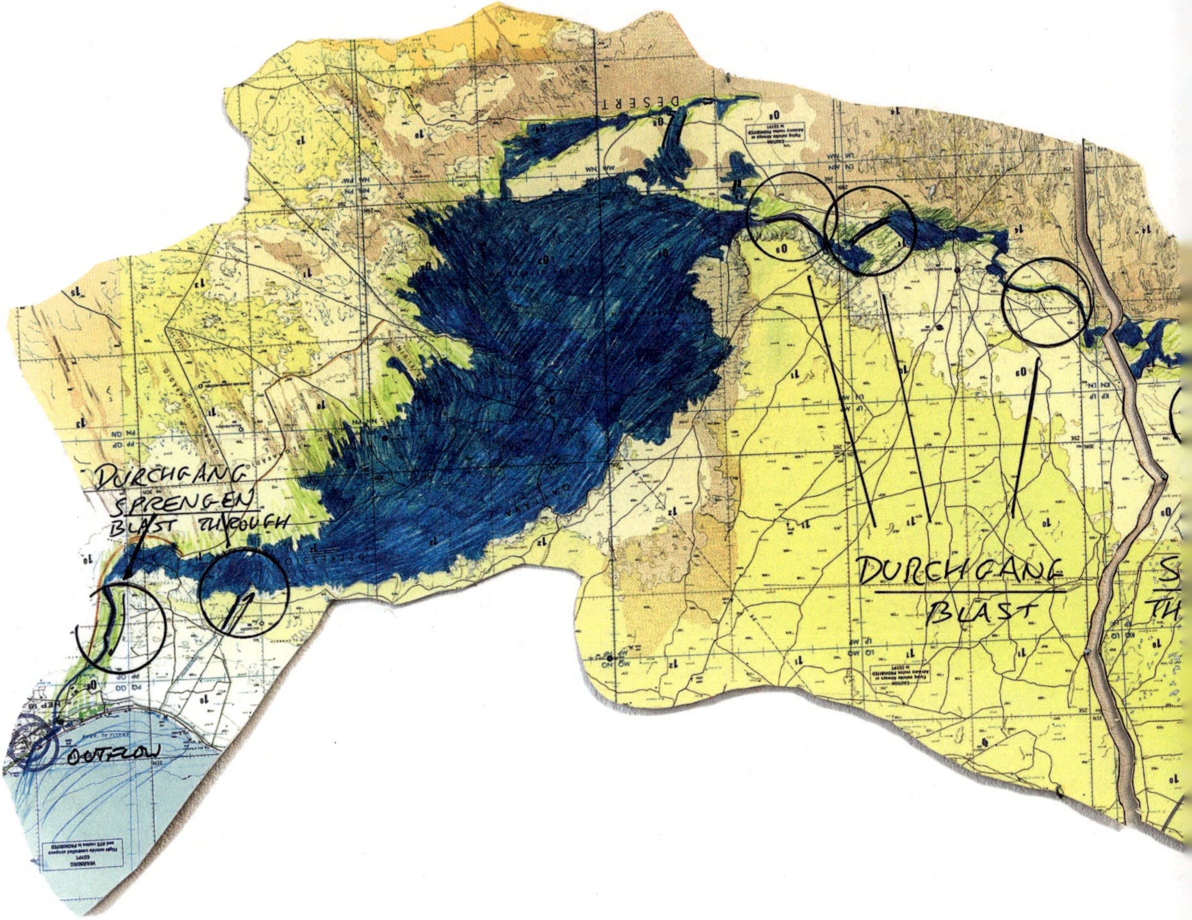

Making Cyrenaica an island, with flows at sea level from Adschdabiya to El-Hamam. These links made the decisive battle sites of the desert campaign in World War II. The relationship between the fighting and the seawater pockets is surpassing.

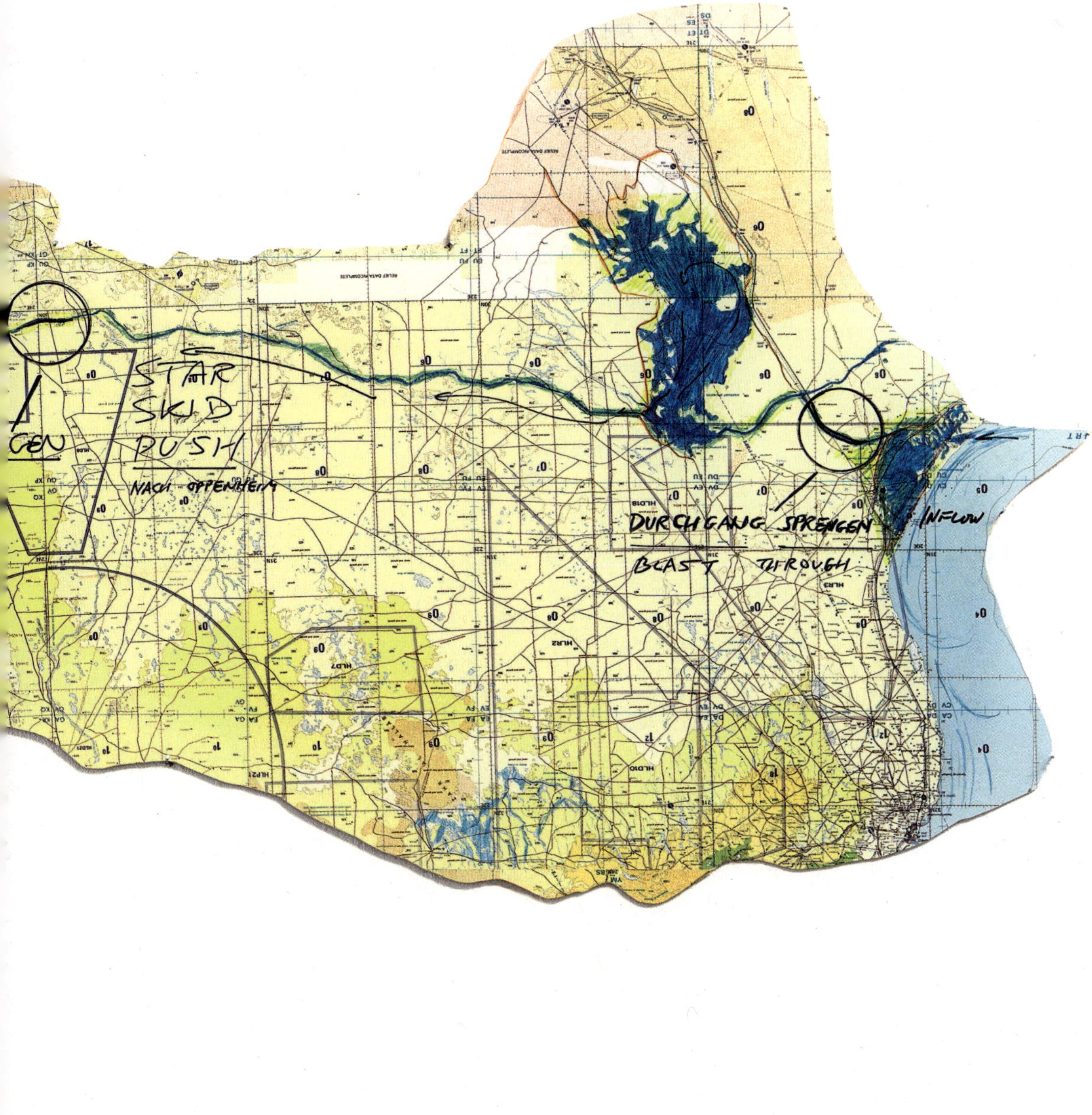
STAR
SKID
PUSH
NACH OPPENHEIM
GEN
DURCHGANG SPRENGEN
BLAST THROUGH
INFLOW

REPLACING THE
BELT AND ROAD
INITIATIVE AS
BEZOS FANTASY
FAST DELIVERY
FOR CONSUMERS
IN EURASIA OR
AFRICA, AS IF
THAT'S NEEDED
FOR WELLBEING
A 2050S DREAM
"MADE IN USA"
UPDATED BY XI
WITH THE SAME
OLD INDUSTRY:
OIL, NUCLEAR,
HIGH DAMS AND
SOLAR "FARMS"
AND NO FUTURE
FOR US HUMANS
WITH MEANS OF
PRODUCTION AS
KNOWN OVER 50
YEARS, ALWAYS
BLOCKED, EVEN
IN U.S.-CHINA
COLLABORATION
FROM 40 YEARS
AGO, BY THUGS
IN BOTH CHINA
AND THE U.S.,
ALONG WITH UK
DEFENDING THE
DOMINATION OF
WILD ANIMALS,
PEOPLES, EVEN
PLANTS, AS IF
THAT'S HOW TO
LIVE ON EARTH

BUILD UP BIRD
FISH & INSECT
NUMBERS, THEN
CREATE PLACES
WHERE MAMMALS
CAN LIVE WILD

WORK IN THREE
SWATHS: EAST
ASIA, AMERICA
AND EURAFRICA
SPLIT EURASIA
IN TWO HALVES
EAST ASIA AND
EURAFRICA, SO
THAT NATURE'S
RESTORED WITH
THE MIGRATING
ANIMALS GOING
NORTH & SOUTH
FOLLOWING THE
SUN, A SOURCE
FOR ALL OF US
XI JINPING IS
OVERLOOKED AS
WE RELY AGAIN
ON WILDERNESS
FOR SALVATION
HIS OBSESSION
WITH POWER ON
EARTH BECOMES
RIDICULOUS AS
WE EXPERIENCE
A CORONAVIRUS
PANDEMIC, ALL
DUE TO SLOPPY
AMBITION, ALL
DUE TO TRYING
TO OVERTAKE A
LONG-AGO PAST

READ THE BOOK
THAT OUTWATER
WROTE, AS THE
CALL FOR WILD
NATURE AROUND
US EVERYWHERE
FOR A DURABLE
WEALTH, VIGOR
AND EVOLUTION
MIMIC NATURE,
NOT LONG-DEAD
EMPIRES; DROP

MEMORIES OF A
SILK ROAD, OR
MONGOL REIGNS
RESTORE NORTH
SOUTH TRAFFIC
OF THE BEASTS
WE DEPEND ON,
HUNT, EAT AND
JOIN IN DEATH
ALWAYS LIVING
IN NEW BEINGS
POST-PANDEMIC
ACTION NEEDED
DO IT NOW, IN
ITALY WITHOUT
CHINA BUT VIA
BIRDS OR BUGS
WITH AFRICA'S
HUGE LANDMASS
USE IMAGES BY
ARTISTS SINCE
ART IS AVANT-
GARDE, A PATH
TO THE FUTURE
BEFORE IT CAN
REALLY HAPPEN

MAKING HISTORY
WITH ART IDEAS
AND NOT WITH A
THOUGHT OF OUR
LONG-DEAD PAST
FAREWELL TO XI
HELLO TO BUGS,
BIRDS AND FISH
ALL AROUND US,
FELLOW MAMMALS
ROVING UNBOUND
THE PROBLEM:
A WIPEOUT OF
MOST ANIMALS
ON EARTH, IN
ORDER TO HOG
ALL THAT CAN
BE TAKEN AND
EXHAUSTED IN

A THROW-AWAY
CIVILIZATION

SOLUTION IS:
RESTORE BIRD
FLYWAYS WITH
INSECTS, TOO

THEN MAMMALS

ALONG ROUTES
FROM JUNGLES
TO TUNDRA AS
BIRDS ALWAYS
DID UNTIL WE
HUMANS OVER-
CUT OR OVER-
GRAZED LONG-
AGO SAVANNAH

WE HUMANS COULD EASILY
BE WIPED OUT, AS OTHER
SPECIES OF ANIMALS WIN
THE RACE TO STAY ALIVE

BELT & ROAD INITIATIVE
IS A RELIC OF THE PAST

III FLYWAY PROJECT SITES

FLYWAY 3
Nigeria to North Cape

Ocean Treaty Organizations:
AOTO and ARTO

Project Site:
BALTIC SEA BASIN; NORTH SEA BASIN

POLAND, SWEDEN, FINLAND DECLARE 'BALTIC UNION'; BID SOVIETS IN REGION TO JOIN 'FREE COUNTRY'

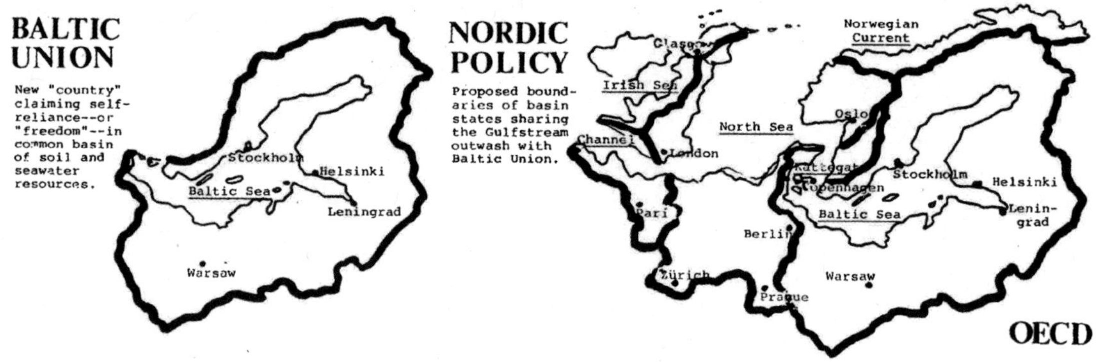

In 1974, in a two-day symposium at the Johns Hopkins School for Advanced International Studies, with luminaries like George F. Kennan and Raymond Aron, Zbigniew Brzezinski suggested that a Baltic Regional Sea Program State be created, with countries like Finland, Sweden, Poland, and Russia as stakeholders, which could provide a way out of the East–West divide. The HQ would be in Helsinki. This would be part of a replacement of the North Atlantic Treaty Organization. At the time, the idea was also applicable to the Black Sea Basin, with a Regional Sea Program based in Istanbul. This was a 1981 scenario, posted on walls near the UN, along with three other fictions. No one remembers what Brzezinski was saying. He seems to have dropped the idea too. Is this possible now?

German Government officials have remarked that what Fend shows about the Baltic Basin, especially, is “known science.” (There’s a slight modification, made in Fend’s scientific paper for the UNEP/FAO conference on “Global Monitoring and Assessments,” in moving the border between the Baltic and North Seas to the Belt Islands of Denmark, as satellite imagery reveals). But yes, the general outline of the Baltic Basin is widely known and scientifically established.

It even can appear in Der Spiegel as standard geohydrology. But then the same officials say that Fend is a “Kriegstreiber,” or warmonger, by suggesting that a political administration be set up for the respective basins, e.g., one for the Baltic and one for the North Sea. Such an administration already exists, under UNEP auspices, with secretariats and international meetings and budgets. Fend only suggests a strengthening of such management. Here’s the question: if what is shown is “known science,” why don’t we act on that? Does adopting scientific knowledge for territorial administration, especially in areas with no war (yet), constitute a threat? Does it need to be blocked? If an artist shows and promotes a scientific fact, is that a crime?

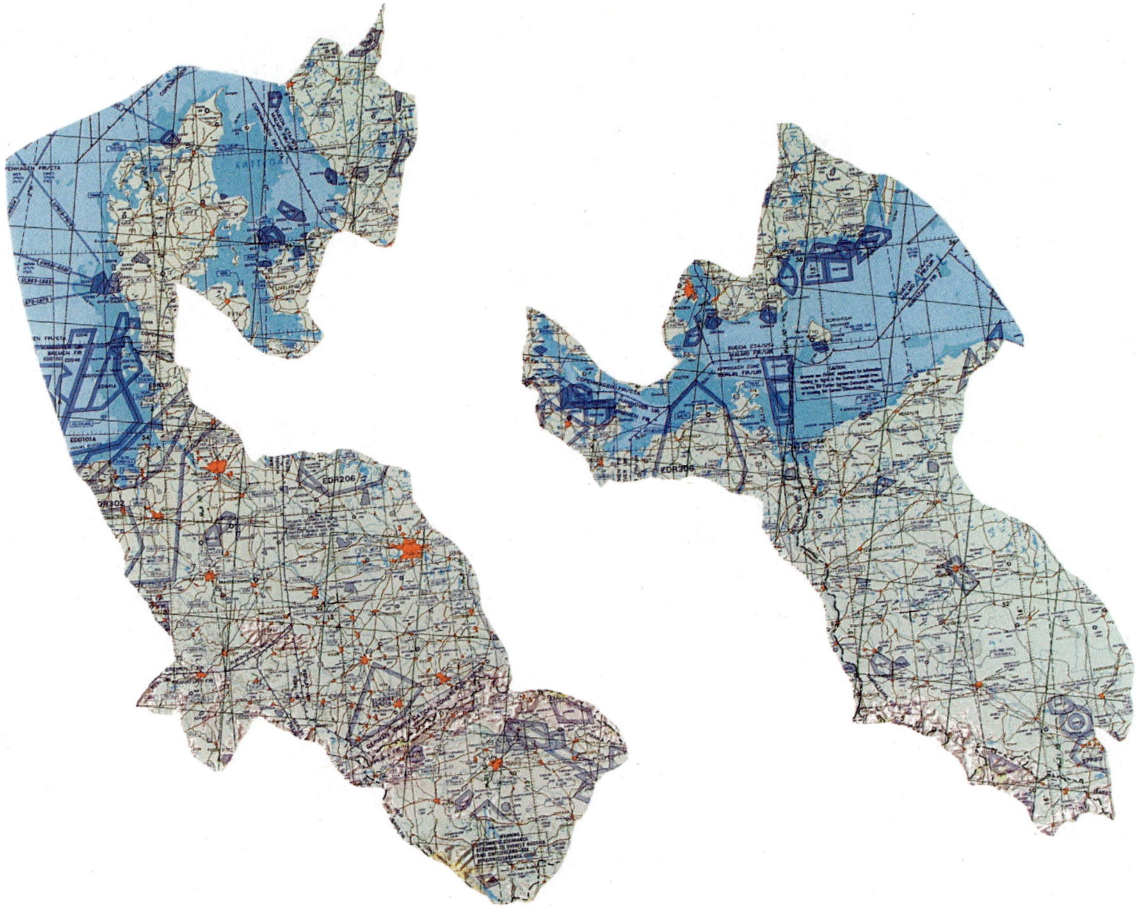

This shows the line of division of what goes into the North Sea and what goes into the Baltic Sea. The German government has said that Peter Fend's thinking about the Baltic Sea is already known science. This division should not only be known, but also acted upon.

ABOUT RAU

In 1993, soon after the "reunification" of Germany, with a commensurate promise to Russia to not push east with NATO, Johannes Rau, then the head of the Ruhr region, and well-known for his attempts to deny Joseph Beuys any political influence, hosted a large art exhibition in Potsdam to celebrate reunification. Peter Fend was invited. He treated the subject literally. He made a terrain model, of cement blocks and dirt, of the entire Elbe Basin. This would include most of the territory of former East Germany, and—very visibly, at highest elevation, beyond a ridgeline, most of the former Soviet satellite the Czech Republic. The visual lesson was clear: Czech and most of former East Germany sloped downhill to the mouth of the Elbe River, entering the North Sea just beyond Hamburg. Fend made a compilation of documents about this. He warned that land use in the former Soviet areas must be improved to prevent floods downstream.

During the opening, Johannes Rau and his entourage walked throughout the exhibition. Fend explained the model to him and his entourage (much as explained facts in Sharjah to the Sheikh). He also gave a dossier to a member of the entourage. To him, this was simply him doing his job. But Rau and his entourage did not do their job. They did not pay any attention to what was given to them. Time and energy were spent on the subject of reunification of a physical body of land to another body of land, including a country called Czech, and what the invited artist did and said was IGNORED. A few years later, after Rau had become President of Germany, a formal role of "cheerleader" for Germany, there was a very big, damaging flood on the Elbe River, especially down by Hamburg. Rau shouted aloud about the catastrophe, as if it were a surprise. As Fend sees it, the catastrophe was entirely Rau's fault. He and staff showed zero respect for what the artist, seen by them to be frivolous, warned them, in employment for them.

Kunst ist kein Dienst?

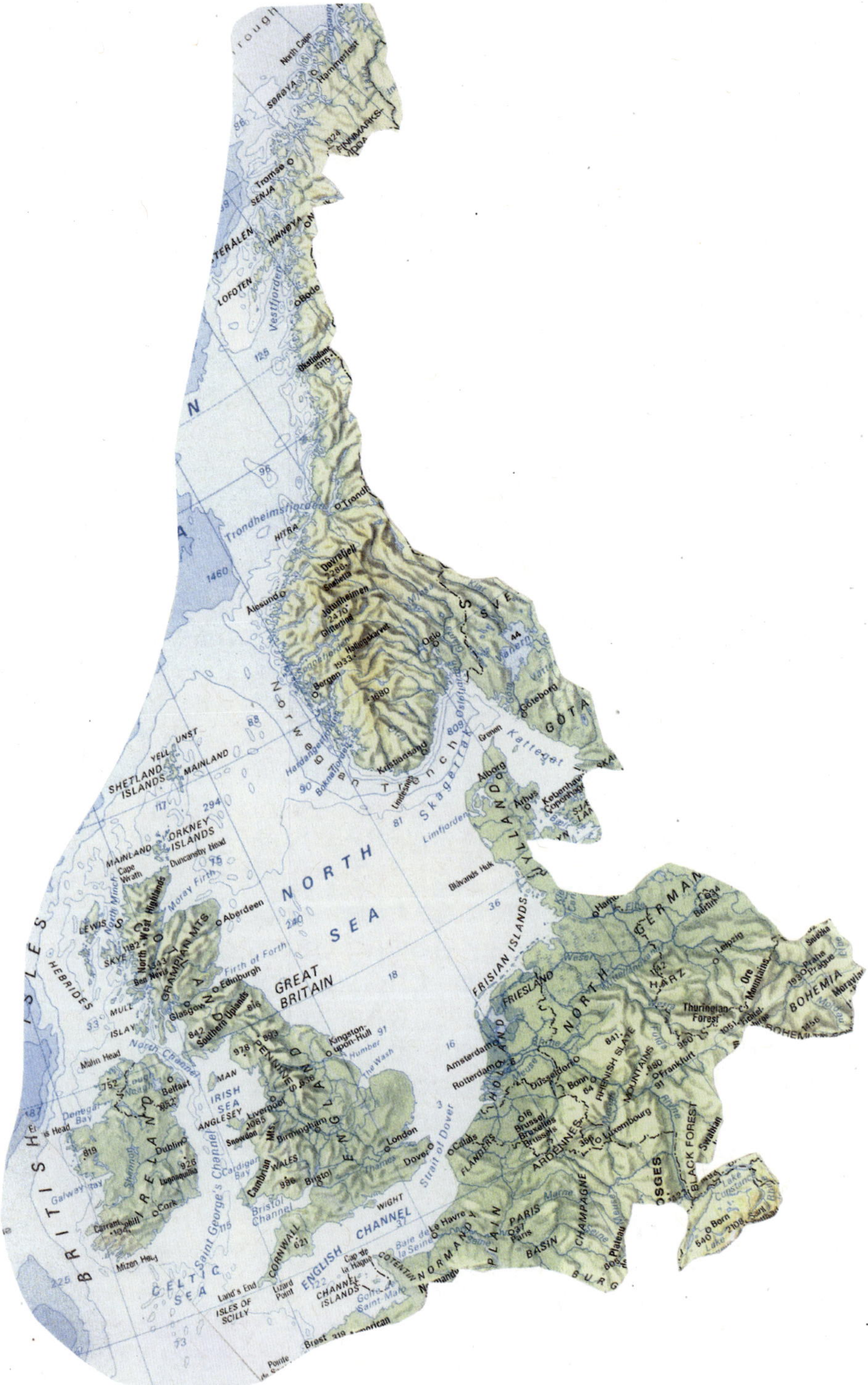

This is the North Sea basin continuing to the Norwegian current. As our satellite imagery of the Danish micro-algae bloom in 1988 shows, there is a massive current flow from the English Channel to Denmark/Sweden/Norway. This means those Scandinavian countries would be the ones affected by any mistake or leak at nuclear reprocessing facilities in France and the UK.

Hand-grab harvest of Fucus inter-tidal seaweeds from rocky shores. What has to be done: collect. Any way you can, as if just to survive, collect the seaweed you can find. Then put the seaweed in sealed containers with anaerobic cultures inside. Thus, produce methane. This is what we will be doing to phase out fossil fuels:

(1) deploy submarines for efficient machine-harvest and gasification, with frozen storage on board; (2) here and there, not everywhere, place buoyed, anchored rope rigs, usually in grids, to grow Laminaria or similar blade kelp; (3) at a local brewery, in Neudorf for example, use fermentation vats, or add more, to convert the harvested seaweed into methane gas; (4) conduct the gas by pipeline to home or industrial users, including an intermediate wholesale outlet, the post-petroleum gas station ("Untankstelle," with no tanks), and symbolize this act with a small buoy offshore, near the beach at, say, Otterndorf, where a stream of methane can burn. The slogan: we are independent. We depend on no one, neither the US/UK nor Russia. We rely on the soil in the sea. (5)Further inland, in shallows where waters are more fresh, vegetation in the water can be collected by gantry crane on slow moving twin-hulled barges. Along the entire length of the Elbe, excess biomass is scooped up. A result appears in the city, in the heart of the financial and shipping district, signaled by buoys.

Action on the Elbe is just a start. We follow the flows out to the high seas. The Elbe and Weser streams pass along the west Danish coast, then get pushed into the Kattegat, the gap between Denmark and Sweden. There, as an Ocean Earth satellite survey showed in 1988, the detritus can jam, then rot, then spark a toxic micro-algae bloom. Large area growth of macro-algae, especially brown kelp like Laminaria, can absorb the excess nutrients better, with no toxic blooms and no eutrophication. Indeed, brown algae are beneficial to fish and shellfish; they prosper together well, with oxygen supply in the water enhanced. So, along the entire Danish coast, extending south to the Belt Islands, extensive brown algae growth protects the sea animals and helps assure strong fisheries. Recall that before the Industrial Revolution the Kattegat and Baltic (East) Sea just beyond were so rich in fish that a spear stuck in the water, anywhere, would make a catch. We aim to make that happen again. We notice where else the outflows from the Elbe go, on to the southern coast of Norway, then west and north into the Norwegian Current—on to North Cape and the Arctic. The entire swirl of waters can be used. We plan now a test for Laminaria. The North Sea has been sweeping sand into a gap there. One can inoculate the sands, let them be absorbed by kelp using solar energy, then collect the kelp—all in a form of preemptive, organic dredging.

Both in the Tees mouth and the Elbe mouth, the harvest areas are influenced by both the river and the salt sea.

GIANT ALGAE SYSTEM

In launching Macrocystis-based industry on a planetary scale, we were advised by world-top algae scientist, Dr. Gerald Boalch, to start in the Southern Hemisphere. That means, in waters spinning off from Antarctica. In 2004, during a residency in Plymouth, Dr. Boalch said, "go to Chile." In 1997, we presaged such a dictum by promoting Giant Algae System, being Macrocystis-based algae industry. We centered this on Antarctica and waters splaying out. Research continued for us in New Zealand and Australia. It could also be conducted in our first satellite-monitoring site: the Falklands. And yes, with two Ocean Earth stakeholders, Eve Vaterlaus and Catherine Griffiths, we'd work with Chilean scientists. But where can such work kick in as imperative economic action? Africa?

A first site for action is South Africa. Another seacoast in the world with Macrocystis as native: western North America, the LA basin. The algae

scientist who advised us the most, Dr. Wheeler North of Caltech, thought we could "start" in the LA basin, then try corollary testing and production in a similar slope, that of Albania.
Why there? He reasoned that such work there could happen in only the winter season, when water is cold enough, and that the isolation and poverty of Albania would make a manual seaweed industry economically plausible.

Now we concentrate on Africa, all linked to Arctic by flyways.

Could socio-political and economic success be proven first in Africa, especially South Africa then at the Elbe mouth?

South Africa has the two submarine shipyards of Africa. Such shipyards are needed, along with good coastal waters, for testing of the seaweed rig and harvesting technology. The rule: always stay in or under the water; never pull things out of the water with surface ships.

Such an industry can extend to the biggest cold-water currents of the planet: Humboldt Current, Leeuwin Current, Tasman Current, Argentine Current.

The three northern hemisphere counterparts are the Labrador Current (to NY), Oyashio Current (to Tokyo), and Irminger Current (to south of Iceland). All such currents dive deep and become very slow-moving masses, resurfacing off Antarctica after one thousand years.

A Macrocystis industry in Antarctica is outlined thus, in a continuation of reasoning about the Antarctica landmass, all sloping to the Southern Ocean, started by Norway in the 1930s. We continue in the spirit of Norway expressed by Roald Amundsen, not Jens Stoltenberg.

All is described in the Giant Algae System text, on the following pages.

GIANT ALGAE SYSTEM

G.A.S.

IDEAS AND MODES OF MATERIAL THOUGHT ORIGINATED IN RECENT ART INCORPORATED BY ARCHITECTS, SCIENTISTS AND ENGINEERS INTO NEW STRUCTURES AND TECHNOLOGIES THAT SERVE CITIES, IN PRACTICAL URBANISM.

HERE, A SUBMERSIBLE FLOATING CAGE, OR OFF-SHORE RIG, FOR PRODUCTION AND HARVESTING OF GIANT BROWN ALGAE, FOR PRIMARY-SECTOR EXTRACTION OF NUTRIENTS ACCUMULATING IN COASTAL WATERS, WITH POTENTIAL TO YIELD LARGE QUANTITIES OF METHANE OR HYDROGEN GAS, FOR A REPLENISHABLE URBAN SUPPLY THAT ASSURES CLEAN AIR. HENCE THE TERM "CLEAN AIR RIG", C.A.R., MEETING THE FIRST CONDITION FOR THE ARCHITECTURE OF CITIES: CLEAN AIR.

OUR PROJECT: TO COMPLETE BUILDING TEST VERSIONS OF THE C.A.R., THEN TEST IT IN A SPECIFICALLY PERMITTED SITE IN NEW ZEALAND, WINTER 1998, USING GIANT BROWN ALGAE—CHIEFLY RAPID-GROWTH MACROCYSTIS.

ALL RESULTS OF THE TESTS TO BE OWNED BY GIANT ALGAE SYSTEM CORPORATION (GAS CORP), THE INVESTMENT VEHICLE, TO BE APPLIED IN SITES AROUND THE TEMPERATE SOUTHERN HEMISPHERE AND PACIFIC NORTH AMERICA WHERE THE RAPID-GROWTH MACROCYSTIS IS NOW PRESENT.

3

The following pages are excerpts from the 1997 report for investment to build and install the "CAR, Clean Air Rig, Carbon Absorption Rig, Cities Architecture Rudiment." This shows the offshore engineering structure for giant algae growth and harvesting by the Giant Algae System Corporation (GAS Corp), a subsidiary of the Ocean Earth Development Corporation (OEDC), New York City.

Towards Ocean Trials of Clean Air Rigs, or Carbon Absorption Rigs, or Cities Architecture Rudiment (C.A.R.)

In the course of queries on how the City shall be supplied with fuel, or how Industry shall be supplied with the rawstuff for production of steel, plastics and numerous chemical goods, the Ocean Earth Development Corporation has reasoned that Algae would be a reliable source.

There can be freshwater algae, such as the Botryoccocus braunii that can grow aviation fuel grade hydrocarbons in its own cells, and there can be saltwater algae such as Gracilaria, which has successfully been grown in the Mediterranean for the absorption of urban run-off with a final yield as methane gas, but Ocean Earth has focused its attention on giant brown algae, to be grown in the open sea in what are recognized to be the world's fastest rates of carbon absorption and solar-energy conversion, or growth. Attention is focused on the open sea, further, only because this is a vast, uninhabited area which, particularly at upwellings (artificial or natural) and near coasts, can be a non-depletable receptacle for nutrients. Crops grown upland deplete the nutrients upland; crops grown at upwellings or coastal waters offshore, if managed well, can never deplete the nutrients offshore.

Taking a large-cycle view of the movement of soil and water, Ocean Earth has focused on developing what can be called the Offshore Soil Rig. Any harvest offshore is a return to upland sites of soil nutrients accumulated offshore or upwelled from sea bottoms offshore. For the public, the term is C.A.R., or Clean Air Rig (as an urban product), also Carbon Absorption Rig (as block against Greenhouse Effect), or still, following Cities Service, the Cities Architecture Rudiment (as an initial act, not sufficient but necessary, for architectural development of a city).

The yield can be an entirely non-polluting fuel: either methane or hydrogen.

The chief dangers to such an industry are:

(1) pollution, which retards the growth of crops and fish;
(2) dams which block the flow of soil nutrients to the sea.

Both dangers are well known. Yet both dangers have not been successfully addressed. There has been some progress on reducing pollution in certain rivers, but overall the oceans of the world, and particularly the regional seas like the North Sea, Baltic and Mediterranean, become more polluted, not less. There is no progress regarding dams: time and again, in country after country, river after river, the building of hydroelectric projects continues, and sometimes accelerates, becoming what is arguably the main cause for the sharp decline in numbers (and size) of fish in the oceans and rivers of the world. One cannot attribute the declines in ocean fertility or fish numbers, and size, in waters off Newfoundland or Iceland to pollution (nearly none), marsh filling (none, either) or overfishing (little change after sharp reductions in fishing quotas), particularly after fishing efforts are cut back. One can attribute these declines to the one industrial phenomenon common to both regions: the damming of rivers.

If there is an adequate supply of nutrients in the sea, and if there is not much pollution, then one can conduct ocean trials in waters naturally conducive to giant brown algae. For now, we focus on the fastest-growth algae, of the genera Macrocystis.

Offshore Soil Rig, or Clean Air Rig

The Rig is submersible, and it is to be built in a shipyard familiar with submersibles. We have discussed this with Australian Submarine Industries, in Adelaide, Australia. They say they can build a submersible rig, which can fall from or return to the ocean surface quickly as wave action increases or declines, for about half the cost—and with more technical expertise—of a conventional shipyard. The time required for production of the first ocean-trials rig, according to this and other firms, has been estimated at 1-2 months. We are aware, further, of Norwegian work with submersible cage systems.

The Rig, which could measure as little as 10 meters in diameter and 10 meters in depth, should be submersible at least an additional 10 meters. It should be set in waters no less than 30-40 meters deep.

First tests should be in relatively calm, sheltered waters, so the depth there can be just about 30 meters.

But more demanding tests, in more exposed, tempestuous seas, where one might need to submerge twice as deep during storms, up to 20 meters, should be in waters with a depth of at least 40 meters.
In any case, the deeper the waters for testing, the better.

Duration of the Ocean Trials need not be long, at least in testing the main points:

submersibility
re-emergibility
survival of the Rig during storms
survival of the Algae during deep submersion

7

survival of the Algae during periods of growth
harvestability of the Algae.

Assuming that the Algae fronds are mature when attached to the holdfasts of the Rig, then the Trials can be conducted within several months.

Fronds would be attached to the holdfasts until after initial growth in a nursery, so there is no need to deal with the full life-cycle of the Algae.

As soon as the Algae have achieved a mature growth rate, of up to two meters per week, then harvesting tests can begin. We propose:

cropping the Algae from below and re-attaching
thinning the Algae from above, at the same time
cropping the entire frond, then attaching new fronds.

A full growing season, of about six months, would be best.

The structural tests, of the Rig and of the Algae behavior as the Rig is submerged and re-emerges, are the most critical.

Harvestability, and various techniques of harvesting, are not as critical. Somehow or other optimal solutions can be found; there has been much experience in this.

There seems to have been no successful experience with a large submersible structure to accommodate artificial beds of giant algae, such as Macrocystis. But we will confirm this with a Chinese source who claims to have grown Macrocystis on artificial structures.

Given the importance of the Ocean Trials, it seems that monitoring should be done continuously. There should be close observation of what occurs, particularly during storms. A sheltered site close to shore is best. The people in charge of the project should be able to get to the site quickly, even from a house or boat nearby, in case of dynamic events.

For monitoring, we recommend:

(1) several monitoring buoys;
(2) an overhead camera, suspended by tethered balloon;
(3) an underwater camera with remote switch-on capacity;
(4) an anchored boat with at least one person, ready to enter the water with scuba gear.

8

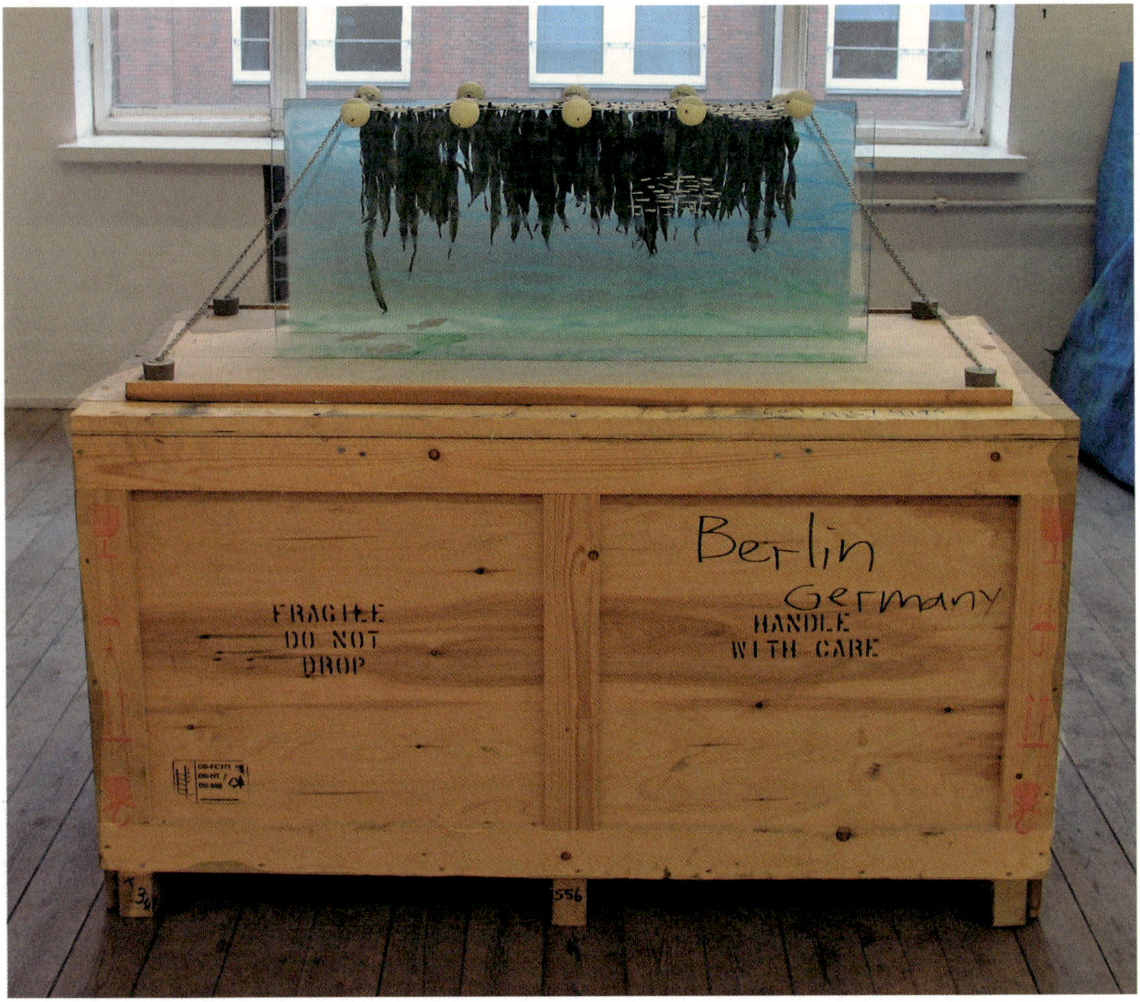

This is a maquette by Eve Vaterlaus for the exhibition at Galerie für Landschaftskunst, then at the Sharjah Biennial, of a rope-rig algae field. This is not in any sense scientific except to say that most algae hangs from a rope, unlike Macrocystis, which is buoyed by its own platters.

ALGAE ROPE-RIG

Just as the tractor has become a fixture of farms, or the automobile of roads, so can the algae rig become a fixture of the sea. It functions to absorb nutrients in the sea for degradation back to industrial methane and other raw stuff. An algae rig, unlike a tractor or auto, can be astonishingly cheap. It can be simple: just a grid of ropes held in place by anchored buoys, with rapid-growth algae attached. That works in sheltered or shallow waters for large kelp, such as Laminaria, or medium–sized tuft algae, like Gracilaria. In East Asia, such rigs are tradition. But what about casting rigs into less sheltered, more open waters? What about making them able to submerge during storms or rough seas to avoid algae breakup? What about making them more seaworthy? And what about speeding up growth and harvest rates with mechanization and regular trimming rather than full-plant harvest? This model here follows drawings of traditional Chinese design, as published in the proceedings of a Chinese–US conference (1983, when they were sharing ideas) on algae-rig engineering for——yes, they were thinking of it then——methane gas production. The model is executed by a founding shareholder of Ocean Earth Development Corporation, Eve Vaterlaus. It models one of the simplest of all rigs.

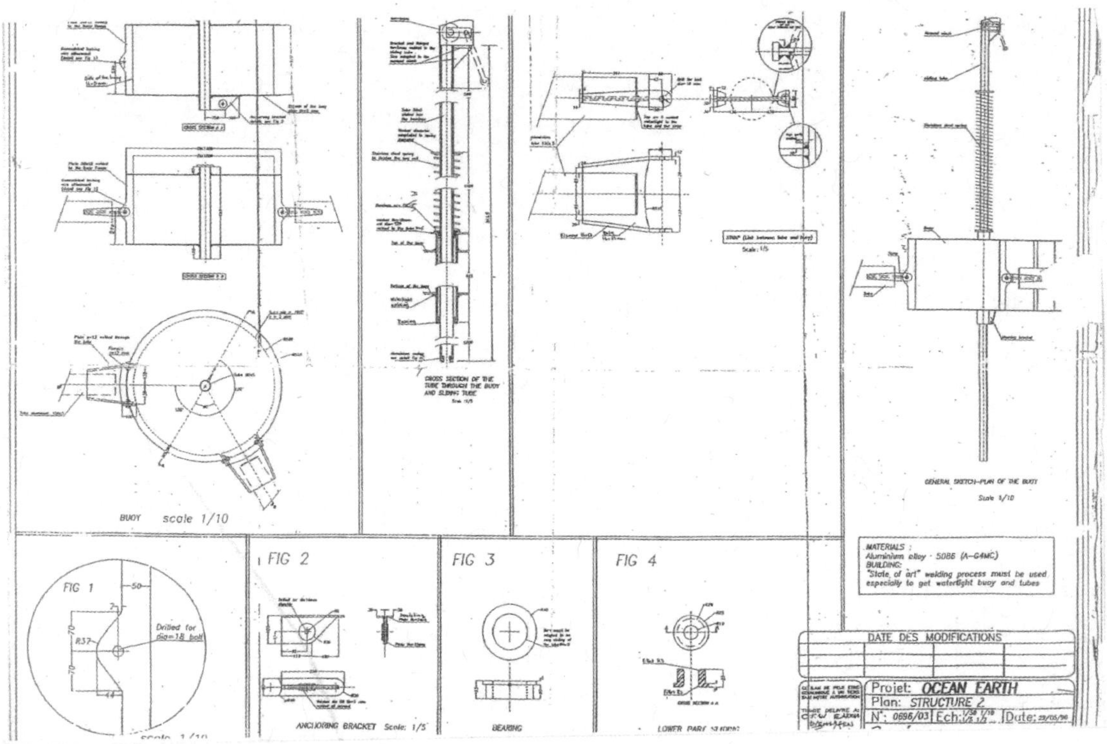

This is one of five sheets of naval architectural drawings by Marc Lombard from La Rochelle, France. He is the inventor of the current formula of America's Cup yachts. He called this project *Hope*.

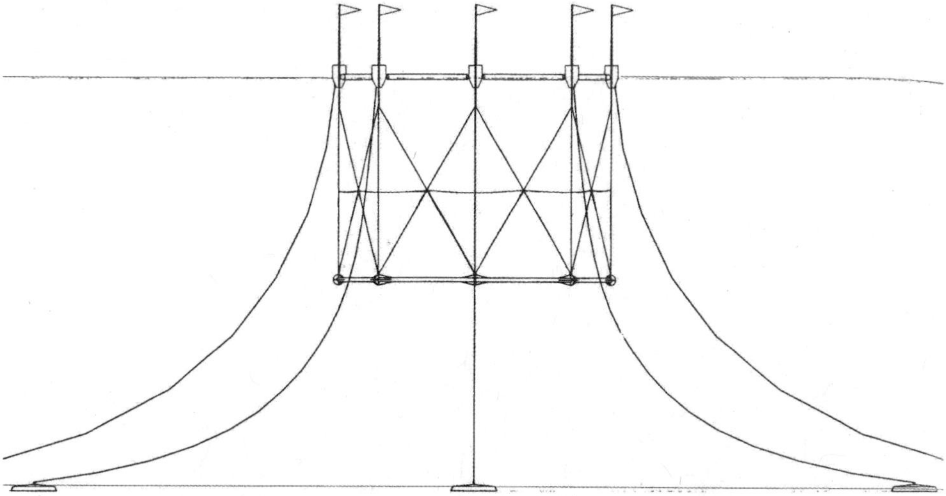

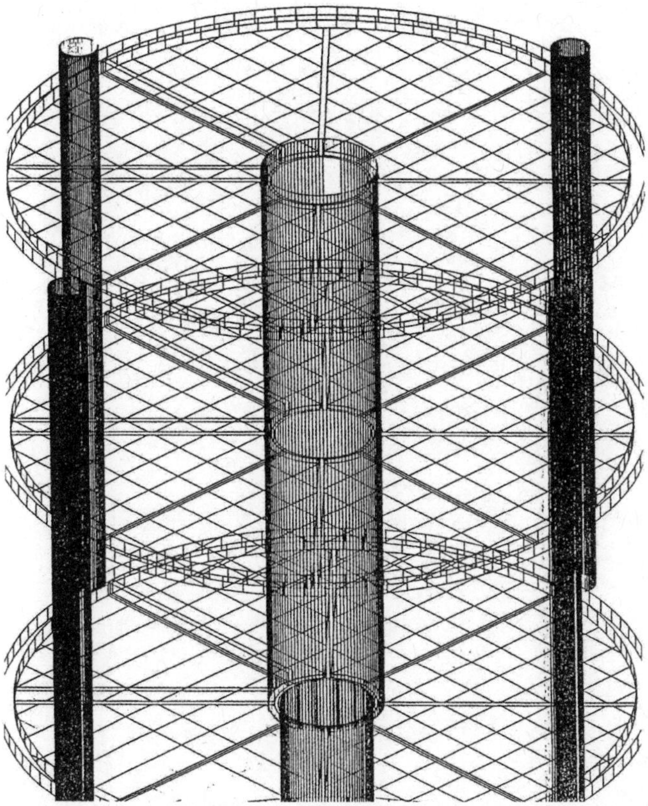

On the top part of the page is an elevation drawing of the final version of a rig designed by Lombard. Each buoy (flagged) has a spring rod extending to the structure so that while they bob up and down the holdfast level, hence the plants remain undisturbed. This presumes waves no higher than the range of spring elasticity: five meters. Lombard recommends sea tests first in a sheltered bay. On the lower part of the page is a perspectival drawing of an early version of rig, upgraded by the studio of Marc Lombard, manifesting Ocean Earth theories about a movable holdfast grid, which can be periodically drawn below, to allow for cutting away from both senescing ends of the Macrocystis, at their biological rates of senescence of up to two meters (one meter at each end) a week.

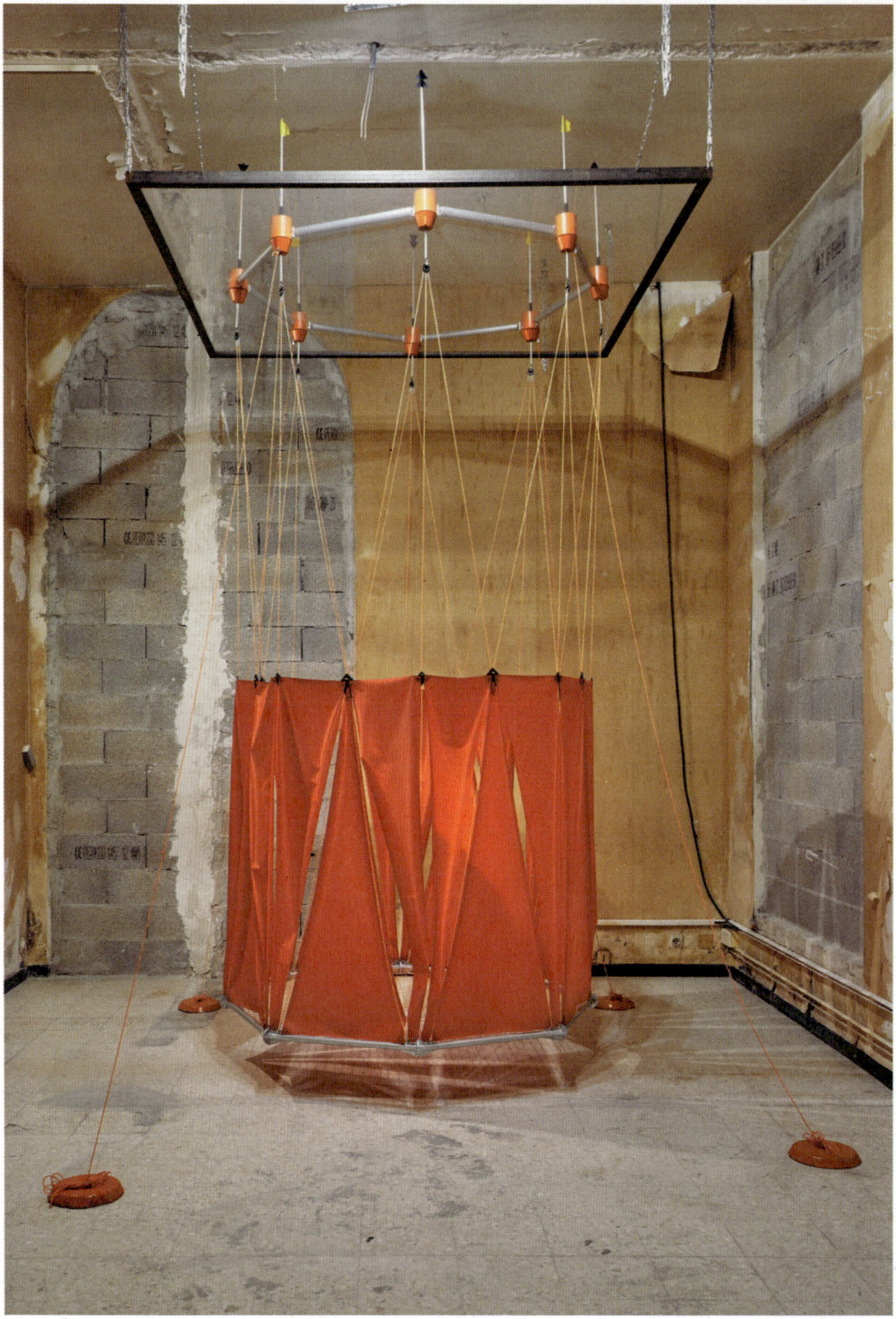

All these structures shown are meant to be submersible during storms and have spring/buoy systems (as shown in the drawing to the left) to absorb oscillation. This needs to be tested at sea with plants to find out how deep the divers have to go and if the plants can survive rapid submersion.

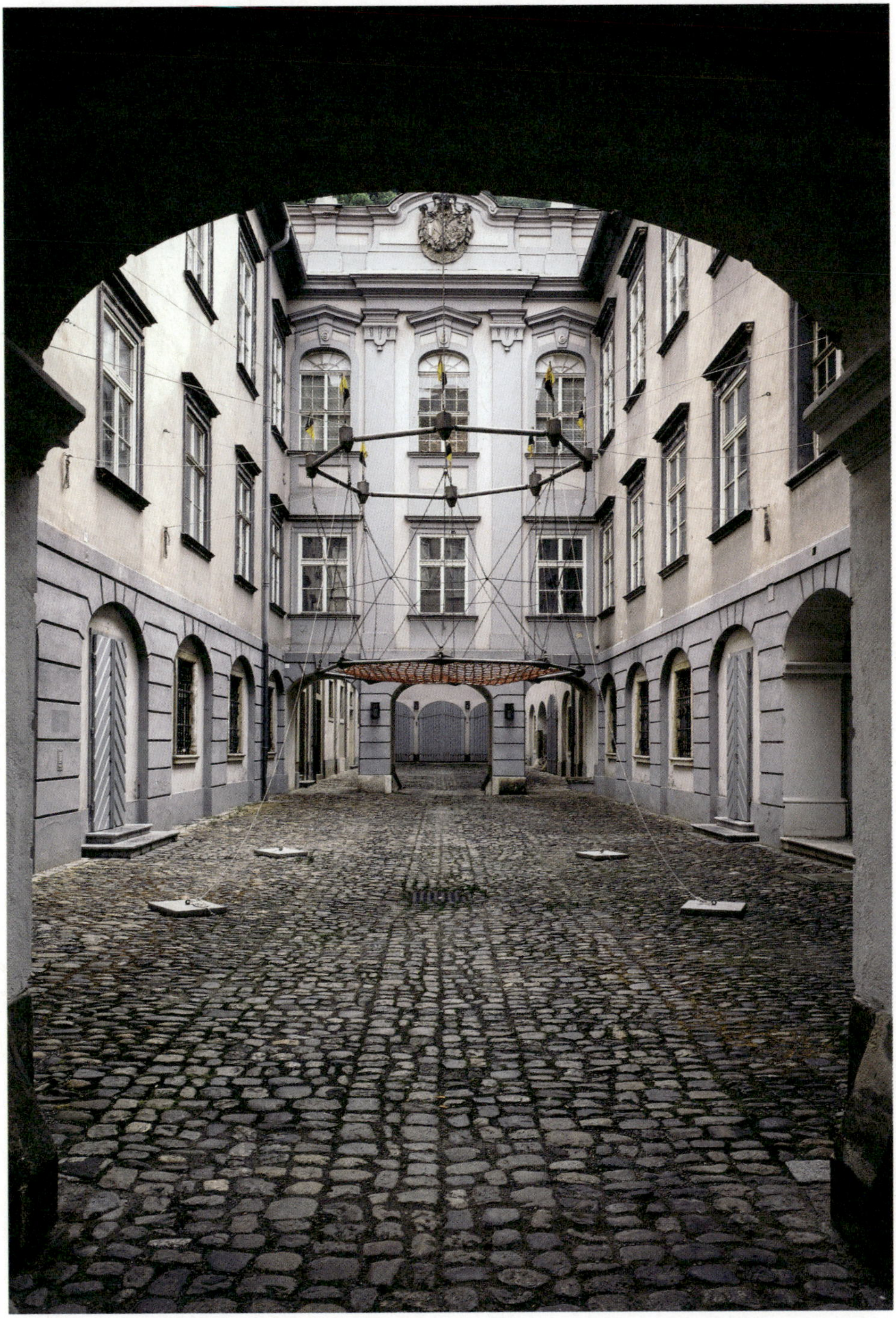

A more realistic version of the Macrocystis bladder kelp rig was commissioned by Peter Weibel in Graz and constructed in a shipyard in Trieste with genuine naval material.

FLYWAY 4
Donau/Oder Corridor

Ocean Treaty Organizations:
AOTO and ARTO

Project Site:
ADRIATIC BASINS; WEST MEDITERRANEAN BASIN

ITALIAN STRATEGY

SURVIVAL TACTICS

The concern of the military is guarantee of the conditions for public well-being. The concern is guarantee of the integrity of home territory.

The home territory of Italy is the Mediterranean.

The Italian Navy sends its training ship Amerigo Vespucci on tour throughout the Mediterranean to broadcast the message that the Mediterranean must be restored.

That is not enough.

If Italians are to survive, if they are to be guaranteed the conditions necessary to their well-being, if their home sea is to be free from dangers of pollution--whether urban waste, fossil fuel, or thermonuclear--these actions will be taken.

1. Italian Navy develops comprehensive monitoring program for the Mediterranean Sea. It begins perhaps with a more-defined sea: the Adriatic. The monitoring begins with sonar bottom-mapping developed by the US Navy. Then it incorporates in that geometry monitoring programs by satellites and aircraft of currents, tidal patterns, pollution, and biological phenomena. The data bases of meteorological satellites, of Landsat scanners, of radar satellites and of the US military's MARS sattelites are combined to gain a complete video-imagable or photograph-printable range of pictures of the Sea.

2. Italian Navy also adopts research program on nutrient upwelling and seaweed harvesting started by, inter alias, Dr. Howard Wilcox of the US Navy. The seaweed harvesting program is made similar to grape-harvesting programs, in rig design, manual attention, and subsequent fermentation. This activity is closely coordinated with ENI, the Italian state oil company, as a practice towards obtaining all required hydrocarbons in Italy as methane fuel, a non-polluting biogas.

3. Satellite earth-imaging by Italian Navy employs technologies and software of Interpretation Systems Incorporated and Grumman Aerospace, who contract substantially with the military. This program is expanded upstream and onto dry terrain as the sources of pollutants, freshwaters or nutrients become subject to the overall Mediterranean picture. In the Adriatic, imaging would soon include all the Po and many of the rivers spilling down the Yugoslav slope from steel mills, say. To understand nutrient and freshwater balances in the Levantine Sea, a satellite-image probe would have to be conducted up the Nile to its source--and then up the Rhone, the Ebro, and into the Black Sea.

This text was written in 1981 for the exhibition "New York/New Wave" and reflected Peter Fend's general view that the chief role of the military is a defense against ecological threats. In his habit of handing out photocopies (Fend's father worked as a research scientist at Xerox) to people (especially at art openings), he also gave David Byrne a copy of this text. Before there were business cards, handing out photocopies was Fend's way of building a career. Though the text had no specific audience, it is part of a continued habit of writing on an electric typewriter and now on a computer in a legal Courier typeface.

4. Biological scientists at Assoreni, the research agency of the Italian state oil company, expand the bioproteins program. The Italian government encourages private research as well, such as that by Liquichimica. Projects are targeted towards developing a nutrient-bomb--a canister or package of easily-dispersed nutrient-rich material which can be spread throughout a marsh, oasis or field, to be taken up by animals, as opposed to microorganisms, and to therefore become an ecosystem-activating agent directly through the animal food chain. Assoreni cooperates with national and federal wastes administrations to determine those pyroloysis or other gas products of urban-waste processing which can be refined enough to become substrates for bioprotein production.

5. Italian Air Force test-bombs bioprotein packages on ecosystems' feeding grounds. As results become predictable, Air Force develops schedule and flightpaths of routine year-round nutrient bombing runs. Paths probably coincide with those of migratory birds.

6. Italian Marines (Lagunari) and Army go to major feeding-nutrient transfer grounds and build up the conditions for species and water/salts circulation. They build lagoons, interspersed marshholes, sinks, backwaters, salt/fresh water mixing continuua, sandbars and spits, inland and oceanshore estuaries, salt-flat underground-animal sites. Sites are identified with help of satellites.

7. Earth observation is consolidated under command of Italian SPACE FORCE. Prime task of Space Force is comprehensive image processing, using great variety of satellite and scanner sources. Future tasks might include asteroid exploration or prototype energy/mining programs--or, similarly, disarming Soviet or US satellites. The Space Force offers services, in league with Interpretation Systems Incorporated, to governments throughout the world. As other governments buy arms, so now they can buy through Space Force its imaging arts. Towards this objective, the Italians launch in 1981 a scientific satellite testing how atmosphere functions and how it distorts scanner readings of the planet. Sales of Space Force hardware expand globally, and soon--particularly through telecasts arranged by Telespazio--the imaging programs become part of television in Italy and throughout the globe. The entire surface area of the globe could become subject to Italian military techniques.

8. As the Sahara and other arid or barren zones become populated with game animals, Army and Air Force coordinate air-ground attack and feeding programs on the animals. Army will [illegible] test structures (e.g., fall traps and guidelanes) for harvest of game) and Air Force will test bombs, bombing techniques, and possible aerial drives of game towards their competition and chase-selected death. Killing structures and practices are designed to leave as much choice as possible to the wiles and strength of individuals within the species, so that evolution continues along the competitive, selective path.

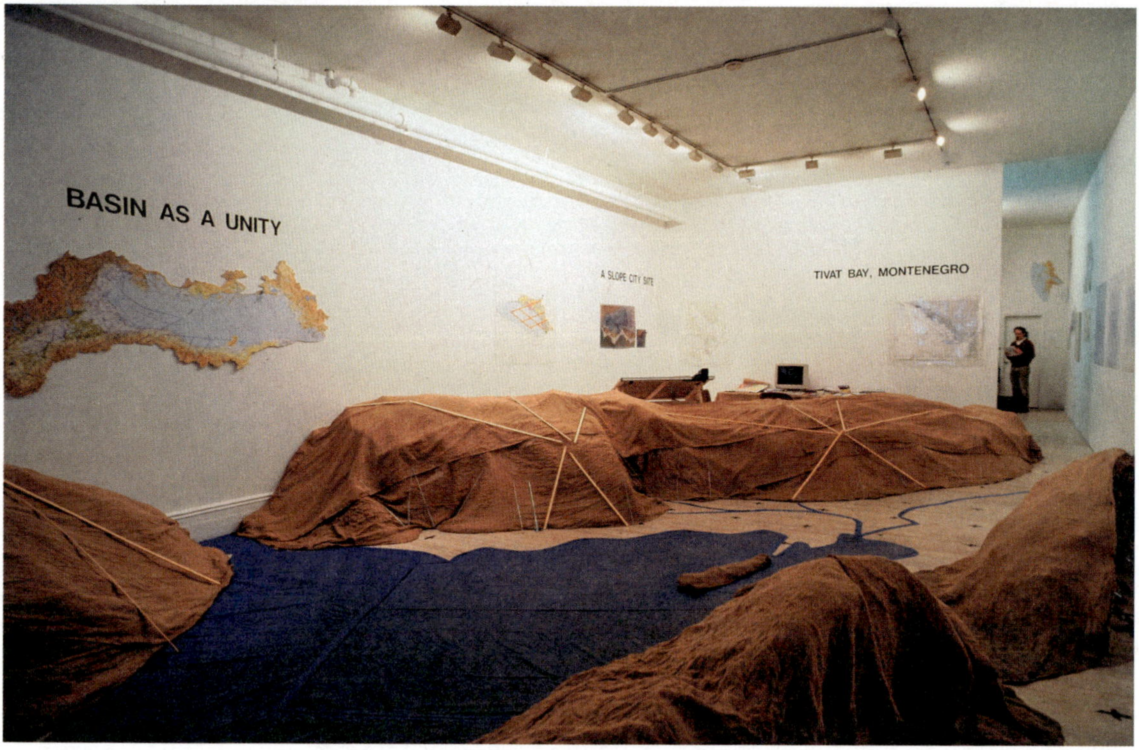

Architecture is made with the body in space, not only by hand. In 1992, *Site Simulator*, a walk-through model of the Tivat Bay urban development area in Montenegro, was installed at American Fine Arts in New York. In that room, three trained architects worked. It was a way to address the challenge of ecological development in an "ecological republic," done with a Yugoslav firm and Kevin Gannon, who had left Paul Rudolph to work with OE. A US government grant was awarded to return there to work with the Institute of Marine Biology.

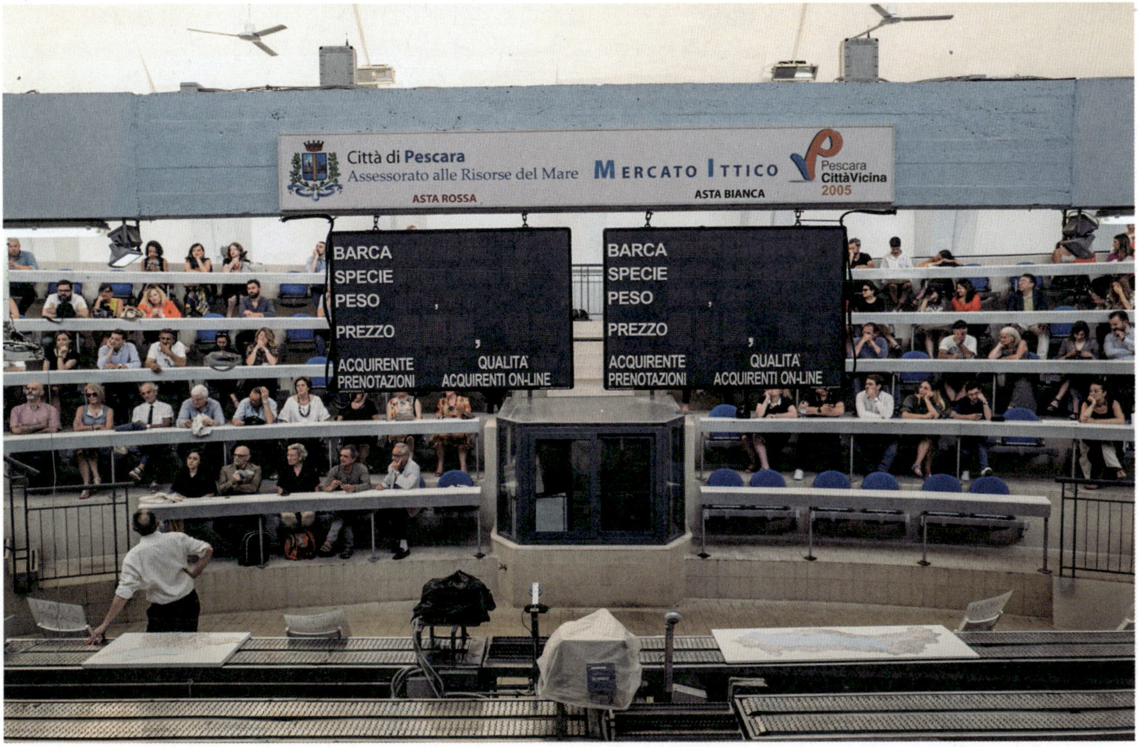

Following an invitation by curator Massimiliano Scuderi and Fondazione Zimei, Fend delivered a presentation to the mayor and city council of Pescara, with live translation, in 2018 at the city's high-tech fish market. This market was much more advanced and fishermen friendlier than the ones on the coast of China. In this case Italy could help China.

The following pages are experts from a barrage of Emails sent by Peter Fend during 2021, which failed to prompt action in spite of Italy leading the UN initiative to organize the UN around the oceans, not nuclear weapons.

ITALY ACTION IN NORTH AFRICA,
DUE TO THE DANGER FROM PLAGUE

CONSTRUCT THE FUTURE
DECONSTRUCT THE PAST

WHAT ITALIANS MUST DO TO SURVIVE

The scenario for human future offered by Bill Gates in a Washington Post Live event in 2021 funded by Jeff Bezos was, as Gates acknowledged, just "1984." Our Big Brothers can be Bill and Jeff.

And it won't work. Because having a database on everyone, and making sure that everyone has scores of vaccinations for every known infectious disease, will not suffice to protect "everyone," or even the human species. As Bill acknowledged, between his many sips of coffee (was he tired?), another variant of an infectious disease will pop up. If the human species tries to survive by fighting off viruses, it will disappear. The viruses will win. They will win because the only secure defense against species wipeout is a massive complexity and diversity of species, of plants, fish, insects, birds, reptiles, and mammals. Survival of humanity requires the vigorous survival of billions of other creatures. We could have learned that from Noah's Ark.

In response to France spending fourteen billion Euro on a "greenbelt" east–west across the Sahel from the Atlantic to the Red Sea, Italy should spend a comparable amount on building up bird flyways north–south across the Sahel and the Sahara, from Sub-Sahara Africa to the Mediterranean Sea, and onward north.

A comparable amount, given Italy's population of sixty million as against France's population of sixty-seven million, is thirteen billion Euro.

Both Italy and France have similar economic losses, in GDP, due to COVID-19, and Italy has fared somewhat worse in infections and deaths.

We can all recognize that plagues are linked to ecological degradation, and that such degradation is a no. One global fact.

Human survival requires the restoration of bird, insect, fish, and mammal numbers from even a generation ago.

Europe is a small place. The President of the European Commission, Ursula von der Leyen, has said that the COVID-19 plague compels member states of Europe to coordinate their actions. If France does one program in Africa to restore animal habitat, then Italy can do a complementary program. We can remember the qur'anic advice, from the Surah Ya-Sin Ayat excerpt, that "waters gush forth" if the numbers of habitat-building animals are sizable. These animals make the muck and mud, and distribute the seeds and fertilizer, and spread the pollen, with which greenery prevails.

Decades of research on bird-insect flyways, and on restoration of deserts to savannah, have been done under the rubric of Earth Art. Much mapping of Africa and the Mediterranean, and even of the destinations for breeding in the Arctic, has been done. All this research can be brought to bear on how Italy would spend thirteen billion Euro to complement what France will spend fourteen billion on. Italian companies and soldiers have a presence already in many of the sites studied. These include: Ghat, Niamey, Misrata, Gabes (extending across the Gulf of Gabes westward to the sub-sea-level salt lakes of Chott Melhrir and Chott el Jerid, Sirte, Bardai, and the Aouzou Strip, Djibouti and the salt lakes that surround it, Uganda, Ethiopia, the Nile Delta. Work in all sites can be expanded to build up water and shade among migratory-flight paths.

Pioneers whose works and designs would be used include: Dennis Oppenheim, Michael Heizer, Walter De Maria, Rebecca Horn, Peter Fend, Robert Smithson. All such people are known as international artists. They are pioneers in material culture, or the technical means of production. Their work can be organized and positioned for sites along bird-insect flyways across North Africa, also in relation to clouds from the south and the west, in the Amazon, all towards an organized follow-through on what France starts with fourteen billion, for a total "one percent for art" cost of what Italy could undertake: 130 million Euro. At the very least, the images produced can be part of project definition, both internally and to the world public. Detailed site work has already been conducted, over three decades, with aeronautical and topographic charts, and with civil-satellite data.

Payment of a "one percent" amount only occurs IF a multi-billion Euro project as we propose even starts. A very substantial presentation of site technologies and site surveys with plans can be made at any time. Already one presentation is scheduled in Vienna at Galerie Georg Kargl.

A multi-billion Euro project, as now proposed for Italy, uses ca. 6.5% of the two hundred billion provided to Italy by the European Union for a response to COVID-19 We believe this is part of a comprehensive response.

Participants in this proposal for Italy, including ENI, the military, any ecological or ornithological program, civil-engineering firms, several art entities and, as the author of the proposal, Peter Fend, of Ocean Earth Development Corporation, first exhibiting the flyway buildup practices for North Africa together with Europe at Caltech in 1978.

AFRICA E ARTICO VIA EUROPA

Five thousand years ago, what had been animal-rich savannah in northern Africa transformed, over about one thousand years, into desert.

Now, due to two hundred years of ever-greater combustion of fossil hydrocarbons, along with vast tracts of monocultured lands, and of buildings in sprawl, the transformation into desert spreads both north and south, faster than ever.

In the past one hundred years, humans have also built a half-million dams, breaking the natural flow of freshwater to the saltwater seas and coastal marshes, nearly wiping out most higher animal species, and disturbing the evolution-established cycles of evaporation and precipitation.

Evidence of desertification is throughout the "temperate" world. One sees it with yellow trees in Berlin and Switzerland. One sees it with locust plagues in Italy. One sees it with unprecedented summer heat.

In Sardinia, where the exhibition "Africa—Arctic Flyway" took place, the annual precipitation has dropped in recent decades by 50%. A summer vacation there becomes risky, due to——every year now——the forests catching fire.

Imperatives become evident.

(1) Replace fossil fuels with biofuels, and energy from other zero-emissions sources.
(2) Replace the dams that cause a sharp decline in life-forms along each river, and then the sea.
(3) Remove excess or fallen, rotting vegetation from anywhere it accumulates, in water or on land.

The first imperative was inevitable. Fossil fuels would disappear within centuries, and then what?

The second imperative challenges common belief: we're all told that hydropower is somehow "renewable," but every dammed reservoir will fill up with detritus, with silt, with pollutants; every reservoir becomes a temporary, and life-destructive, shortcut.

The third imperative confirms what we learned from Adam and Eve: the plants, even animals, must be culled; even in Paradise, there is work to do.

To meet these imperatives only in Sardinia, a professed "Paradiso," is not enough. They must be met along the full length of flying-animal migration through Sardinia, from jungle Africa to tundra Arctic. We show all the places along the north–south route.

We mount this show during the late-fall/winter pause in Sardinia's tourism calendar, during a time when people can wonder, How do we prevent another climate-disaster summer as we had in 2019? There might be some winter sports too, such as alpine and Nordic skiing nearby, and even wintertime surfing on both east and west coasts, but all the time there's a question: could summer 2020 be, somehow, better?

We show how.

(1) The current state-approved plan for "methanization" of all Sardinia, being a regular supply of LNG to a small-scale regasification plant in Oristano (or also Cagliari?), all feeding into a pipeline network aligned with the railroad, and—for remoter areas—to truck transport, WILL NOT, according to calculations by the Union of Concerned Scientists, lead to any significant decline in carbon emissions, or "warming." The "methanization" is arranged by one of the world's largest traders in fossil fuels, based in London. They have "teamed up" with companies from Norway and Switzerland, and then a company in Sardinia, to establish a permanent customer base for imported fossil LNG. This only increases the warming and the desertification. The pipeline would be built from 2020 to 2025, but only for fossil hydrocarbons? The big talk, from London and Rome, has been that Sardinia would become a model of "transition"

from coal and oil to methane gas… but what's the "transition"? Improvements come only with gas from biological sources, based on this or recent year solar influx.

Show ways to reduce hydrocarbon or hydrogen fuels, or even electricity on site, with excess vegetation collected in reservoirs or canals inland, or offshore and (as in Sicily's Marzamemi), on the coast.

(2) The current claims of dams being a "good" source of energy, in not having emissions, disregard what is visible on Google Earth, and what is well-documented by zoologists. The dammed reservoirs appear green, full of phytoplankton and vegetation, while the seawaters appear clear and blue, with very little phytoplankton. But of course, the reservoirs accumulate silts (and pollutants), and these cause an explosion of vegetation in the reservoirs. The explosion depletes oxygen, killing animal life therein. Add to this the blockage of fish movement by the dams, and one reaches a near-total wipeout of freshwater animal species. Any migrating bird seeking freshwater finds, instead, a lifeless zone with few surviving fish and, often, toxins in the water. Immediate action is needed.

(a) Remove the vegetation and algae accumulating in reservoirs.
(b) If possible, convert that removed biomass to biogas, or—as it is crude and unsuitable for pipe-lines?—to electricity on site.
(We have a contract with a chemical engineer for the processes.)
(c) If dammed waters are not clogged and deadly, restock with fish.
(d) Within a year or two, especially now with the low water levels behind dams, start deconstruction of the dams, turning them into terraces with whitewater rapids between levels.
(e) Install run-of-the-river hydroelectric technologies, such as screws or arrays, suspended over the rapids, of Poncelet/Duchamp waterwheels of Ocean Earth design.

A crash program could convert the entire hydroelectric and water storage industry of Sardinia, with more than fifty dams, within one or two years.

(3) Very disturbing, throughout Italy, or any professed vacationland, has been the dominance, in every cafe, bar, and street corner, of people, especially men, who have nothing to do. What are vacationing children to learn from such a sight: that getting drunk at ten AM is fine? And that gambling on machines in every shop for the rest of the day is a life? Even in Paradise, Adam and Eve had to work. They had to clear away the excess growth, or the fallen growth, in the forest, in the meadows, in the lakes and sea. They had to patrol their Paradise. This should become the honorable work for all the people, in an alleged Paradise like Sardinia. Fuel and fiber can be found everywhere in Nature. Convert the found surplus into biogas, or simply firewood, or electricity. The opening scene of “Der junge Karl Marx” shows what is to be done: the people of the countryside, and maybe the professionals alongside, for a few hours a week, all work regularly on clearing the countryside of its excess and rotting vegetation.

Ecological management can be conducted on regional scale, with practices from Physiocracy. This is the generally-recognized first manifestation of economic theory. It starts with the proposition that all wealth in an area is based on the land (and water) of that area. The proposition may seem quaint. But it becomes “modern” when we consider that since the eighteenth century, when it was pioneered, the notion of wealth from the land (and sea) has been hugely modified by the use of fuels and materials from mineral resources BENEATH the land, namely coal, oil, gas, and uranium. Such use of resources from beneath the land was condemned by the Native Americans, and it was condemned four hundred years ago by poet John Milton, who predicted “Pandemonium” therefrom, but it proceeds at ever greater volume on the planet, despite all the talk about windmills, solar panels (also extracted), and biofuel airplanes. If we are to assume that any mineral source of fuel will harm the life forms of Nature, and if we are to assume that any dam will harm the river-to-sea habitat, then we must surrender to the eighteenth century realization that all wealth lies in the land and water, or what is beneath our feet. All commerce and manufacturing afterwards is dependent on what's beneath our feet. Such a fact was forgotten in ancient Mesopotamia, in ancient Afghanistan, in the Mesa Verde region of the American desert, in the Sahara five thousand years ago, and in the overgrazed sheep lands of New Zealand, with its massive wipeout of birds, in our century.

Revenue for administration comes from three sources in line with what is outlined under Physiocracy: (1) a tax on property, according to its "vegetation vitality," or wilderness-intensity, such that urban areas have maximum tax, farms less, wilderness very little; (2) a tax on each bay basin, or—with dams—each dam catchment upstream, in the unit, to finance projects for better function within that catchment, and (3) a tax on moving land, being vehicles, boats, aircraft, according to size, fuel type, distance moved. The means of administration are generally accepted "technical means of verification," e.g., civilgrade observation satellites, river monitoring instruments, and "moving land" assessments. We can start demonstrating this prospect in a single dam catchment.

For those who wonder about locomotion, we offer the zero-emissions vehicle slated for manufacture in Sardinia, very close to Orani. We also promote electric vehicles, assuming that the electricity comes from local sources (and not power plants far away). And we promote biofuel or hydrogen vehicles, which depend on local infrastructure, usually under ten thousand Euro in cost, to function.

These imperatives can be met along the full length of annual insect and bird migration, at least as it has been, from the Gulf of Guinea, in Africa, to the northern tip of Norway.

V. "Electric Field with Snares"
Plan
Pitfalls with water attract land animals; cages over waterholes attract air animals; in the competition for space, predators take advantage. Evenly-spaced electroconductive poles effect an immunological structure.
Concepts: De Maria, Denes, LeWitt, Oppenheim, Smithson

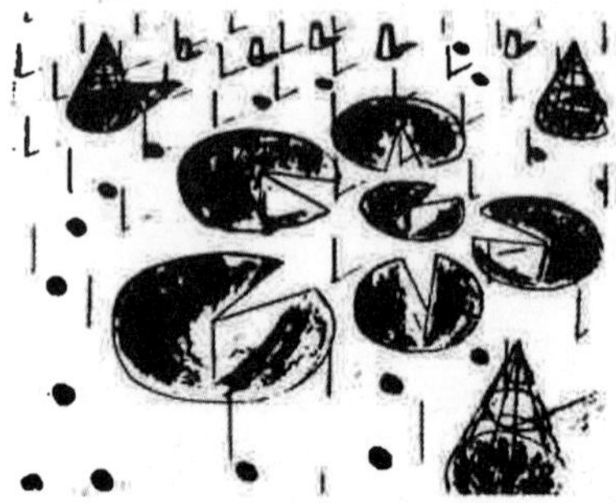

VI. "Assembled Spirals"
Low-angle aerial photograph
River is channeled into hillside, ponding there among spiraled holes and snares. Unsopped water flows gradually downward in reverse-S up the valley and onto the opposing slope, where a second spiral receives it.
Concepts: Beuys, Oppenheim, Smithson

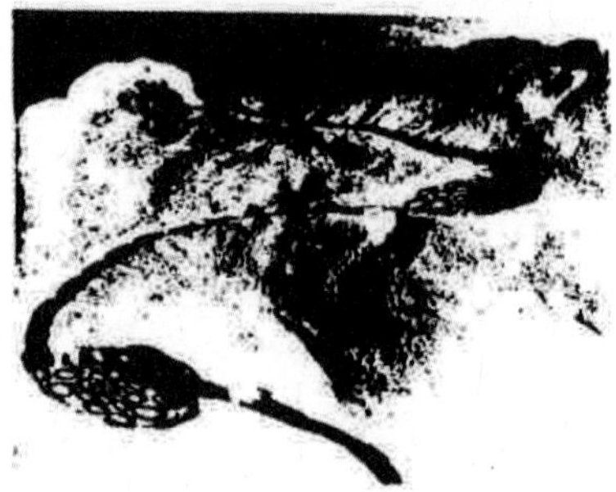

VII. "Production Lines"
Ultra-high aerial photograph
Aerial migration routes bind sites in Eurasia with sites in Africa, transferring to the uplands nutrients from salt waters. At stops, species intersect, marshes form and grasses spread, making possible the sustained harvest of mammals on land and of kelp, degradable to methane, in the sea.
Concepts: Haacke, Oppenheim

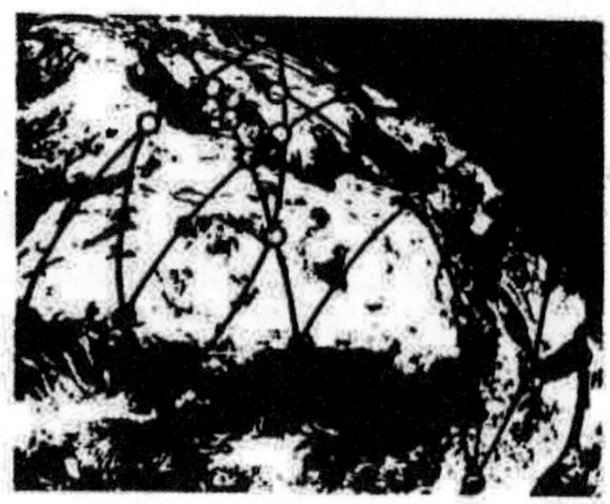

details from *Earth Net: An Economic System*, 1977-78

The above is a page from the catalogue accompanying Caltech's Baxter Art Museum's 1978 exhibition "Earth Net: An Economic System." The third image outlines the function and importance of aerial migration routes, or rather bird flyways, drawing from ideas by artists Hans Haacke and Dennis Oppenheim. This display was praised in the student newspaper as the only work in the exhibition dealing with reality.

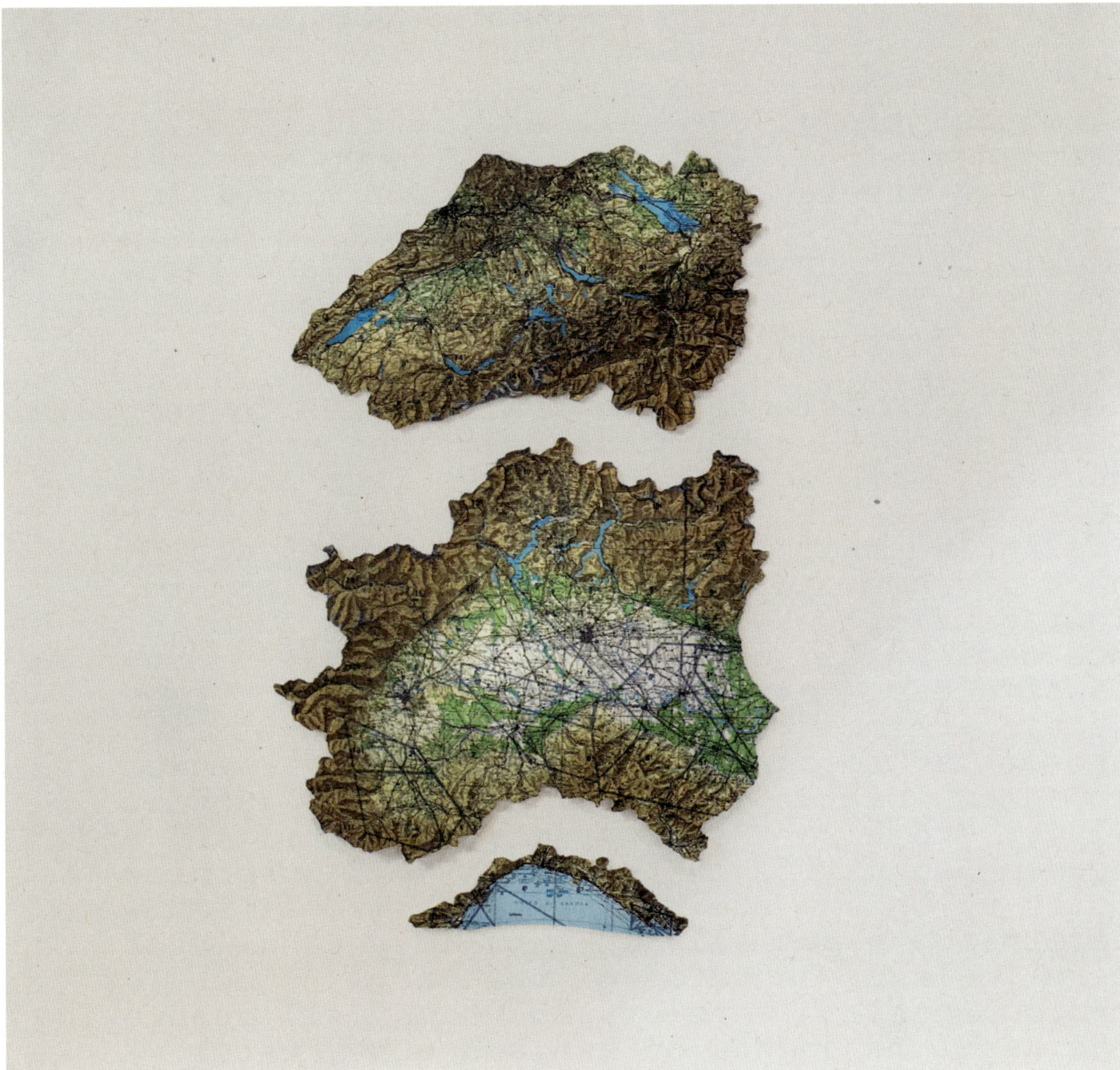

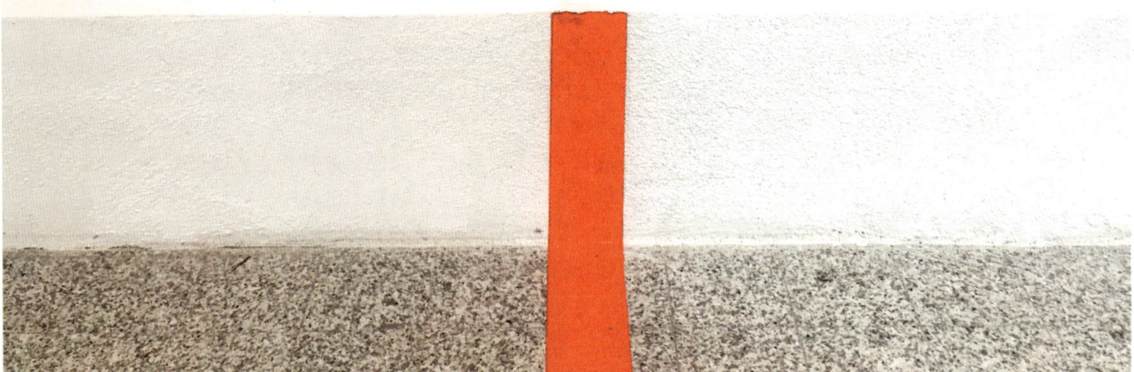

Bird flyway route from Sardinia into Europe on display in the exhibition "Africa–Arctic Flyway" at Museo Nivola in Orani. Which means bare chemical plants, highways, trucks, giant cities. It is a tough trip for birds. It is not that easy. Europe should make itself agreeable to the birds traveling through to their breeding grounds.

SARDINIA CHARTING FOR SALT-SEA RESTORATION

Sardinia, since 1978 with an installation at Caltech called "Earth Net: An Economic System," has been treated as a stopover for migratory birds and insects between Sub-Saharan Africa and the Arctic. Vast numbers of such birds, and all the fish, insects, bugs, or rodents they feed on are the sine qua non.

Dividing up islands into their slopes to saltwater bays began, as systematic practice, under a contract with Icelandic citizen Inga Svala Thorsdottir. The division lines coincided with Icelandic tradition: each fjord or bay would have its own management. The now-husband of Thorsdottir, Wu Shanzhuan, asked for an opinion on the decision to be made then, in 1993–4, about a massive dam project in China, at Three Gorges. Wu was a member of the Chinese Communist Party, and he had to cast a vote. Months of research led to an exhibition of scenarios for the Yangtze River, and also the Nile, Tigris–Euphrates, and Aegean Sea basin, in London (1994). Suspicion built up on why the numbers and size of fish were declining, especially in a plainly unpolluted area like Iceland, centered on the large numbers of hydroelectric diversions and dams, all destroying the usual movements of fish and other water organisms from land to sea.

Dams, not overfishing or pollution, were seen as a No. One reason for fisheries' decline. Coastal wetland removal or drying up were also seen as reasons, but much of that could be attributed to changes in water quality caused by dams upstream.

In 2000, following travels down much of the Colorado River to the Gulf of California, and noticing a parallel with the Tigris–Euphrates in the Persian/Arabian Gulf, rivers began to be divided up into dam catchments. Every dam, in blocking the movement of soil and life-forms, was reducing the river to a lifeless flow of H20.
In the two decades since, any island or peninsula,

such as Italy, Sicily, or Sardinia, would of course be divided up into their bay catchments. This confirmed with an Irish law of 1959, learned about in a residency in Ireland in 2003, which calls for each bay, from outermost point to outermost point, to be treated as a "hydrometric area." The law is similar to traditional border rules in Iceland and other Viking lands, and—due to a Shinto religion centered on water—in Japan. Since 2009, all of Italy, Greece, Finland, Japan, China, Korea, and elsewhere have been divided up into bay basins, including all the land sloping into the bays. Government officials have often said that including the land sloping into a bay, or a regional sea, or a single stretch of ocean current, can be impermissibly "political." But it's a scientific and physical fact, unrelated to politics.

An invitation for a one-person show in Sardinia, at the Museo Nivola deep in the countryside, led first of all to dividing Sardinia into its bay catchments as defined by the Irish hydrometric area law of 1959. Much more was discovered while on the island. There were many dams, with reservoirs among the biggest in Europe. And the scientific literature about the dams, which curators Lennart Wolff and Elisa R. Linn tracked down, showed that they were gravely harming wildlife populations, including fish and birds. Much was also written about how the dams, by greatly reducing nutrient runoff into the sea, were reducing the coastal wetlands, and therefore both fish and bird populations. With the Museo Nivola show, running from late October 2019 to February 2020, began a systematic separating of each dam catchment on any river in any bay basin. The hydrographic map of Sardinia was being splintered further into many still-smaller soil/water units. A poetic term for each unit could be Dennis Oppenheim's term, also about trapped waters, called "Shape Collectors."

The first show in response to Wu Shanzhuan, showing earthwork alternatives to dams and canal diversions, was attempted a second time at the Smart Museum of The University of Chicago, with one month allowed for research at the University. The research yielded this discovery: a 1905 conference of the American Society of Civil Engineers, deciding on whether to endorse an efficient waterwheel designed by Jean-Victor Poncelet of France, or an even-more energy-yielding, but river damaging, technology of high dams with turbines, led to this outcome: the high dams being chosen.

The result has been a global disaster. Country after country went on a dam-building binge. Sun Yat-sen, then Lenin and Stalin; FDR; Hitler; Franco; France after the World Wars; Italy; all adopted the 1905 decision of the American Society of Civil Engineers, and we now have in the world five hundred thousand high dams with turbines for conversion at 95% efficiency of falling-water power to electricity. China built on its Three Gorges Dam decision to become the world's biggest builder of dams, always with disastrous consequences for the life in rivers, and then the coastal wetlands, then the Ocean. The waterwheel alternatives, or maybe screws, or other micro-hydro technologies, are not high-tech, not big, not comforting for technocratic egos.

For a while, we settled for the usual large-size wheels of three-meter diameter. Then an idea came from Marcel Duchamp: use bicycle fork-mounted waterwheels, and produce such waterwheels in the multi-billion volume that normal bicycle wheels have. Scenarios for massive arrays of waterwheels were conceived and drawn up for low-rise dams and waterfalls in the Lake District, UK and on the homeland river of my paternal grandparents, near Augsburg, Bavaria: the Lech. This low-tech solution, with nonetheless sophisticated Poncelet curve blade array on the rim, has been contracted inside Italy, for marketing from Italy worldwide, with the type of company that would sell such Duchamp/Poncelet waterwheels: Sardinia Cycling, headed by Giovanni Lamieri. All these arrangements were made for the exhibition at Museo Nivola, Sardinia, and they were continued for display and development in the Manifesta 13, as part of an answer on why the river waters arriving in the saltwater lagoon next to Marseille, the Etang de Berre, are so devoid of salts, nutrients, or life forms. A global industrial campaign had begun.

Only COVID-19 got in the way. Many further plans, including work with Finmeccanica for mass production of the Poncelet curve blades, collapsed in the face of near-complete economic shutdown. Now, delayed by a year and a half, we resume. The task includes translating the mathematics (let alone the French) in a 130-page report by Jean-Victor Poncelet, who was distinguished in the nineteenth century as an early head of France's MIT, the Ecole Polytechnique.

We intend to continue in our own corporate integrity. We do not bury the three decades of discovery and, let's say, ideational gestation, that we, very uniquely, have experienced. Sardinia as we have mapped it, and now mapped it in its dam catchments, each set subordinated to a bay basin, is handled by us as a business corporation over forty years old. If the rivers of Sardinia can come back to life, functioning like blood-streams into the larger field of life, the sea, then we can restore what should be a sizable fisheries and biomass industry off the shores of Sardinia. A starting point for proof of concept could be: Alghero. The town is named after what has long been prolific there, but now no more: macro-algae, with fish.

Over the long-term, our clients, the ones who benefit from our work, will not be Sardinia only, or Italy only, or any country or territory only. It will be the migrating birds and circulating fish upon which our existence on the planet depends. Sardinia, or anywhere else, should be a paradise for migrating birds, insects, and fish. Not what they have become: a place of starvation and death. We can all remember that a pandemic exists continuously and ever worse, on the Earth: the human race with present-day technologies of land use. We seek a massive change in those technologies, despite the power-hungry behavior of most governments.

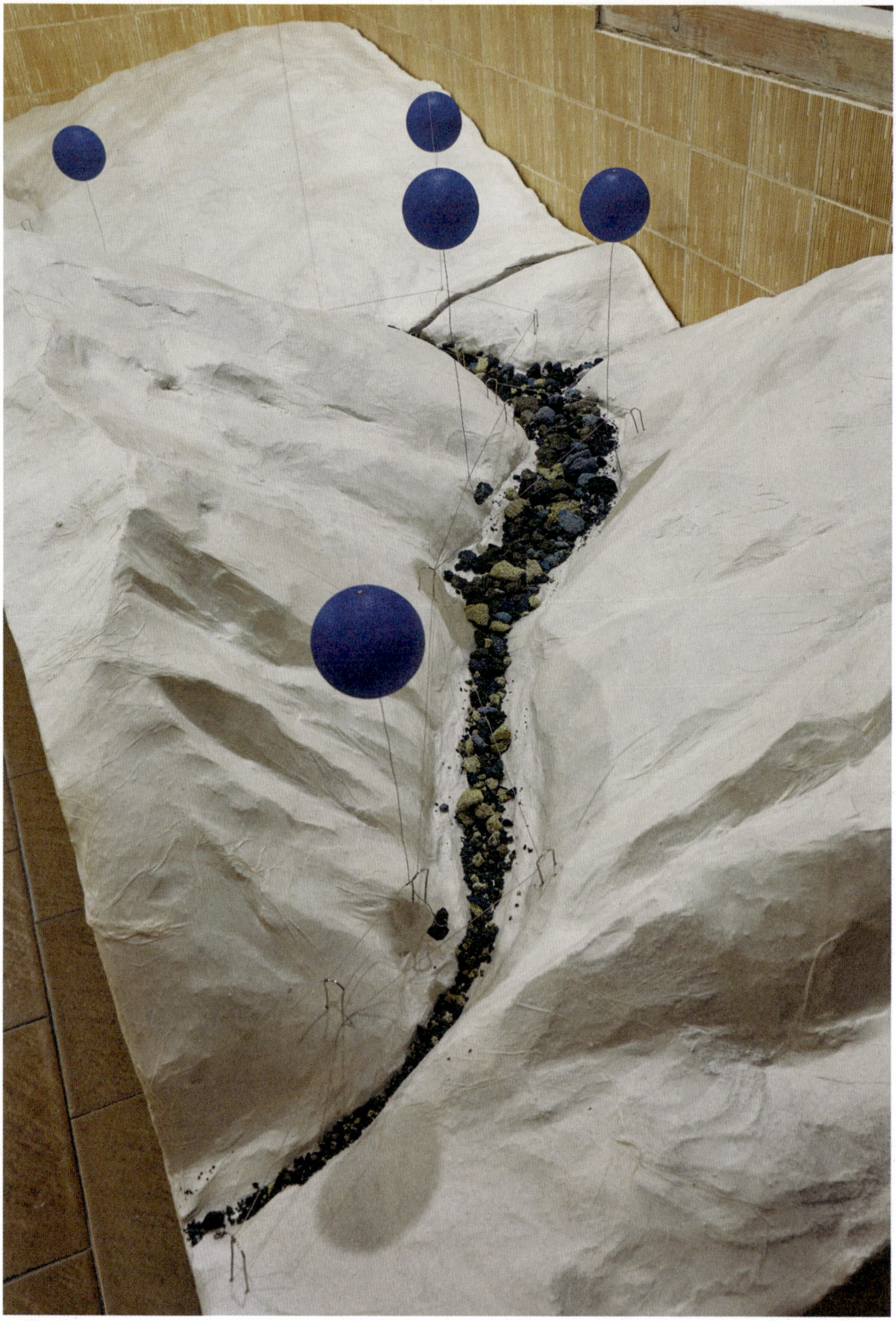

This shows rubble and pieces of a deconstructed dam being lifted out of the depression using balloons.

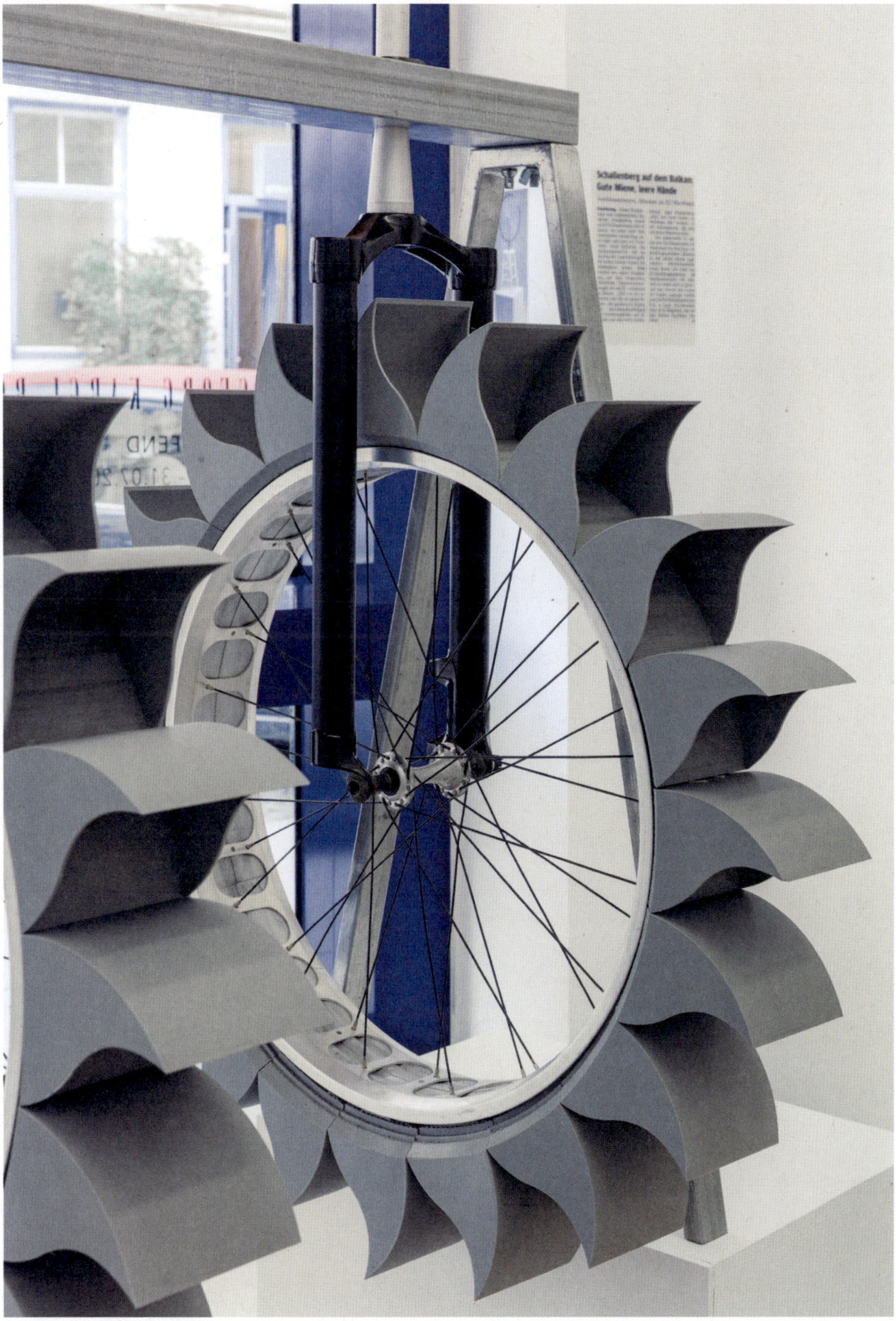

This is a maquette of a Duchamp/Poncelet waterwheel mounted on a bicycle fork and wide-rim bicycle wheel.

EXCLUSIVITY PROTOTYPE AND DISPLAY-STRUCTURE
PRODUCTION AND DEVELOPMENT CONTRACT BETWEEN
SARDINIA CYCLING, WITH GIOVANNI LAMIERI,
AND OCEAN EARTH DEVELOPMENT CORPORATION, WITH PETER FEND

1.
The Parties to this Contract are Sardinia Cycling and, as a person, Giovanni Lamieri, and Ocean Earth Development Corporation and, as a person, Peter Fend. Mr. Lamieri is an Italian citizen; Mr. Fend is a US citizen.

2.
The jurisdiction of this Contract is Italy.

3.
The initial term of this Contract is One Year, being from the date of signature by both persons.

4.
The Contract is subject to prolongation or renewal at any time. The Contract is also subject to amendment or thorough expansion according to developments and new intentions.

5.
Under the Contract, Mr. Lamieri and Mr. Fend will exchange any and all information, discoveries, contacts and possible sources of finance about a Research Project ("Project").

6.
The Project is for an industrial use of wide-rim bicycle wheels when mounted on a fork suspended from a perpendicular rod, bar or beam.

7.
The Project is for industrial use of a version, or ideation, from Marcel Duchamp's "Bicycle Wheel" (1913), but upside down, or—in bicycle-use orientation—correct side up.

8.
Under the Contract, a Display Structure (being at least one wheel, maybe several, set in forks suspended from a tube, bar or beam ca. 1.5 meters long, each end held up by an A-frame or saw-horse array in metal or composite. Standard bicycle-shop technology and parts are used. The wheel, or wheels, are able to spin freely.

9.
The Display Structure is produced before Wednesday night, 23 October 2019, and is delivered no later than Thursday at 1300 on 24 October 2019 (or is picked up by a person reporting to Fend) to Museo Nivola, via Gonare 2, 08026, Orani, Nuoro Province, Sardinia.

10.

The turbulence of world politics—particularly about energy policies, but exacerbated by crises in Africa, the Middle East, Myanmar, and the European Union vis-à-vis China and Russia—compels a very rapid campaign for replacing dam-turbine hydropower with undershot waterwheel, screw, and other non-blockage systems of hydropower. Any technology developed and displayed under this Contract is meant to affect the deconstruction and replacement of over five hundred thousand dams. Towards that end, funding is sought for as much as bearable without slowing down the overall progression of Ocean Earth in its site work.

13.
Other engineering efforts on the bladed wheel, as by a Mr. Zuccoti, are not, for now and in this Contract, expected to meet the industrial standards envisioned by, and prescribed precisely by, Poncelet, and also Zuppinger.

14.
What information will be made public, and will be announced in any exhibition and for the press, will be decided by Mr. Fend and Ocean Earth, chiefly for business-security reasons. Copies of related documents are provided to Mr. Lamieri and Sardinia Cycling.

15.
A confidentiality and trade secret agreement is to be signed by 1 April 2021, or before any further exhibition, whichever comes earlier.

16.
Further drawings or photographs, as they are made and ready for exhibition, will be sent by Mr. Fend to Mr. Lamieri, and by Mr. Lamieri to Mr. Fend.

AGREED TO BY MR. FEND AND MR. LAMIERI ON OR BEFORE 1 MARCH 2021.

Peter Fend, Ocean Earth, in NY   Giovanni Lamieri, near Cagliari

FLYWAY 6
Nile–Moscow corridor

Ocean Treaty Organizations:
AOTO and ARTO

Project Site:
GULF OF ODESA; CRIMEAN COAST ON BLACK SEA; SEA OF AZOV

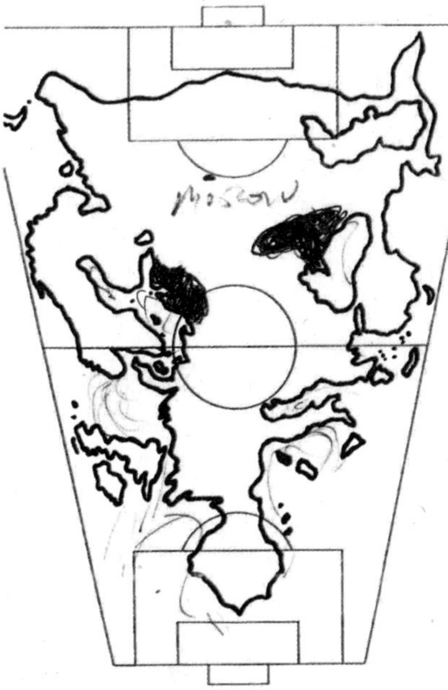

East vs. West

Russia Threatens To Deploy Troops Near U.S.

Moscow weighs sending its military to Cuba, Venezuela as Ukraine talks stall

Russia's deputy foreign minister said talks with the U.S. over the security situation in Ukraine had stalled and suggested that Moscow could dispatch a military deploy-

By Ann M. Simmons, Courtney McBride and Laurence Norman

ment to Venezuela and Cuba, as the Kremlin seeks to pressure Washington to meet its demands to halt Western military activity that Russia claims pose a threat.

Deputy Foreign Minister Sergei Ryabkov said Thursday that Moscow couldn't exclude dispatching "military infrastructure" to Venezuela or Cuba if tensions with Washington—which have soared in recent weeks over a huge buildup of Russian troops on Ukraine's border—continue to rise.

"I don't want to confirm anything, I will not rule out anything....Depends on the actions of our American colleagues," Mr. Ryabkov told privately owned Russian-language television network RTVi in an interview in Moscow. Mr. Ryabkov said he saw no immediate grounds for fresh talks with the U.S., after several rounds of negotiations this week yielded little progress in defusing the crisis in Ukraine.

In Washington later, White House national security adviser Jake Sullivan said U.S. and European officials would confer in the coming days, but that no dates have been set for further

Please turn to page A8

JAN 14, 2022

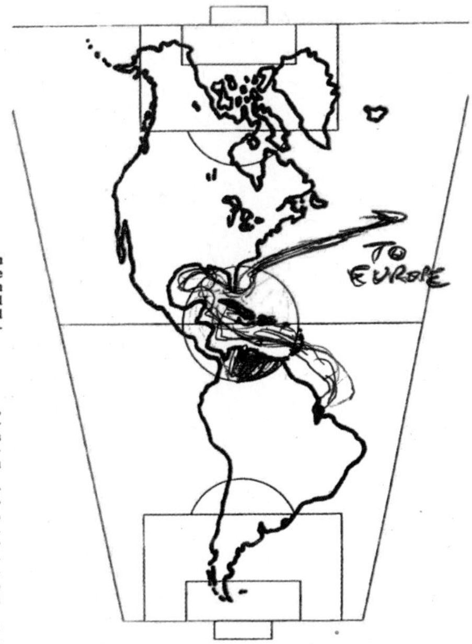

North vs. South

In these geostrategic football fields, which are trapezoidal, there is a constant struggle for control over the middle. The NATO expansion, the push east beyond Poland into the Sea of Azov is seen as a major aggression by the other side. Russia will always be the other in the geostrategic football game. Such an interpretation is not meant to be funny, but rather dead serious.

WALL BETWEEN EAST AND WEST

As surely as there's a difference between North and South, so there's a difference between East and West.

The Equator is the barrier between North and South.

The Lomonosov Ridge, crossing the Arctic Ocean and becoming massive in Greenland, is the barrier between East and West.

As with a prior notion of barrier between East and West, in Berlin, so the natural barrier between East and West, the Lomonosov Ridge through the North Pole on to Greenland, is claimed by… Russia.

The Berlin Wall was a misplacement of the barrier.

Now we have the Lomonosov Ridge to recognize.

That was already done in East Berlin, part of East Germany, back in the days of the Wall, or even earlier, at Alexanderplatz. A giant clock mimicking the world was placed there, in Alexanderplatz, and on that clock are named the prominent locations in each time zone. In two such time zones, there is only one name up high.

In one, it's West-Groenland.

In the other, next to it, is Ost-Groenland.

We of the planet can divide the world at Greenland, into East and West there, and then proceed across the North Pole to around the world.

WHO IS
ON TOP
TODAY?

RUSSIA
TURKEY
FRANCE
THE UK
THE US
CHINA?

WHO'LL
BE THE
WINNER
IN THE
CRISIS
ZONES?

UKRAINE
WITHOUT
ANY WAR

This was made for Peter Fend's daughter to display in her Harvard room during her online class activity in 2022.

OCEAN EARTH

Ocean Earth Development Corporation

1392 Madison Avenue, # 173, New York, NY 10029
www.ocean-earth.net

Peter Fend
A founding shareholder
fend@ocean-earth.net
Tel. 1 646 512 1781

18 January 2022

Permanent Mission of Ukraine
to the United Nations
220 East 51st Street
New York, NY 10022

To the Permanent Mission:

Over two decades ago, your Mission received a large compilation of documents about attempts to cover up and distort facts revealed with civil-satellite observation of the Chernobyl region, all in relation to a visit to Kiev of a nuclear-industry delegation from an EU-member state.

You are provided now with a copy of the cover letter, duly blacked out in accordance with a high court ruling in that EU-member state. Our own government, that of the United States, was actively involved in the coverup and distortion of facts.

Our discoveries then led to abundant analysis of the hydrology of Ukraine. Proposals have ensued for profitable and ecological management of the seaweed resources and upland soil resources of Ukraine's region. Three saltwater basins are singled out: Gulf of Odessa; Crimea coast on Black Sea; Sea of Azov. Maybe such thinking, scheduled to be published by Random House this year, can be of benefit.

Sincerely yours,

Peter Fend

This letter was hand-delivered to a soldier at the Ukrainian mission to the United Nations in New York.

OCEAN EARTH

OCEAN EARTH DEVELOPMENT CORPORATION
Incorporated in New York State

Office of Record for Official Filings
1560 North Sandburg Terrace, 905 James
Chicago, Illinois 60610 USA

Office in New York City
149 Ludlow Street
New York, NY 10002
Tel 212 533 3054 Fax 212 274 8706

Peter Fend
President

July 7, 1999

Permanent Mission of the Ukraine
to the United Nations
220 East 51st Street
New York, NY 10022

Ladies and Gentlemen:

We write you in view of tomorrow's scheduled visit to the Ukraine an entourage from the

We understand from news reports that the entourage might raise proposals for the construction and management of new nuclear energy power plants.

We are no experts on nuclear power, but we have had substantial experience with agencies of the regarding our widely-published efforts at satellite monitoring and site analysis of the Chernobyl reactor-complex. These agencies include: , ; the , and apparently several other agencies attached to the Embassy in Washington, DC. Our experiences with these agencies, occurring mostly during 1986 but continuing in years thereafter, have been negative.

In sum, what occurred was this. When news first appeared of the Chernobyl accident, our company, true to its then four years of business practice, sought to obtain Landsat and Spot satellite data for the site, with the intention of processing the data with expert scientists near Washington, DC . One of our co-workers, was persuaded by his to let them "help" us in the task of analyzing the data and shipping it to , specifically to a facility with which we had contracted called the . What resulted, however, was fairly much the opposite of "help." Even though we are responsible for all the costs of the data, for all the costs of shipping the data, and for all the costs of processing the data, both in Washington and in Munich; and even though by satellite-industry rules we are therefore entitled to the control of all such data and the publication of all results: agents of the and so on have caused in our gaining access to this data, at least in , and have caused a permanent loss of access to or property rights in the data not long afterwards. In effect, they have from us. This includes all the half-dozen data tapes purchased by us and delivered (sometimes with much delay) to our contracted processor, . Our use of the data tapes did yield some publication under our control, with substantial revelations, all very different from what was appearing with official-source photographs.

Proof of the quality of the work appears in the decision of the European Space Agency to publish the analyses which we contracted for in its Earth Observation Quarterly. After the publication, the attempted which had been published, but we were able to convince the European Space Agency that we had the legal right to control of those photographs, as we had already secured the legal right to control of the computer tapes from which the photographs were produced.

Even though our data were seized, the photographs which we managed to publish—despite many obstacles from elsewhere, e.g., at the

This letter was blacked out in compliance with a court decision of the Oberlandesgericht Düsseldorf in 1988, saying that any work Ocean Earth did with satellite data would be of no interest to any government agency.

Open University in the United Kingdom, to purchase the same data and conduct the same researches we had commissioned, to see if our conclusions were correct. One team of scientists found our conclusions to be correct, indeed, and they arranged for a news article in the London Times, coinciding with our own publication at a conference sponsored by the United Nations Environment Program and UN Food & Agriculture Program in Venice, Italy in 1989. A copy of the published news article is enclosed.

Our conclusions, in sum, were that the nuclear-reactor complex at Chernobyl was built on a landfill, and that as such it was vulnerable to continual pressure from the main vector of the Pripyat River. We supposed that this pressure may have caused certain dislocations which led to the breakdown in water supply necessary for reactor stability. We affirmed that, in any case, the site would remain under hydrological pressure, and that all of it should be sealed off as well as possible and be abandoned. We argued that the area should be evacuated. We proceeded, in subsequent years, to propose a diversion of the Pripyat River around the reactor complex, to be built in Belarus. We proceeded also to suggest strongly that the Ukraine concentrate on deriving energy from gas, including natural gas piped through from points east, and including new, upcoming sources of renewable gas, such as on-land cellulosic biomass or offshore algae, potentially plentiful in the Ukraine Black Sea. These proposals have been developed fairly elaborately, and testing in now being contracted in New Zealand, Iceland and Montenegro.

Our aim in this letter, however, is not to suggest what the Ukraine should do in its energy future.

Rather, our aim is to inform you that agencies of the [redacted] have acted [redacted] in relation to a private effort at satellite study of the Chernobyl mishap. [redacted], [redacted] of scientifically-verified findings based on data which a private party purchased. They have also [redacted] data of the private party. [redacted]

If you need to know more, we can respond.

Sincerely yours,

Peter Fend

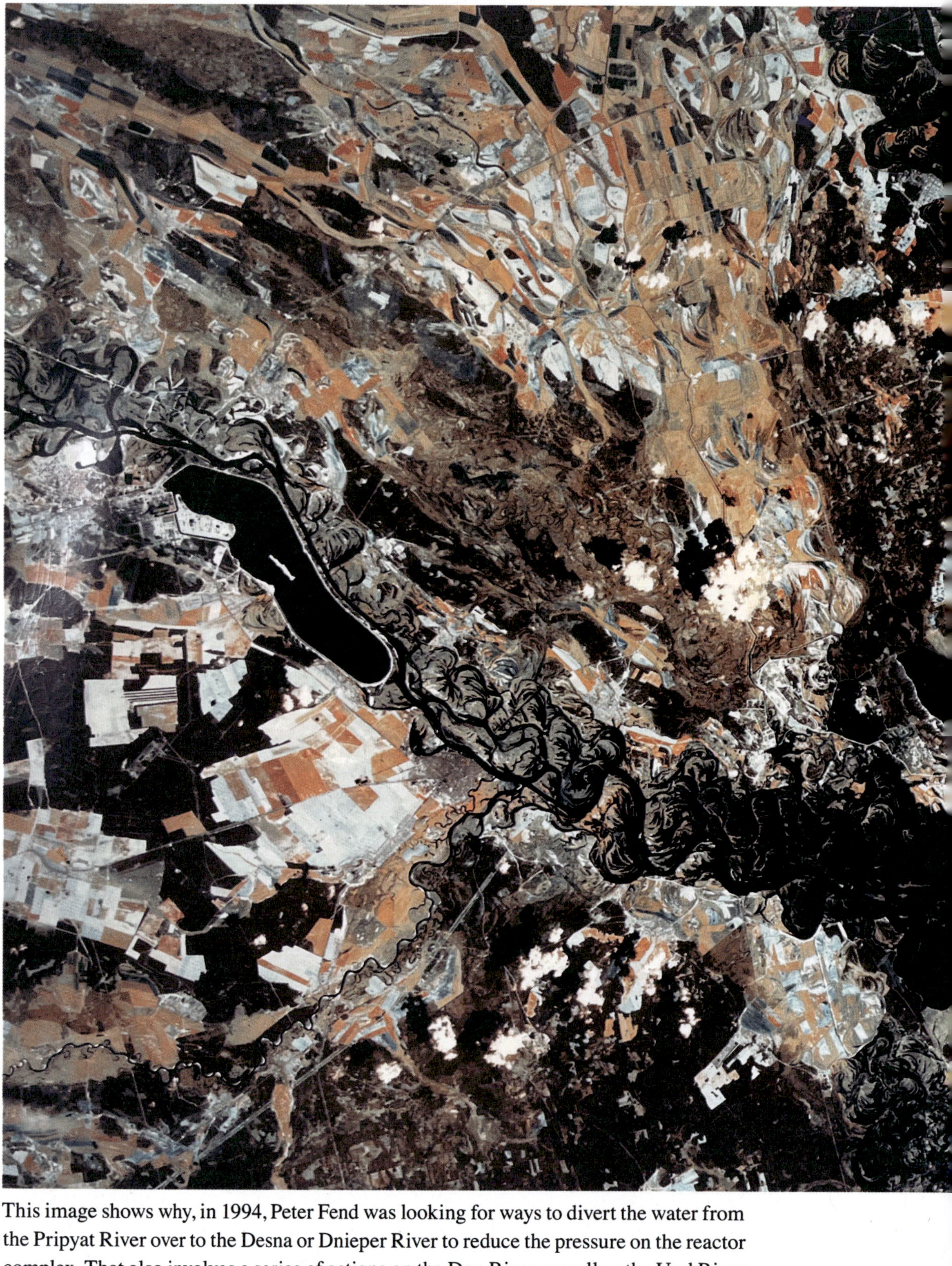

This image shows why, in 1994, Peter Fend was looking for ways to divert the water from the Pripyat River over to the Desna or Dnieper River to reduce the pressure on the reactor complex. That also involves a series of actions on the Don River as well as the Ural River vis-à-vis the comparative salinity of the Caspian and Black Seas.

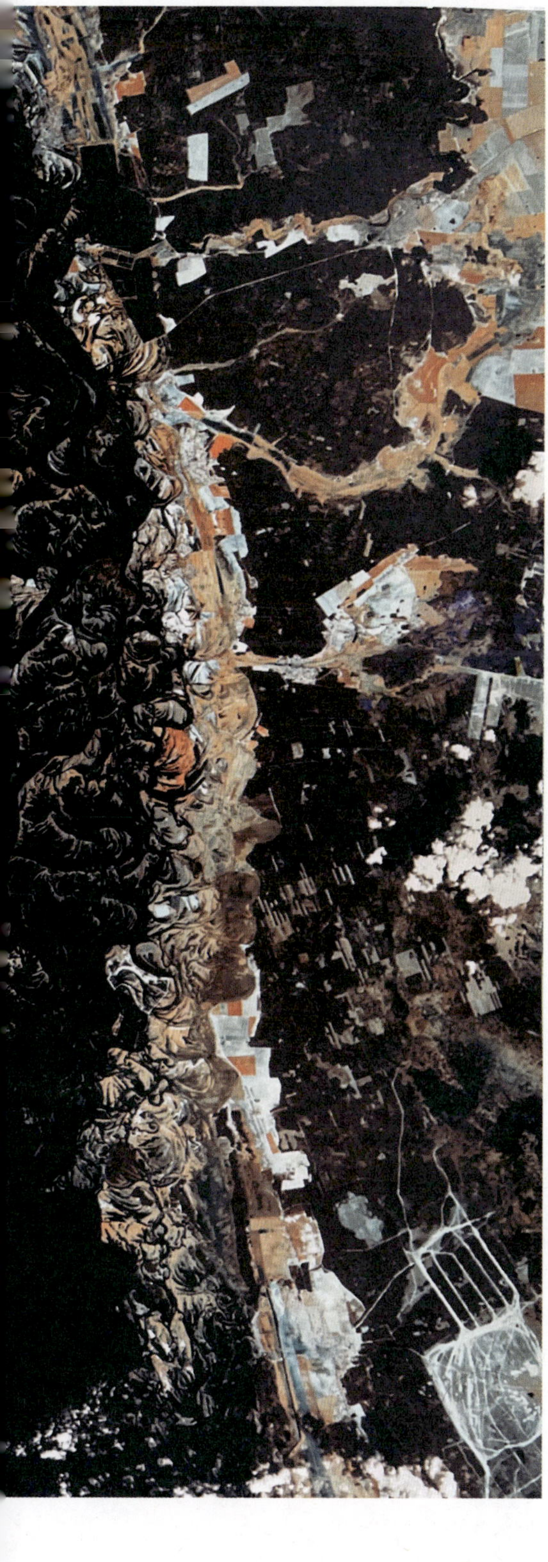

Ein privates Forscherteam legt neue Aufnahmen des Reaktor-Unfalls vor: Was wussten die Amerikaner?

Tschernobyl-Katastrophe: Die Satellitenbilder

theorie von OECO

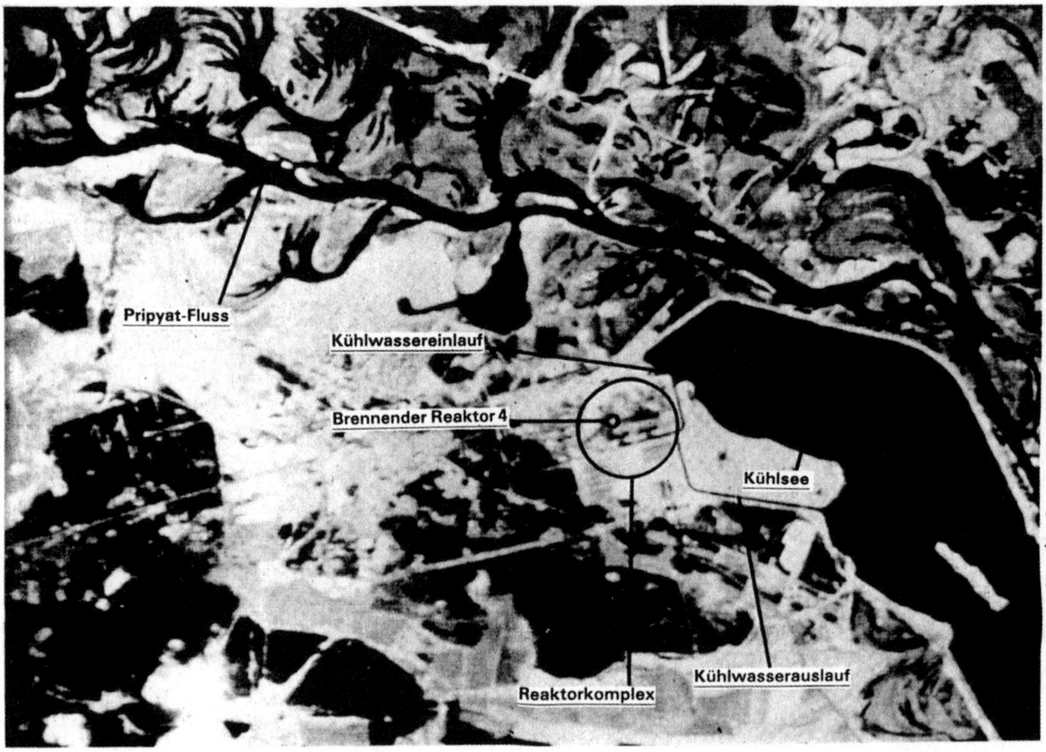

Alle KKWs benötigen Unmengen Kühlwasser. Tschernobyl baute man deshalb am Ende eines künstlichen Teichs, wo das Wasser einfliessen und flussabwärts erwärmt wieder abfliessen kann; die Insel verbessert die Strömungsverhältnisse. Das KKW steht auf künstlich aufgeschüttetem Land und hebt sich von den sumpfigen Flussauen und den natürlichen Feldern ringsum ab. Die Aufschüttung erlaubt es, den Baugrund zu entwässern und trocken zu halten, doch sind Aufschüttungen auch stärker hydrologischen Kräften ausgesetzt. Am 29. April, dem Tag, an dem diese Aufnahme entstand, führten die Flüsse wegen der Schneeschmelze mehr Wasser, was Grundwasserspiegel und Bodendichtigkeit beeinflusste und den Reaktor im Übergangsbereich von natürlichem und künstlichem Terrain verschoben haben könnte.
Bild: Ocean Earth/Sipa

At the time—May 1986—of this article, Ocean Earth began to identify the problem of the landfill and artificial lake, which would not be stable during any spring. So the errors were not primarily of works at the site, but of the siting of the Chernobyl plant in a middle of a riverbed that is mobile every spring.

Landslip was factor in Chernobyl blast, expert says

By Nick Nuttall
Technology Correspondent

The Soviet nuclear disaster at Chernobyl was caused by land subsidence and mistakes in civil engineering rather than by scientists involved in unauthorized experiments, an expert on satellite imaging claimed yesterday.

The new evidence contradicts the official versions of the world's worst nuclear accident. Mr Peter Fend, an American expert in satellite imaging, who presented the evidence to a gathering of United Nations-backed scientists in Venice, said the explanations given by Soviet and Western governments were crucially flawed.

He also alleged that there had been a deliberate cover-up to suppress the truth, particularly by West Germany.

Mr Fend claimed the German authorities had confiscated satellite pictures, providing crucial evidence that official versions were wrong, from one of their own scientists.

Various reasons could lie at the heart of these attempts to hide the truth, he said – not least the risk posed to a string of other Russian reactors along the banks of the Pribyat river, where Chernobyl was built, by land slip and subsidence. He feared they, too, had been built on unsound ground and might have shaky foundations.

According to scientists at the Open University in Milton Keynes, Buckinghamshire, Mr Fend's New York-based company, Ocean Earth, is recognized internationally for its supply and analysis of satellite images of river and ocean basins.

Evidence for Mr Fend's claims are based on a series of satellite pictures taken before, during, and after the Chernobyl disaster in April 1986. The shots reveal a dark line cutting across the reactor that officials, including the US Geological Survey Department, maintained was the shadow of a smoke plume cast across the area as the nuclear pile burned.

Mr Fend, however, is convinced that the dark slash is a fault in the land, which gave way under the weight of the Chernobyl plant, causing the collapse of Reactor 4. He said the prevailing winds at the time were blowing in the wrong direction for the contention that the dark line was a smoke shadow to be sustained.

Mr Fend argues that the line was still in place more than two weeks after the explosion, although the fire had long since been extinguished.

Further evidence that planners in Moscow sited the plant on unsafe ground comes from scientists at the Open University. Dr Steve Drury, of the Earth Sciences Department, said yesterday that his researchers discovered that the dark line was faintly but clearly revealed in satellite photographs taken before the accident.

Dr Drury said this refuted the smoke plume claim, and a subsequent claim by Soviet authorities that the dark line was caused by blast damage.

There is a growing conviction among scientists that the expanding dark line is evidence of water seepage from the river into a land fault, and that this was what triggered a land slip. The sand and clay ground probably also had peat deposits that made it unstable.

The Health and Safety Executive's Nuclear Installations Inspectorate in London disputed Mr Fend's claims, saying its officials agreed with the International Atomic Energy Authority, which backs the Soviet Government's explanation that human error and unauthorized experiments were to blame.

The Times, London 27 September 1989 re Fend and Ocean Earth

The story is somewhat inaccurate: the fault, or error, was not a problem of geology but one of hydrology. A large building requiring a stable foundation was placed in the middle of a river path, on top of an artificial landfill, with the meandering river being diverted and, to further weaken the site, a large reservoir placed immediately downstream, as a cavity subject to distension. Fend was never interviewed for this story, which was followed up elsewhere.

The authoritative imagery appears in the Oxford University Press and European Space Agency publications on Chernobyl.

Nuclear energy requires perfection. Human beings are not perfect. As we see very dramatically in the war in Ukraine that is going on at the time of publication (2022), that if something goes wrong, it is beyond control. This kind of high-tech is not safe.

CHERNOBYL
INSTABILE

A new town that did not work: the industrial settlement just upstream from Chernobyl. The reason for failure: poor siting.

To gain access to large volumes of water, a massive reactor complex—with its own requirements for secure foundations—was built on a shallow landfill on top of a river bed, in the middle of meanders. Downstream and alongside, a giant cavity was excavated from the mud of the river bed so that a water supply for the steam driving the turbines could be recycled. This seemed to be a clever arrangement, for the complex could be isolated among marshlands far from any prominent river, far from view. Forgotten was the fact, plain to any child, that mud in a river bed will tend to ooze downstream, particularly during spring floods, and that anything siting on a tongue of mud just upstream from a giant excavation can expect to be moved. As French and German nuclear authorities have confirmed to us, quietly, this happened. A shifting foundation led to dislocations of external water supply, hence to an unexpected shutdown of the reactor—during which 'the operators on site' made a mistake.

These photographs, from a French satellite passing over the site several weeks after the accident, then four months later, show evidence of the cause. From left to right, along the axis of the Pripyat River, with meanders about equidistant on both sides, the later image shows massive new plugs of concrete. The diversion itself is caused by concrete embankments. Then, in a line, appears: (1) the broad flat concrete square, holding rigid the waters a meander that—unlike others—forms (2) a curious bulge; just downstream, at (3), a flat hollow once filled with water is dried and later plugged in with concrete: (4) downstream, parallel to the lake divider, more concrete emplacements: at the downhill side of the reservoir, where pressure to dislocate might be greatest, appears (5) a new, 200-meter long concrete buttress; and further down, by Chernobyl itself, (6) appears another concrete emplacement. All changes align with the Pripyat, as revealed in larger satellite views; the alignment passes directly through the fatal one reactor, No. 4.

A clue of the problem appears as the dark tracery at right angle to the river axis from No. 4. With the first public Chernobyl imagery, this tracery was attributed to smoke. But evidence from before and here, much later, shows a continuing presence. The dark line appears more as a fissure, or upwelling of moisture, in the landfill—a point of dislocation perpendicular to the line of movement.

The disaster was architectural. Given that the entombed reactor will be hot for a hundred years, and that the concrete plugs into the river channel are not expected to last nearly that long, more drama may yet ensue—not just for the Ukraine, but for most of Europe.

Kenzo Tange once designed a Tokyo Bay megastructural city that any satellite would reveal, and any Doxiadis-scale thinker would undertake. But the buildings envisioned were to be set over water, on artificial ground, in a region vulnerable to earthquakes and tidal waves. How stable could such giant structures be? How stable, by comparison, would be the structures evident from satellites to lie on faultlines, like Indian Point nuclear power station? With satellites the crucial site and foundation research, preliminary to any major project, can be economic—and customary.

Peter Fend /91

TEXT FOR AMERICAN FEDERATION OF ARCHITECTS PREVISIONING FUTURE

George Chaikin, teaching architecture at Cooper Union and busy with Ocean Earth, arranged for OE to participate in an exhibition on computer architecture with OE's satellite imagery from Benghazi, Chernobyl, and SS20 missile bases in the Soviet Union.

UKRAINE SALTWATER BASINS

The current borders of what's labeled as Ukraine were decided on, rather hurriedly, at the end of the civil war throughout what had been the Russian Empire, in 1922. A reincarnation of that Empire was formed, called the Union of Soviet Socialist Republics. Since then, especially after the Chernobyl disaster, much of the Union broke apart. We now have more or less sovereign states called Kazakhstan, Estonia, Georgia, and Ukraine. Fighting has broken out here or there, most recently inside Azerbaijan, due to ethnic and religious differences. No one can pretend that the USSR was one big united states. It was, in fact, many disputing states which, under Leninist and Stalinist pressure, plus World War II, somehow cohered.

Nowadays, with the loudly-proclaimed need for moves beyond fossil fuels, it makes sense to adjust borders, according to ecology and hydrology, for efficient management of renewable fuel resources. Didn't everyone agree at COP26 that serious, on the ground action, not just on paper, must be done towards replacing fossil hydrocarbons with renewable ones, in turn convertible to hydrogen or electricity?

Such a change can occur in saltwater basins. Nearly all of Ukraine's territory drains into the Black Sea, which has UNEP Regional Seas Program headquartered in Istanbul. Of that territory, there are three major coastal-water zones: (1) the Sea of Azov, (2) the southern coast of Crimea, (3) the Gulf of Odesa.

Each of these zones has a very different biology. The Sea of Azov, shallow and sandy, has much green algae, like Ulva lactuca, which can eutrophicate. The Crimean southern coast, with much deeper and colder water, has largely brown algae, like Laminaria, which does not eutrophicate. The Gulf of Odesa, with more confined waters, and many inlets, fosters red algae, like Gracilaria. The management and harvesting of algae in each of the three coastal-water zones, and the control of any inflowing waters or pollutants, would each be entirely different. The drainage basins, or hydrometric areas as defined by a 1959 Irish law, can easily be identified. Two of them have been preponderantly Russian, in their ethnic mix, and one—for the Gulf of Odesa—has been preponderantly Ukrainian. Much of the fighting and disputation has been about who controls the first-two described areas.

Ocean Earth proposes to handle the Azov Basin, the Crimean Peninsula, and the Gulf of Odesa as neutral regional-bay states, or hydrometric areas, subject to Physiocratic rules of administration.

If the West wants to assert a voice, they can call not only on an end to the disastrous war but upon both Ukraine and Russia to diligently work on post-fossil hydrocarbon and hydrogen production from the Sea of Azov, with its huge amounts of green algae, and from the colder coastal waters of Crimea, with also huge amounts (as remarked upon during the Yalta Conference in 1945), of Laminaria.

We, Ocean Earth, would be glad to be involved in development of such industry in the Sea of Azov, south coast of Crimea and the Gulf of Odesa particularly for control of what flows inward from the land.

In the Gulf of Odesa, a chief worry comes from the many dams built by the Soviet regime on the main rivers. These dams have provided hydroelectric power, but in a very unnatural and not-so-"socialist" way. They have also caused a ca. 90% decline in bioproductivity of the Gulf of Odesa. Longterm, the dams should be replaced with other, much more benign, technologies of hydropower. We are contracted with an Italian company to replace all the dams with much more local, simple, and "democratic" forms of hydropower. Can this be a long-term benefit to the Ukrainian people?

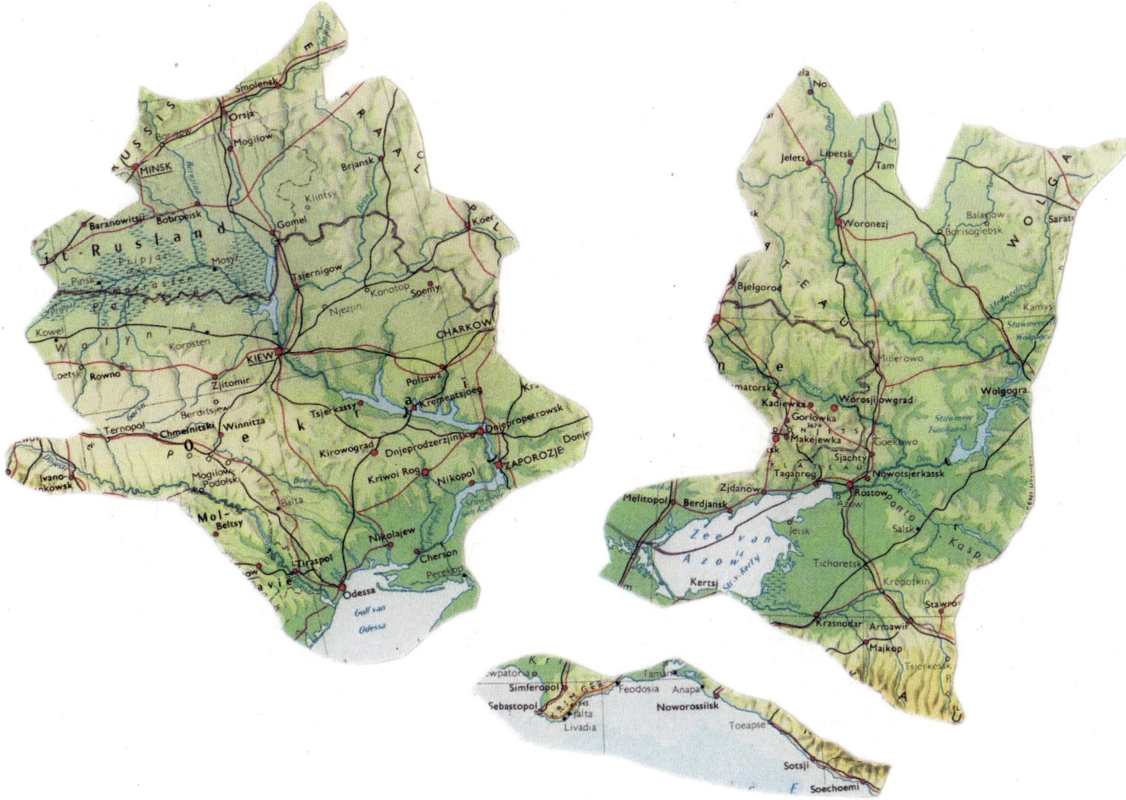

This kind of thinking, Ukraine in its saltwater basins, was already on display in an exhibition in 1994 in London and was removed the day after the opening. Many art dealers continue regularly very effectively, censoring or blocking initiatives by OE and Peter Fend, or simply deciding not to exhibit consigned works. Putin trying to take over all of Ukraine discredited any attempt to accommodate or befriend Russia. These two main facts alter everything.

NET-ZERO GAS SUPPLY FROM A PHYSIOCRATIC STATE

written February 1st, 2022

It's now acknowledged that a major part of the tension about Russia–Ukraine relations resulted from fears that a dependence of Western Europe—especially present-day Germany (which morphs with every generation)—on Russian fossil methane could cause subordination to the will of Russia.

Why not creates zones, even "pockets," of net-zero fuel supply. These zones would have fuel come from marine or aquatic plants, yielding methane, or hydrogen, or at-site generated electricity.

In the Sea of Azov, there are few if any sources of fossil methane. But there's much potential for methane, or hydrogen therefrom, or electricity therefrom, with the huge quantities of Ulva lactuca seaweed that annually grow, and can be managed to grow much more, in the Sea of Azov.

We propose a Sea of Azov administration, towards production of only net-zero energy.

And we propose the same for the Gulf of Finland, in the Baltic Sea basin, the adjacent Gulf of Riga, and even—for publicity purposes at least, the Greifswalder Bucht, where the Nord Stream II pipeline is meant to arrive, with fossil methane from Siberia.

Why, amidst the very evident change in world climate, with a prospect of all the permafrost in the Arctic ring melting, releasing huge amounts of methane and carbon dioxide, neither good for any of us, and needing to be absorbed by marine plants, is there so much brouhaha about who gets a not very-ecological fuel sent by pipeline from Siberia. We saw the same drama in Sardinia in 2019. The managers of fossil-fuel deposits want very much to prosper, at the expense of the planet, and at risk of a war.

We propose action this spring and summer in the Sea of Azov, and along the coasts of the Baltic States, to show that the days of fossil gas supply from Siberia by the likes of Nord Stream II are… ideally… few.

After hearing an interview of a Washington Post lead columnist with Kaja Kallas, prime minister of Estonia, with 1.3 million people, but big coastal waters.

FLYWAY 8
Eastern Gulf Corridor

Ocean Treaty Organizations:
IOTO and ARTO

Project Site:
BASIN OF THE GULF

Peter Fend 40 Lispenard Street New York, NY 10013 431-1645

1 July 1981

Mr. Sirri Altikriti
Iraq Mission to the United Nations
14 East 79 Street
New York, NY 10021

Dear Mr. Altikriti:

As an artist concerned with architectural questions, I have made regional planning maps for most of the world which organize terrain according to hydrological drainage--not into rivers only but into saltwater bodies, including the salt lakes, seas and bays of the world.

As you may recall from our conversations last Fall, I have prepared videotapes discussing how these regional mappings relate to historical processes, including the present conflict of minorities within Iran. These tapes can be lent to your Mission or the Interest Section on Washington for your review, or they can be viewed at the facilities of a business partner of mine. In the meantime, I would like to disclose the mapping.

The mapping of saltwater-centered regions has not so much been "art" as a combination of oceanography and topography. While it has appeared in major art shows, it has also--more importantly--been solicited by scientific and geographical organizations. The Lamont Doherty Geological Observatory of Columbia University reviewed the mapping and encouraged its continuation since, it seemed to them, no one else had so systematically done it. The United Nations Regional Seas Program is receiving a map from the Centre d'Art Contemporain in Geneva, where I just exhibited, and they would like a complete packet of information. The United States Geological Survey is circulating copies of the maps in its hydrology section, and a scientist there who specializes in satellite-monitoring is arranging appointments for me with the heads of the International Division and the Earth Resources Observation Satellite Program. Meantime, the Lamont Doherty Observatory--impressed by the geographical and satellite-imagery studies I have made--is recommending to the Arctic and Antarctic Research Institute of Leningrad that I and my artist-partners produce images of ocean circulation for their upcoming joint expedition to the Southern Ocean.

This letter was written in 1981 to the Iraq Mission to the UN in New York, a Mr. Altikriti, as part of my general sales campaign for saltwater basins. Over the years, there were roughly twelve visits to the Mission of Iraq (along with the embassy in Washington) and almost as many to the Mission of Iran.

Within the art community, I have presented historical discussions that relate patterns of human settlement and migration to the physical framework of saltwater basins. It seems that a remarkable number of events in history become explainable when viewed with the basin maps. Recent events include: the internal fragmentation of Afghanistan and Iran; the Muslim revolt in northern Nigeria; the secessionist efforts of the Basques, Bretons, Catalonians, Welsh and other European peoples; the Kusovo uprisings in Yugoslavia; the resurgence of Great Russian nationalism, exclusive of other nationalities, within the Soviet Union; the separatism of British Columbia and the Pacific United States; the claim for repossession by the Palestinians at least of their Dead Sea Basin homeland. A most prominent example, of course, is the effort of Arab peoples to form a confederal union around the Arabian Gulf, an effort rising to a head in 1917 and being manifested now most plainly in the struggles of Arabistan.

But ecology is my primary concern, not history: I map the world to try defining the separate catchments into which soils, salts and pollutants collect and circulate. The Arabian Gulf and the lands sloping into it are an ecological unit: it circulates nutrients and waters much as a biological organism would. The Gulf Basin is a sort of super-organism. It can be conceived, monitored and managed as a single ecological system.

As an ecological system, the Arabian Gulf is in jeopardy. Already overgrazing and desertification have through centuries desiccated most of the terrain, greatly reducing drainage and evaporation. Now, industrial pollutants and agricultural chemicals threaten biological existence in the Gulf itself. But if that biological existence were strong and manifold, the Gulf could sustain a substantial biogas, seaweed and fisheries industry. According to Jacques Cousteau, it could yield enough biogas to meet all future hydrocarbon needs after the fossil fuels are depleted. And if the lands sloping into the Gulf were comprehensively monitored and managed for diverse yields, they could be restored to ecological productivity. The Basin altogether could become a self-sufficient ecological and economic system. But present land-use practices and resource-extraction practices bode ill for the Basin. The Arabian Gulf is in danger, and so are the peoples on its slopes.

Fortunately, as is true in most basins of the world, the peoples of the Arabian Gulf Basin are generally of one nation. They are generally Arabian. They share a common culture and a common language.

Fortunately too, there is a project of the United Nations Regional Seas Program drawn up specifically for the Arabian ("Persian") Gulf. The project, like similar projects for the Mediterranean Sea, Caribbean Sea, Gulf of Guinea and Red Sea, has legal authority to include within its plans all the lands which actually or, with de-desertification, potentially drain into the regional sea. It is now being determined whether the maps I have prepared for parts of the world, including the map for the Arabian Gulf Basin, could serve as functional maps for the U.N. Regional Seas Program. If so, then there would be United Nations sanction of comprehensive observation and management of the terrain with each of the maps I have prepared, including the map of the Arabian Gulf Basin.

Because I would like to bring these maps into administrative reality, at least under the authority of the U.N. Regional Seas Program, I am interested in parts of the world where such a reality seems to be within reach. I believe that the Arabian Gulf is one such part of the world. The breakdown of Iran into its ethnic parts, whether or not under Iranian administration, was proposed by me when I began the mapping with earth artist Dennis Oppenheim in 1978. I saw a distinct ecological argument for a separate administration of the lands draining into the Arabian Gulf, including Arabistan. These lands of present-day Iran could be conjoined with other states within the Arabian Gulf Basin--including Saudi Arabia, Syria, Jordan, Arab Turkey and Iraq--in a common ecology and resource program. And all of this conjoining could be sanctioned under the supra-national jurisdiction of the U.N. Environment Program, parent organization of the U.N. Regional Seas Program.

A number of pioneers in video, film and photography have joined with me in formation of the Ocean Earth Construction and Development Corporation. We have the capacity to produce mosaics of film or video images, all derived from digital-data computer tapes relayed from multispectral scanners on satellites, of the various saltwater hydrological basins which I have mapped. These mosaics can be updated weekly. In a rapidly-shifting range of color interpretations of phenomena on the ground, the mosaics can show the dynamics and processes now ongoing in various basins. The images are both beautiful and accurate: they record the splendor of water and soil action on the planet. For the Arabian Gulf Basin, such images would demonstrate incontrovertibly the natural logic of including Arabistan and other Arab parts of Iran in the general planning and overview of that Basin. Perhaps your Mission, or other official agencies of Iraq, would be interested in discussing the possible production of such a mosaic of a distinctly-Arab ecological entity.

Sincerely yours,

Peter Fend

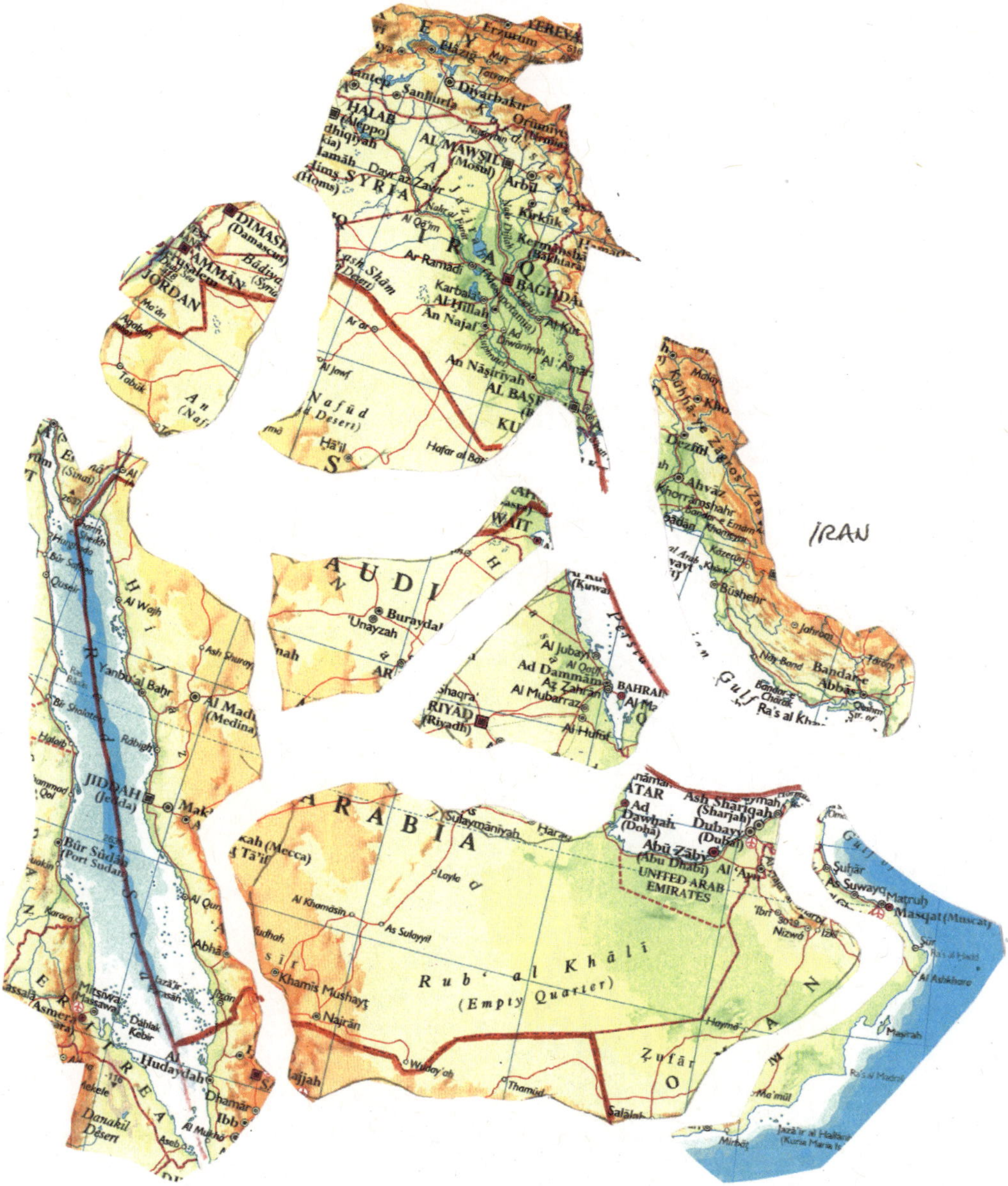

SEA BASINS OF THE GULF COOPERATION COUNCIL

In 1917, if Duchamp's urinal was as popular and understood as much as pop music now is popular and understood, then the Ottoman Empire would have organized its Arabian Peninsula (with Red Sea) in this way. It would have also made a deal with the Persian Empire about Khuzistan and the slope to the Gulf, but at the time, the British were moving in and were already in dominance in southern Iran, so no such understanding or application of art was possible. All for ecological restoration of that region? This is a working document, produced from 1:12,000,000 map stock (IGN France) in 2021. This is also what Fend would bring with him and lay out on a table if there were a meeting with Saudi Aramco on how to spend a chunk of its one hundred billion profit this past year, in eco investment.

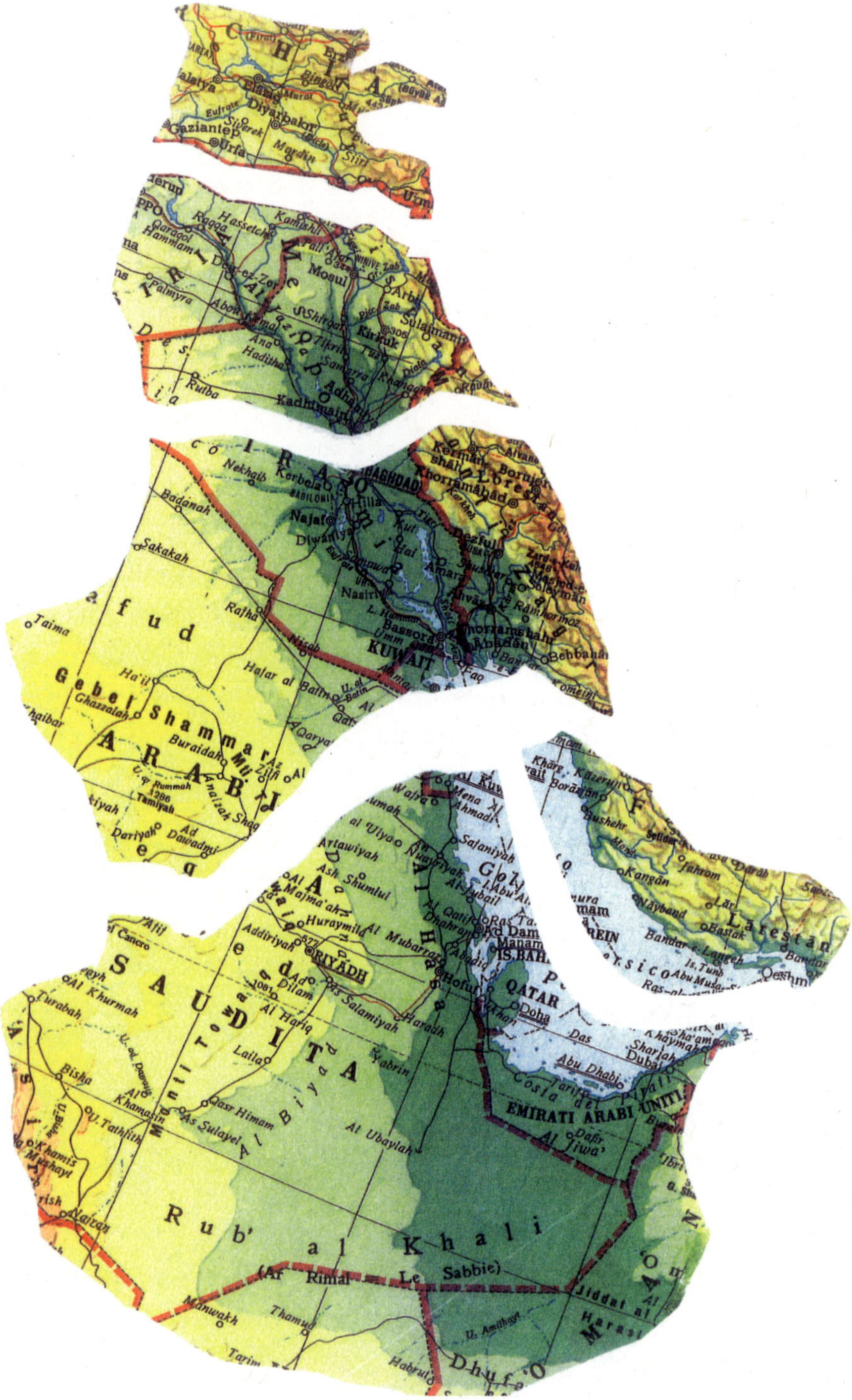

What drains into the coast of UAE was of great interest to Eva Scharrer, the UAE curator, but was deemed to be too political. These images were produced for Tue Greenfort in hopes of a convergence of practices by him, Peter Fend, Tomas Saraceno, and Marjolijn Dijkman in 2008.

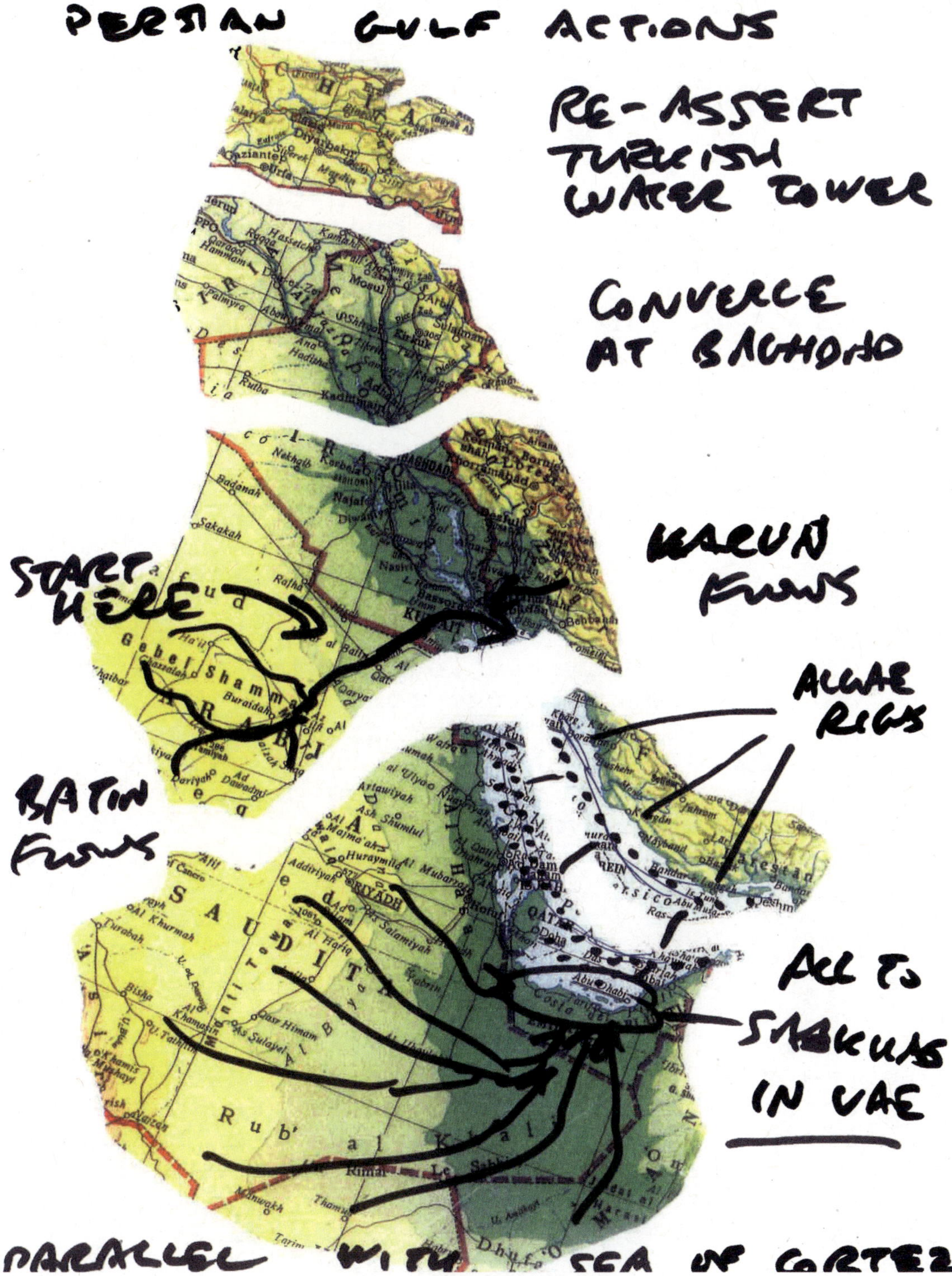
PERSIAN GULF ACTIONS
RE-ASSERT TURKISH WATER TOWER
CONVERGE AT BAGHDAD
KARUN FLOWS
START HERE
ALGAE RIGS
BATIN FLOWS
ALL TO SABKHAS IN UAE
PARALLEL WITH SEA OF CORTEZ

FLIGHT TRANSECT BASIN OF THE GULF

The immense wealth from geological deposits of petroleum generated in the past century, and possibly still generated for another century, gives those living in most of the semiarid or arid regions where petroleum is found—namely Arabia and Iran—an opportunity unique in human and geological history: to return what is now desert to savannah, to increase seaweeds and fishes in salt seas, to restore hordes of wildland animals. This opportunity is available to the entire Persian Gulf basin.

The wealth generated can be invested in a broad array of construction and engineering projects, inland, along the shore, and offshore. Large structures can be built at the head of the Gulf, as recent history shows, most dramatically in the 1980s. But large structures can also be built along the rivers and wadis feeding the Gulf, from southeast and northwest, deep inside Saudi Arabia or Iran. And even with the concavity of lands tilting and, if watered, draining into the United Arab Emirates, into the south coast of the Gulf, a ten or twenty year program can be conducted to restore the water cycles, both in the air and in the ground, for a gradual recovery to ancient fecundity.

In 2007, for Sharjah, physically, I focused on a very small concavity within the Persian Gulf basin. The concavity is a small part of an intermediate basin, that of all lands draining into the coastal saltwaters of the United Arab Emirates. The concavity comprises just two ephemeral river basins, or wadis, flowing on occasion to the Gulf from the mountain ridge less than one hundred km east of Sharjah. A thorough trek was made over these two wadi basins: Wadi Yuddayah, sloping into Sharjah; Wadi Lamleh, sloping behind a low ridge northwards to the coastal shoals of Jazirat al Hamra.

During the trek, I was finding out how and in which sequence structures derived from Earth Art can be installed in the wadi basin or offshore, to induce more animal habitat, largely underground, stronger water cycles, and the return of nutrients offshore to human use as methane gas. The produced methane gas can be distributed using energy supply points developed under the RAPID Brand.

The governing paradigm for continuous exchange between methane, oxygen, and carbon dioxide comes from Joseph Beuys' sculpture "Fat Corner." The molecule essential throughout this exchange is water. The means of assuring its presence, in line with "Water: A Natural History," is provided by those activators of the soil with water: animals.

In the United Arab Emirates, I first exhibited and then corresponded with curator Sheikha Hoor al Qasimi on ways to make the entire Gulf, including its insloping lands, become a verdant place. It could be a healthful stopover for aerial animals flying between Africa and Asia.

On meeting with marine scientists in the UAE, I learned that the oceanography of the Iranian side of the Gulf is very different from the oceanography of the Arabian side. Along the Arabian side, from the mouth of the Shatt al-Arab and Tigris–Euphrates on to the Straits of Hormuz, there is a constant pressure of sediment-laden waters against the shore. This pressure becomes greater along the southern coast of the Gulf, the coast of the UAE. The pressure is physically manifested in accumulations of crushed seashells. What follows here is a version of what had been started thirty years ago. I intend to resubmit this proposal to Iraq, and to Iran, and to all the countries around the Gulf with the potential for a closer-knit Gulf Cooperation Council. For now, this GCC works largely on petroleum and nuclear-fuel power. We of Ocean Earth would race forward with new but simple technologies, employing hundreds of thousands of now-unemployed youth. The chief aim is post-petroleum and post-dam energy production, superseding the huge dependence, in the Arab (and Israeli) world, on a very temporary source of wealth.

Page 8

UN Investigates Charge That Military Data Was Passed On to Tehran

By Warren Getler
International Herald Tribune

LONDON — UN officials are investigating allegations by the president of a company specializing in analysis of satellite data who says he gave valuable military intelligence to Iran this month under the impression that he was giving it to the United Nations.

Peter Fend, the founder of Ocean Earth Construction and Development Corp., acknowledged that he was "naive." But he said in interviews that he approached the United Nations in New York out of a spirit of idealism and because his company was looking for "constructive" business.

Mr. Fend said his company, which is based in New York, believed that its satellite data could be used by the United Nations in monitoring a cease-fire in the Gulf War.

Instead, he said, a senior UN official from Pakistan, Iqbal Riza, organized a meeting at UN headquarters with two officials of the Iranian Foreign Ministry. They were identified as Mojtaba Mirmehdi, deputy minister for legal affairs, and Mohammed Mahallati, director general for international affairs.

[illegible] knew he would be meeting with Iranian officials [illegible] said he assumed the meeting would be held under the auspices of the United Nations and monitored by its officials.

Instead, Mr. Fend said, the only UN representative present was a videotape technician.

A UN spokesman, Joe Sills, said the organization had begun an investigation of Mr. Fend's allegations.

"The matter regarding the relationship between the UN and Ocean Earth is being looked into by senior officials," he said.

Mr. Riza, a director of the Office of the Undersecretaries-General for Special Political Affairs, confirmed that he had put Ocean Earth in touch with the Iranians.

"I did arrange for the meeting in the UN," he said in a telephone interview. "The UN is a public place."

Mr. Riza said the link between Ocean Earth and Iran, as far as he was concerned, was merely commercial. "It is between them and the Iranians," he said.

Mr. Sills said Ocean Earth contacted the United Nations a couple of years ago about the possibility of using satellite photography for monitoring a cease-fire.

"We looked at it, but did not feel it would be of use," he said. "This year, Ocean Earth came back to us with some updated material, and they also requested that they be placed in touch with the Iranians.

"We did so and arranged for them to show a tape on Friday, Oct. 9, at the UN using UN screening facilities," he said.

"Officials from the Iranian UN mission had asked us to set up the screening," Mr. Sills said. "If an[y] member of the UN asks us to d[o] this, we normally would comply, i[t] would be routine. There was never supposed to be a member of the Undersecretaries-General office in attendance. What happens between Iran and this company is totally their concern."

Mr. Fend said that the Iranian officials asked Ocean Earth to deliver a 30-minute videotape of images from the Shatt-al-Arab waterway, which lies on the front with [illegible] they wanted the images for military purposes.

"We told the Iranians that we were not here to do business with Iran, we're here to do business with the UN," Mr. Fend said. "Nothing is going to be delivered to anybody except through the UN, and that means Iraq and all other UN members would have access to the material."

Nevertheless, Mr. Fend asserts that valuable information was passed to the Iranians, including details of recent Iraqi fortifications.

He said "it could be very useful" for missile targeting and other military purposes. The meeting "ended up being an intelligence transfer to Iran — courtesy of the UN."

Images shown during the meeting, Mr. Fend said, included video recordings of photographic displays obtained from the U.S. civilian satellite, Landsat, and from Spot Image SA, the French civilian satellite agency.

He said that the Ocean Earth analysis of the data from the Gulf War zone reveals, among others things, construction of an Iraqi canal that bypasses Fish Lake, a strategic barrier along the southern Iraq-Iran border, where most of the ground fighting is concentrated.

Ocean Earth has retrieved land images, including those of war zones and environmental hot spots, such as Chernobyl in the Soviet Union, from civilian satellites since the early 1980s. It has sold the data and analyses to news media and research institutes, including the British Broadcasting Corp. and CBS Television. Governments have not been among its customers, Mr. Fend said.

Mr. Fend also accused Mr. Riza of passing on to the Iranians an earlier videotape of satellite images from the war zone that his company had made for demonstration purposes. He is demanding that the United Nations pay $30,000 for the tape.

If such were the case we would be jailed in the US.

NOT TRUE. THE INVOICE PRESSED BY RIZA PRIOR TO THE IRAN MEETING WAS FOR $3[illegible] FOR ALL THE MATERIAL.

10 OCT 1987

A COPY OF ALL THE MATERIAL WAS THEN FURNISHED TO THE EMBASSY OF IRAQ. THEY TOLD US THAT FROM THEN ON THEY WOULD NOT TRUST THE UN.

This came out after consultation with the Council on Foreign Relations in New York. It exposed aspects of Iran–Contra, or US-covert assistance to Iran in maintaining a "balance" in the Gulf, preventing any scheme by Iraq. Two press conferences were initiated by the press agencies of three UN member states, the first (1987) by Russia and the US, the second (1991) by Turkey. The day the article appeared, also in the *New York Times*, with international press following up, a UN confidante explained that a major political cataclysm had been exposed: nothing may be said in public. The hydrological scheme, which could have benefited the entire Gulf, has yet to be allowed. Participants in the press conferences included (1987) Sante Scardillo, Joan Waltemath, Fend, and (1991) Scardillo and Fend, with Oppenheim and art dealer Colin de Land present, to promote further construction of the intended Iraqi earthworks, apparently in line with Earth Art logic.

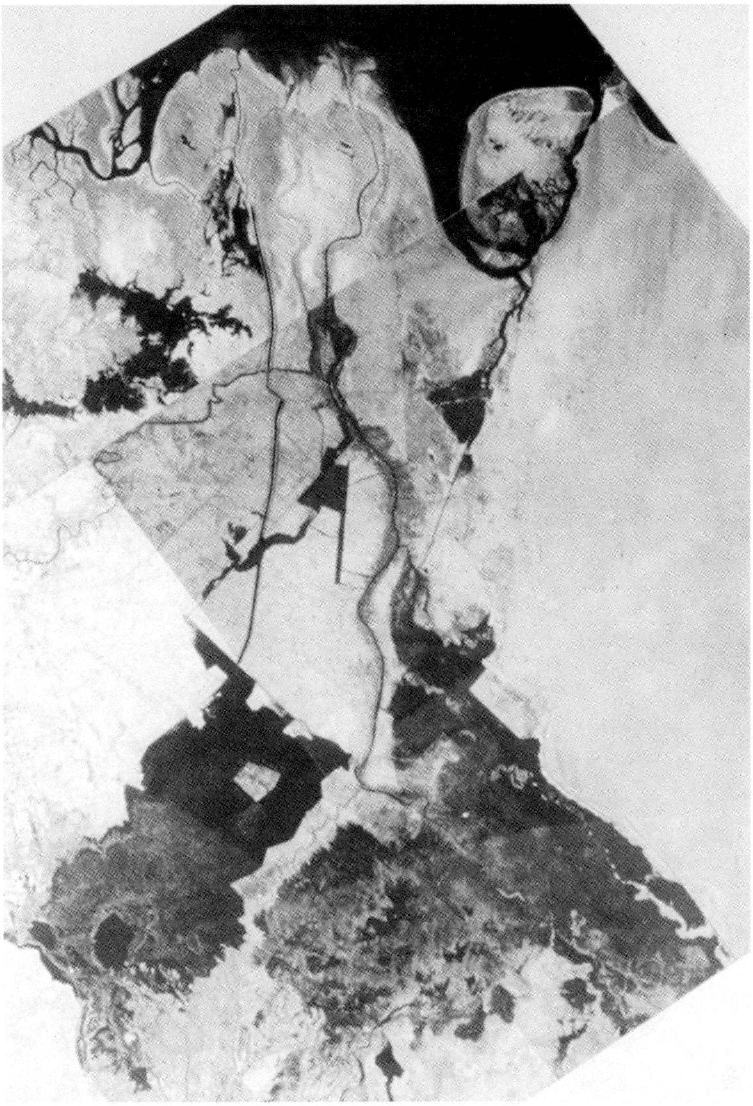

This shows the continuation of sinusoidal flows of the Tigris (east) and Euphrates (west) down to the Gulf, intended by Saddam Hussein's Iraq in the 1980s, but blocked by a secret provision of detailed satellite imagery by a UN official to Iran, exposed in October 1987. The attempt would have assured through-flow of river waters, with nutrients, to the Gulf. Oceanographers in the UAE described this phenomenon as the two faucets of a bathtub. The enormous bioproductivity of saltwater in the Gulf would have increased. All was set forth in large panels at American Fine Arts in 1988, accompanied by a soundtrack of the press conference at the UN about the UN official who incorrectly gave our imagery to Iran, sponsored by the Russian and US press agencies. The show was called "Body," since the sinusoidal flow of the Tigris and Euphrates aligned with the form of a Persian fertility goddess, Anahita. Attempts to review the show were frustrated by Western authorities.

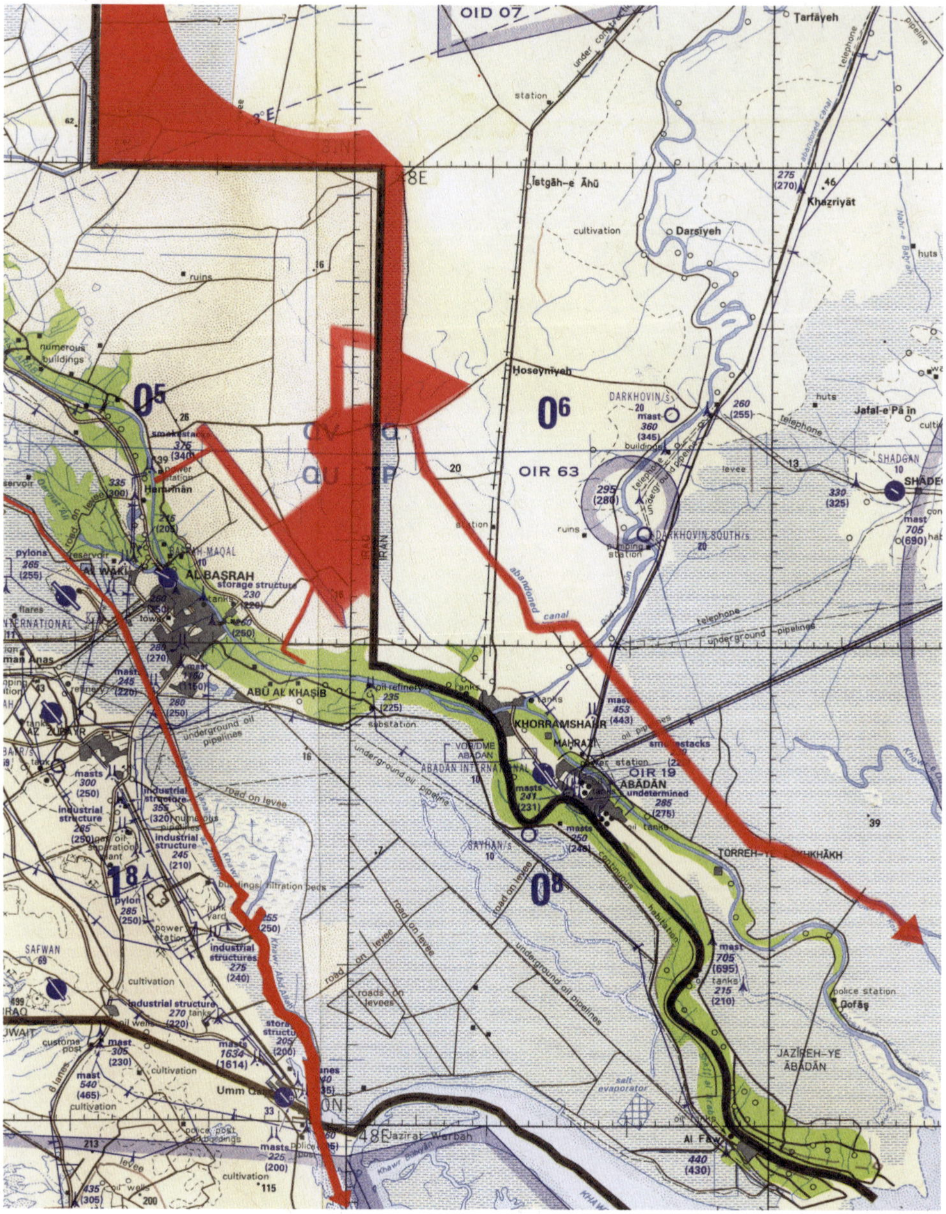

As aeronautical charts show, traces remain of the massive water structures built during the Iran–Iraq War. So, they could function again. Red here shows what could be re-built as waterways. Should something like that happen? Ecologists can decide. The Tigris and Euphrates would be pulled apart to receive inflows from the Karun-Karkheh and Wadi al-Batin on opposite flanks. This allows a flushing-out of the alluvia accumulated in the converging mouths of all four rivers. For armistice purposes, the zone between an eastward-placed channel of the Tigris and the current Iran–Iraq border, which separates two different time zones, could be given a name, and concept, from Dennis Oppenheim: *Time Pocket*.

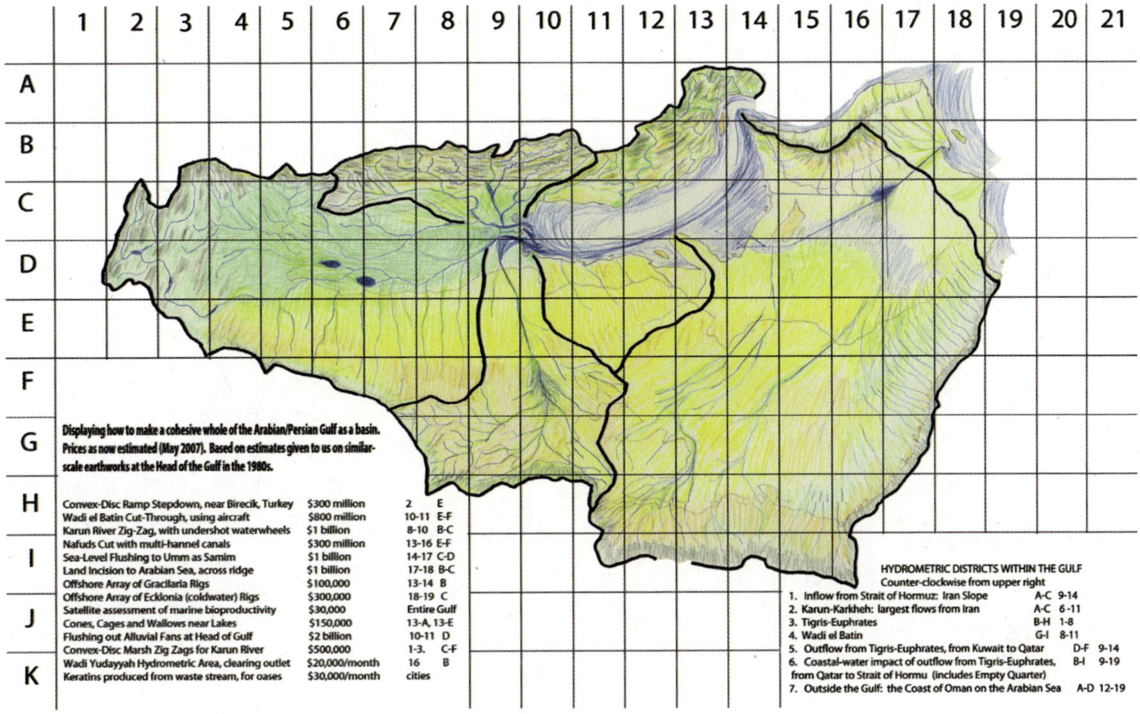

Workers from Peshawar got excited by the models shown in Sharjah in 2007, as ways of restoring the wadi, a dried river bed, especially near the sea, and they built a terrain to show this. They also helped me at the mouth of the Wadi Yuddayah, the main river of Dubai. A further collaboration between the workers and Fend on the Indus River was prohibited by the UAE officials for racial and social class reasons.

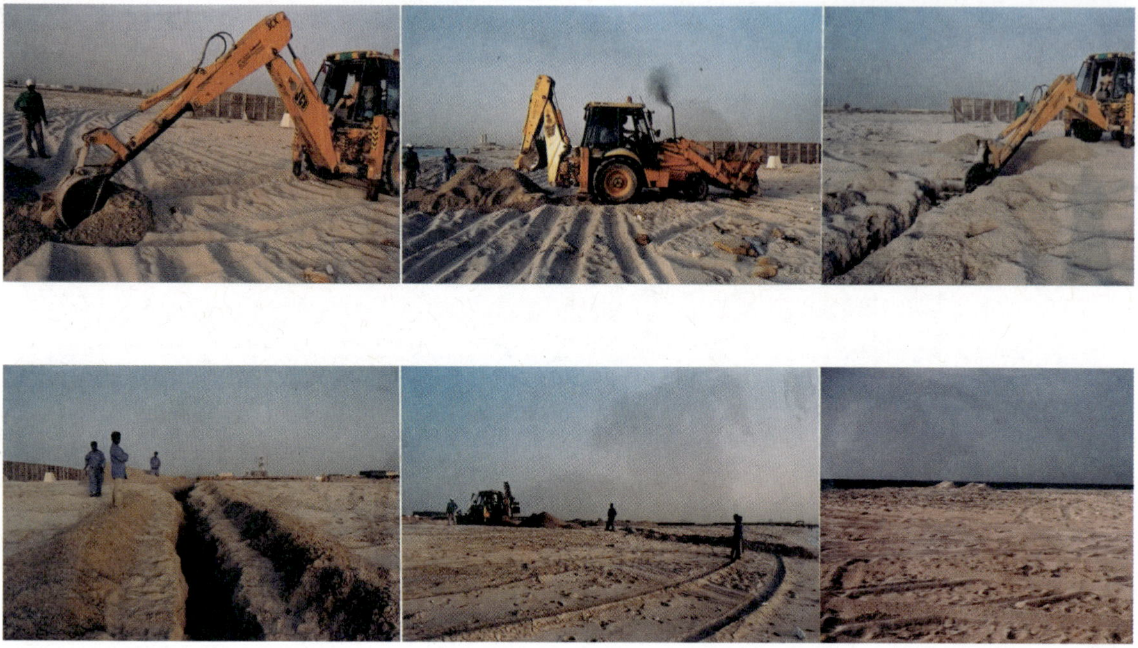

At the mouth of the Wadi al Yuddayah in the UAE, I make cuts to reconnect the Gulf with salty depressions blocked off from the Gulf by… not sand, but crushed seashells. The Gulf is very alive: given the ambient temperature of 35–40 degrees Celcius, ideal for biomass fermentation to yield gas, one can expect a surfeit of hydrocarbons. Funded by the Kunstverein Heidelberg, 2008.

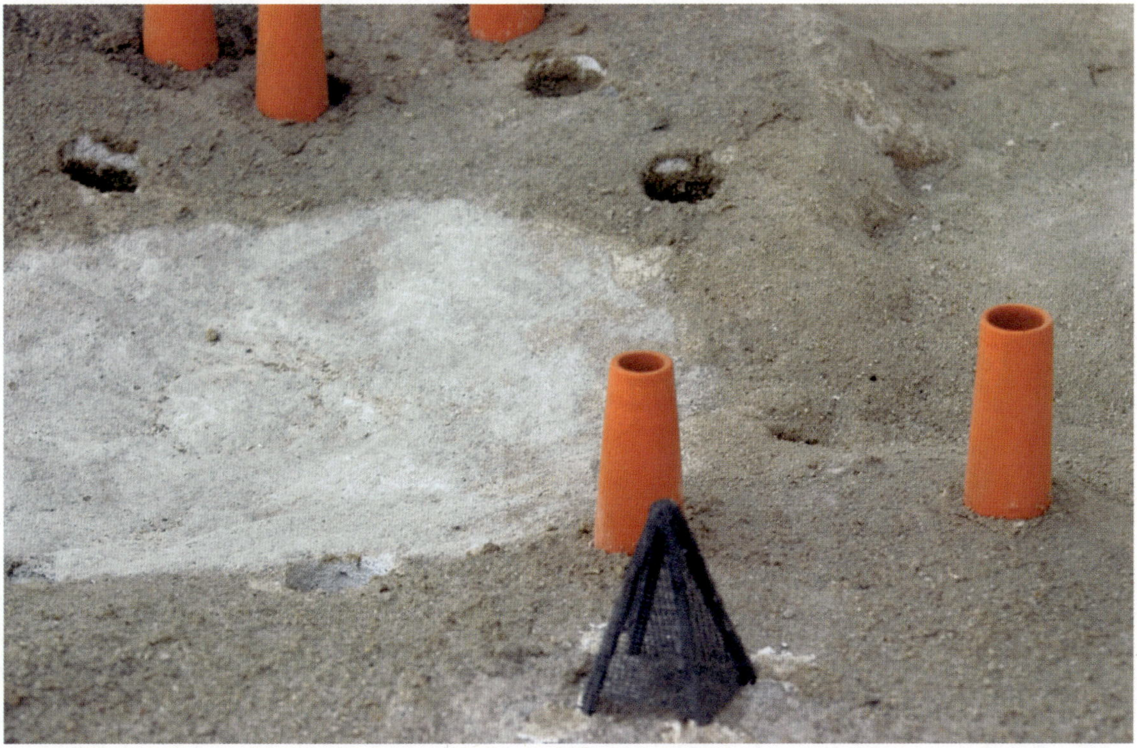

Near where underground freshwaters reach salty or brackish waters, and before those waters become salty too, one can build freshwater wallows. These could attract birds and insects. Upright cones create micro-habitat, and cages shelter birds. In concavities and holes, keratins from waste streams can be deposited. After a few seasons, vegetation builds up. These sites are linked with similar wallow-buildups along migratory flyways. Produced for Georg Kargl Fine Arts, Vienna.

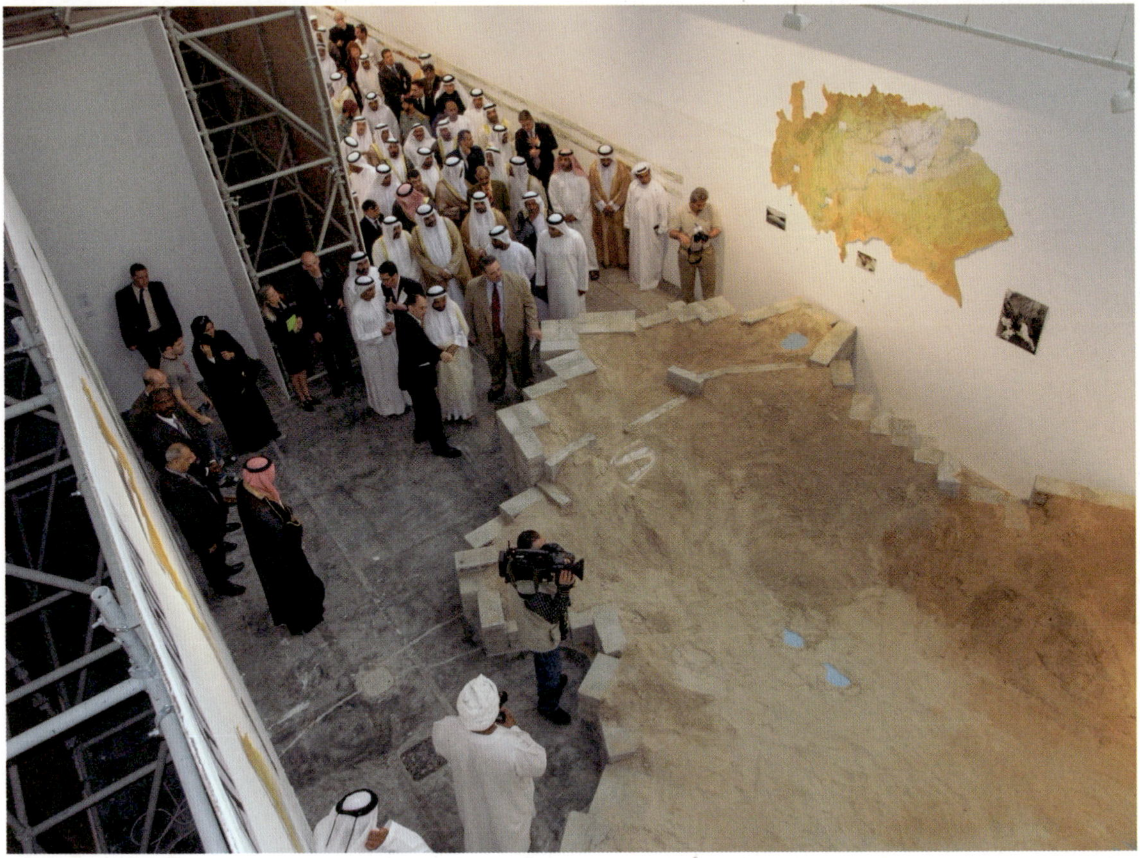

The installation at Sharjah Biennial 2007 shows what's on the map of Saudi Arabia in hydrometric areas or basins: the Red Sea, Gulf of Aden, the Tigris–Euphrates basin (originating in Turkey), and the flanks of the Persian/Arabian Gulf. The most significant part, aside from the Tigris-Euphrates, is what slopes from Riyadh into the coast of the UAE. In effect, the UAE is the largest territory and most suitable for large-scale ecological development. In the middle of the installation, in the Gulf itself, Fend placed a model of a macro-algae rig. Water temperatures in the Gulf seem ideal for macro-algae growth and harvesting. Also, there's no lack of nutrients. A zero-emissions biofuel industry could start inside the Gulf.

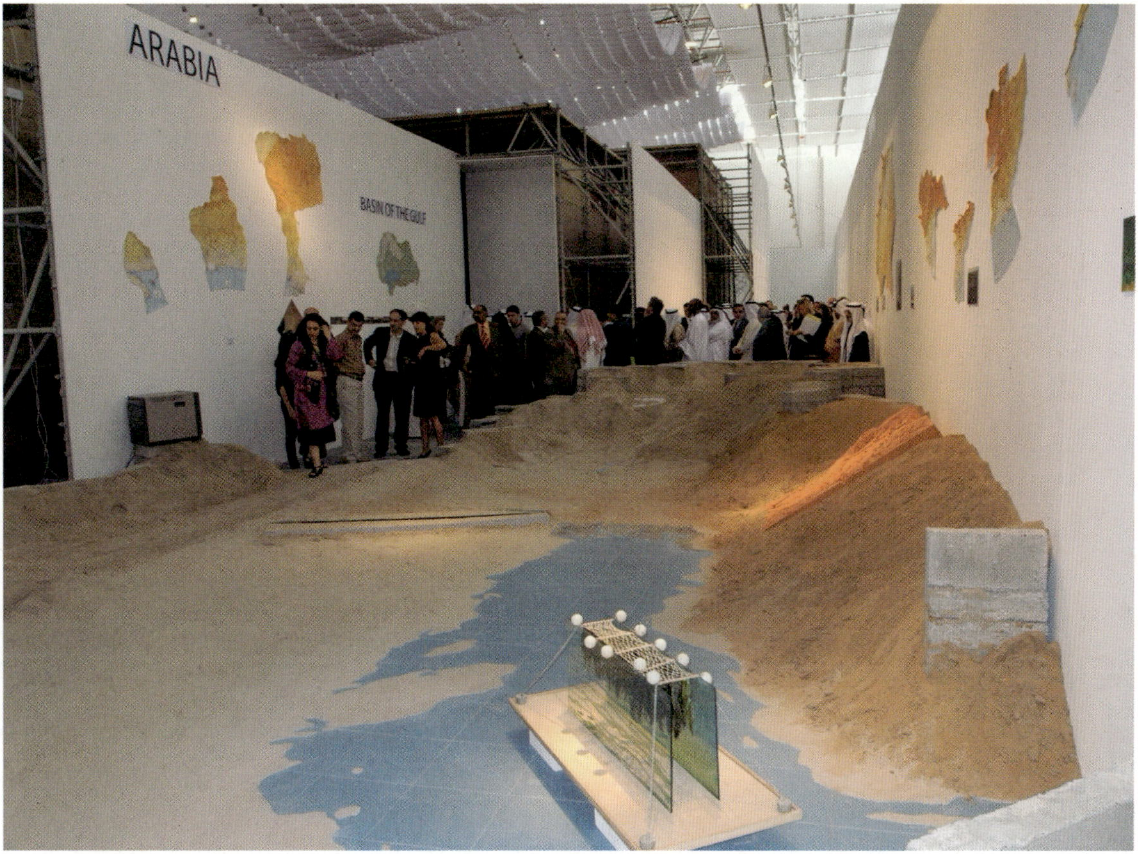

While showing around the Sheikh of Sharjah and his entourage, the US consul to the UAE was grinning all the time and slapped Fend on the back, saying, “We’re glad you’re here.” Based on Fend’s talks, in Dubai, with the UAE Minister of Environment, it seems very useful to adopt a scientific attitude towards the basins, especially as they impact seawaters, without all the inflated attention to “geopolitics.” The Gulf Cooperation Council, based in Riyadh, Saudi Arabia, exists for this purpose.

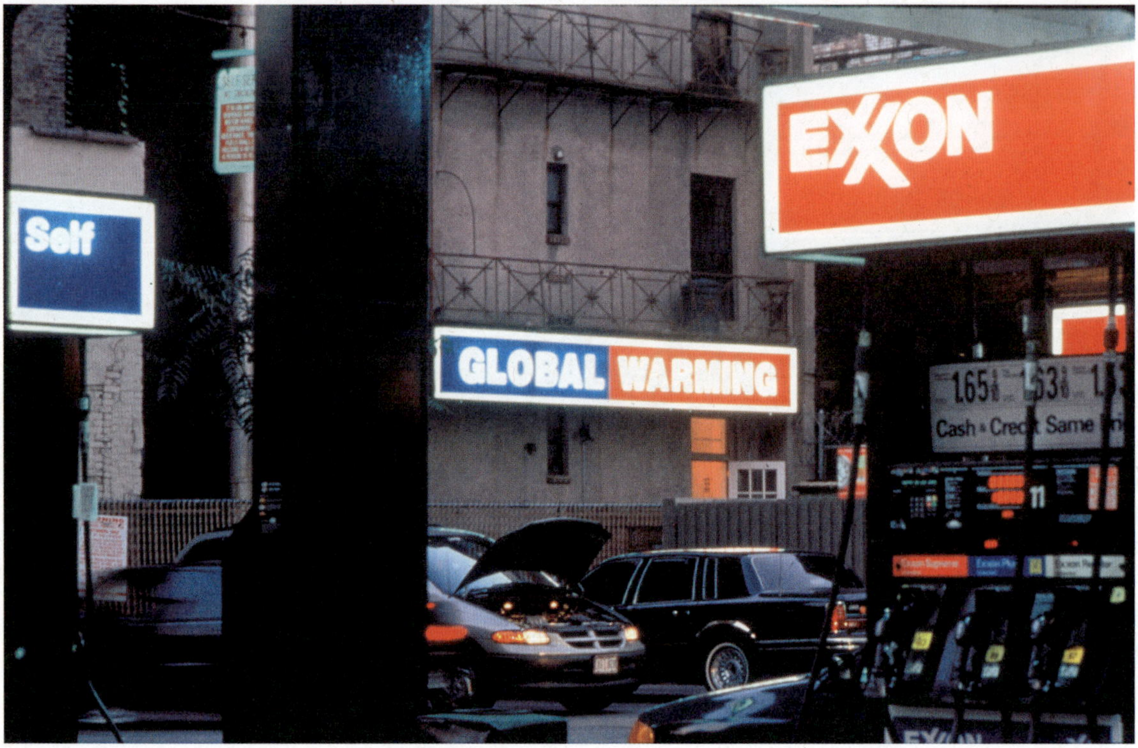

The problem lies in the oil companies' control of the oil fields and their determination to decide on any energy future at risk to the planet. This gesture was made on a very hot summer day in New York in 1999, in anger. It has often been misdescribed as a sculpture but is a graphic meant to be part of a real signscape. Its architectural rationale builds on what Robert Venturi and Denise Scott Brown have described in *Learning from Las Vegas* as the signscape as an architectural reality.

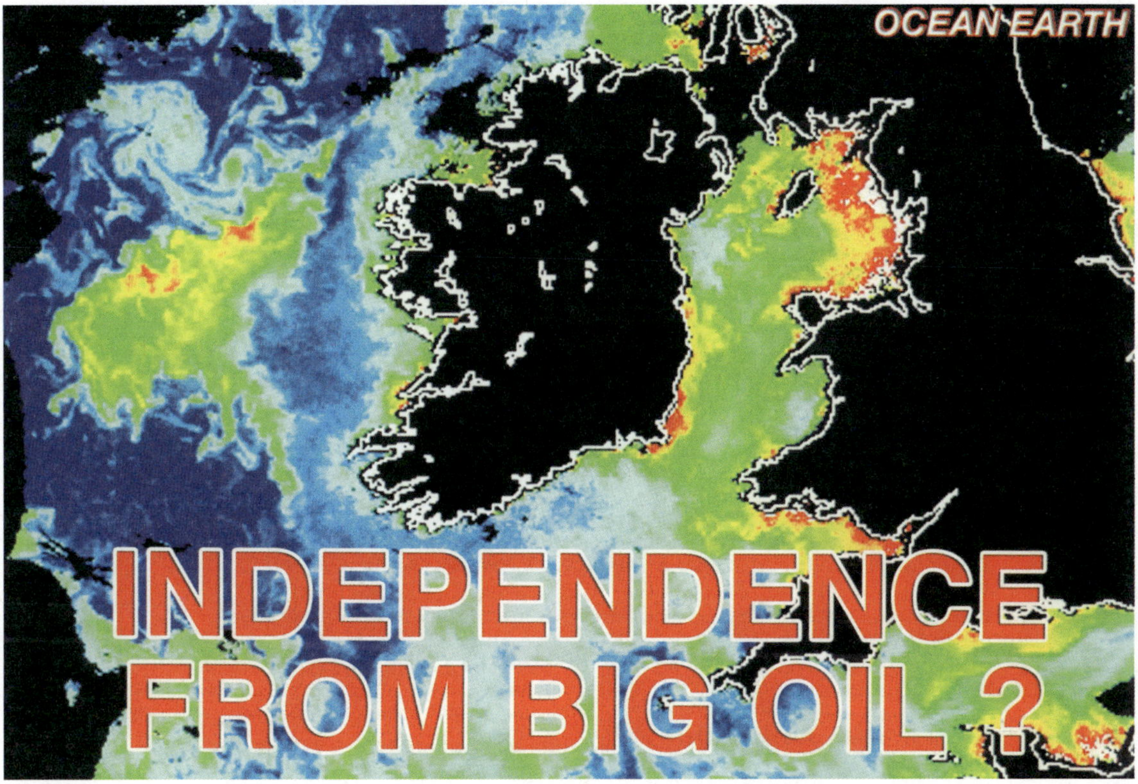

This was made in Ireland in 2003 and was part of a poster campaign on mass transport systems in Dublin.

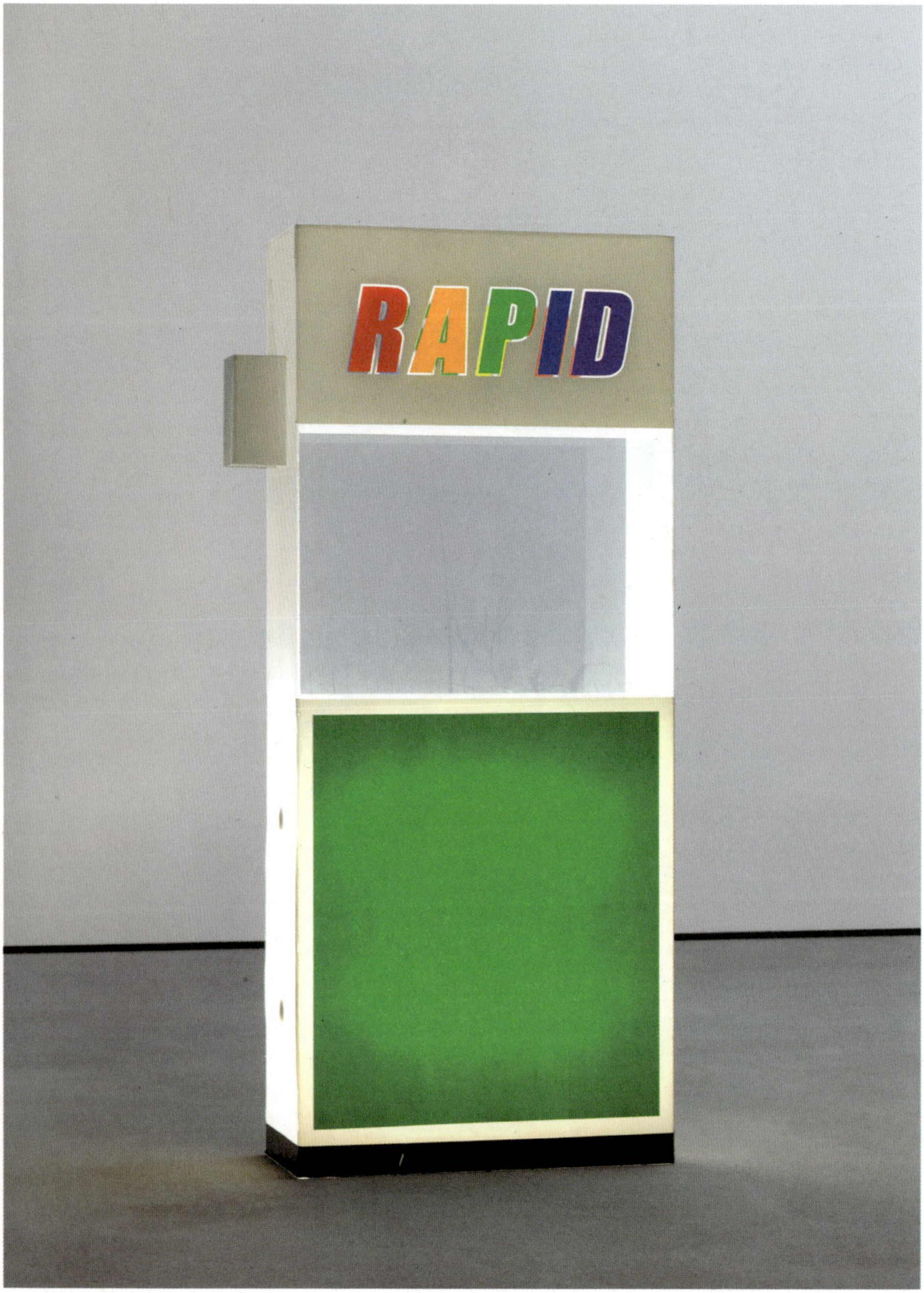

RAPID Methane Gas Station for biofuel from local sources in hydrometric areas. This was made in 2000 and is now in the collection of the Migros Museum für Gegenwartskunst , Zurich.

ARCHITECTURAL DESIGN CONTRACT FOR THE "RAPID" BRAND PROPOSED IN 2000 AT THE AMERICAN FINE ARTS COMPANY, NEW YORK, BETWEEN PETER FEND, OF OCEAN EARTH, AND JORDAN REUTER, AN ARCHITECTURE BA HOLDER AS OF WINTER 2021, IN NEW YORK STATE, USA.

1.
The "RAPID" brand proposed at American Fine Arts in New York, with publicity in numerous art journals (lead review, Art in America), and with public display and website promotion in 2020-21 at the Migros Museum, Zurich, has no legal registration or corporate ownership at this time. Initiators were licensed architect David Cook, now with Grimshaw Architects, licensed architect John Voss, and five artists, Bill Meyer, Christine Cobb, Julia Fischer, Peter Fend and Christy Rupp. Payments and acknowledgements have been made to these people, due to the intellectual property being collected and displayed, with much effort, including a trip to Washington, DC, and meetings with ecological organizations like Environmental Defense Fund, NY, all of which led to a Business Concept.

2.
The Business Concept is for a energy-supply point for transportation equipment (cars, trucks, airplanes, boats) which includes no gasoline or fossil fuel, and is unconnected with any fossil-fuel company such as the "energy majors." Energy can include biomethane, biokerosene, bioethanol, ammonium (a Japanese choice), hydrogen (a German choice), bioethanol, or plain electricity generated therefrom or coming from another source. To avoid dependence on "energy majors," the RAPID brand would produce all fuels at or near the outlet, largely from methane and electricity on the grid or in gas mains, and also from fields of biokerosene sources, such as Botryococcus braunii, at the site.

3.
Declarations by automobile manufacturers such as GM and Ford that they would produce only electric vehicles by 2035, which are contradicted by declarations from Daimler-Benz and some Japanese firms, leave the world fairly uncertain of just what will be in demand in the coming decades, even after 2035. It seems safest to be extremely flexible. This is possible with the equipment now available for conversion of gas-main methane into a variety of fuels, including hydrogen, ammonium and electricity. The source of the gas-main methane could be fossil, which undermines the ambition of post-fossil capability, but at least has few pollutants. The RAPID brand has the main business advantage of not depending on truck-deliveries of fuel from faraway to the outlet. RAPID relies on fuel from on-site or very-energy sources.

4.
Whether RAPID can safely and efficiently provide electric recharge for

In 1999, collaborators Christina Cobb, Julia Fischer, and William Meyer Fend launched RAPID: Post-Petroleum Fuel Stations. The RAPID brand can deliver locally harvested renewable fuels such as methane and biogas, allowing for a "democratized" energy supply independent from big oil and gas companies, Russian or Qatari.

EVs is not clear.

5.
Safety is the top priority. Any of the fuels suggested are dangerous and explosive, and in some cases toxic even to skin, and no mixing can occur, nor accidents of spillage or explosion be serious. If any accident were to occur, the design of the RAPID outlet must prevent a catastrophe. Assuming a dependence on methane supplied from a gas main, the input AND all equipment for any conversion to a fuel type, plus all equipment for supply of other fuel types, like biokerosene, muust be protected by earthen slopes and moats. This occurs with CNG fueling stations in Finland.

6.
Design of facilities for safe handling of separate fuel types, including maybe even electric charge, requires thorough study of the dangers and of how equipment for conversion from inputs into marketable outputs can be located, always with safe barriers between fuel types.

7.
The "genius" of the RAPID brand as Business Concept consists in the design of physical facilities that allow for (1) avoiding tanks and storage of trucked-in fuels, and (2) ability to provide whatever fuel is in demand. What is available and what is in demand can vary hugely from one place to another. In Armenia, for example, most vehicles would use CNG from methane or biomethane. In Japan, the fuel most sought could be ammonia, from what source? In many countries, hydrogen might be most sought.

8.
Local supply of fuel, and of electricity for any fuel-production on site, is central to the Business Concept. We map local supply sources within dam catchments and the hydrometric areas including dam catchments. Local labor and logistics is promoted. The global distribution practices of the "oil majors" are avoided.

9.
Intellectual property in developing this Business Concept, including all designs for each and any fuel or energy outlet, belongs to Ocean Earth Development Corporation. Assertion of this property relation must be completed by October 1, 2021. Regardless of how the property relation develops or is defined, the intellectual property belongs to RAPID as a brand, including the original participants from 2000 at least as stakeholders, and to Ocean Earth as the overall proprietor. Intellectual property is not held by any one person. If the Business Concept is found to not work, or be safe, or be profitable, then it becomes part of the history of Ocean Earth Development Corporation and, if publication of such occurs, American Fine Arts Company.

10.
Jordan Reuter can work on this Business Concept however he likes,

and with payments or percentage stakes from any funding that may arise, and with credit to him as a designer where his design is singular, identifiable and agreed in writing to be his, either alone or in collaboration with other named persons.

11.
All designs are subject to thorough review by a licensed engineer or chemical-industry safety specialist before publication or exhibition. A certificate of safety, or at least a professional opinion as to safety, must accompany any exhibited or published plans.

12.
Copyright will be assigned to RAPID as a subsidiary of Ocean Earth. The precise wording must be determined no later than October 1, 2021.

13.
Due to the extreme uncertainty on fuel types for transportation equipment in the coming decades, from 2021 through 2050, and due to the likelihood of very different fuel or energy choices in different locations on Earth, all making the Business Concept very speculative, Jordan Reuter agrees to a trade-secret agreement and non-competition agreement, with all public releases going out solely through RAPID or Ocean Earth Development Corporation, or any legal successor, and not through him, for twenty years from the signing of this agreement, in February 2021.

14.
The twenty-year trade-secret agreement and non-competition agreement applies regardless of the fate of RAPID or Ocean Earth. This rule results from the extreme slowness and unpredictability of ideas generated in the art world. A similar delay, for twenty years, occurred with the ideas worked on by Gordon Matta-Clark, as permitted by his widow, Jane Crawford.

15.
In the event of a demise of RAPID, or Ocean Earth, or Peter Fend, Jordan Reuter can proceed with publication or exhibition, or business development of any drawings and plans developed by him, alone or in co-signed collaboration, but with reference to the original authorship of the Business Concept of RAPID, as a subsidiary or operation started in 2000 of the Ocean Earth Development Corporation, itself founded in 1980. All such rules result from the unique conditions of art history, including architecture history.

16.
This Architectural Design Contract can be exhibited and published at any time under the authority of Peter Fend or Ocean Earth. The purpose would be art-historical and architecture-historical vindication of what was started in 2000.

17.
The jurisdiction is this Contract is New York State, USA.

18.
A copy of the Contract is filed with every art dealer or museum handling or exhibiting the work of RAPID or Ocean Earth.

Read and agreed-to by Jordan Reuter, with signature also of Peter Fend, founder of Ocean Earth and initiator of RAPID.

	2.23.2021
Jordan Reuter	Date
	FEB 28, 2021
Peter Fend	Date

NO ONE WORKS
FOR RAPID, BUT
WORKS WITH IT

"EMPLOYMENT"
REPLACED BY
CO-OPERATION
IN THE RIVERS
AND THE SEAS

WHAT IF ART HAD ITS WAY

ARTISTS' INITIATIVES WITH PETER FEND

Abramovic, Marina
involved in "Arms" debacle with Rob Scholte and Fend

Acconci, Vito
praised Fend megastructures in Times Square show, despite their being kicked out of show

Armleder, John
invites Fend to role in political-idea journal

Azizov, Ziegam
invites Fend to show in Aberdeen on petroleum; showing earthworks for Arabia and Persia

Barker, Noah
pursues setting up offices with Fend in Libya House

Basquiat, Jean-Michel
asked Fend to produce a basin work about Haiti

Beuys, Joseph
asked Fend to come to Duisburg for Ruhr action

Burden, Chris
arranged for Fend to appear on LA artists' radio, then published in "High Performance"

Byrne, David
asked Fend to produce a map of the world, for him

Cattelan, Maurizio
invites Fend to role in his magazine(s?)

Center for Land Use Interpretation
invited Fend, with fee, to work in Harper Dry Lake; later in Lake Ivanpah for show at University of Nevada, Las Vegas (Coolidge, Tang)

De Maria, Walter
tells me of scientists' interest in "Lightning Field"; says I should proceed on reviving that; we were corresponding when he died

Denny, Simon
invited Fend to do TEDx talk in Liechtenstein

Dickson, Jane
invites Fend to do stretch-fabric on scaffolding, as space-shaping project, Forrest Avenue Maze, Forrest Avenue School, South Bronx

Fekner, John
launched Fend at PS1 Clocktower, and in Jamaica Bay project (Queenssites)

Fischli, Peter
had Fend do his class at Staedelschule for a week; handles works sold to David Weiss

Fitzgibbon, Coleen
video-recorded Fend frequently, collaborated in The Offices and Ocean Earth

Ganahl, Rainer
buys much work; flies China flag in Shanghai; invites Fend to do a "windows" theme show with Roger Pailhas, and Fend makes a spinning room film

Geller, Matthew
invites Fend to compete for slot at The Kitchen; starts "Art of the State"

Goldman, Bobby
asks Fend to produce basin piece about Indonesia

Greenfort, Tue
asks Fend to show three drawings in Braunschweig promoting Dijkman/Fend/Greenfort/Saraceno venture

Grond, Walter
in Absolut Homer fiction, chapter on "Fend"/Libya

Guenther, Ingo
late in 1983, started working with Ocean Earth; (facts may not be made public for 1984–8)

Halley, Peter
invited Fend to an East Village show, had Fend publish in "New Observations," interviewed him

Harrison, Rachel
co-interviews Fend for October, with David Joselit; repeatedly recommends Fend for shows

Holzer, Jenny
started The Offices of Fend, Fitzgibbon, Holzer, Nadin, Prince & Winters; offered to be "media director" of legal successor Ocean Earth; invites what becomes OE at Chase Manhattan Plaza

Hybert, Fabrice
invited to participate in French Pavilion, Venice Biennial; actions there win Best Pavilion

Kippenberger, Martin
bought piece from "Kleine Fragen"; had Fend do a guest-talk, etc. at Staedelschule

Koether, Jutta
after much effort, publishes re OE in Persian Gulf

Kluge, Alexander
buys OE telecast videos, other satellite products

Koons, Jeff
hosted three "power breakfasts" on mass media, evidently (Cicciolina) took Fend's advice

Loebs, Jason
starts a "dialogue"; intends to publish it

Locher, Thomas
puts Fend in "Aperto," 1993 (Bourriaud tried that role also)

Matta-Clark, Gordon
asked Fend to join him in a new architecture firm

Meckseper, Josephine
publishes Fend story re Rob Scholte car-bombing

Mosher, Kirsten
invites Fend to publish re satellite experience

Munro, Shane
sets up corporation structures, and scanning actions; invites Fend to session at Staedelschule

Nadin, Peter
shows Fend twice in Peter Nadin Gallery, 1979–80

Nechvatal, Joseph
invites Fend to perform "End of LA"

Oppenheim, Dennis
had Fend take his slot in talks about Willoughby Sharp; recommended Fend to Matta-Clark, Sharits and others; had Fend advise on earthworks for Iran

Orta, Lucy
offers to "collaborate" with OE on "Habitus" at Galerie Anne de Villepoix, Bourriaud notices; offers Antarctica expedition, from 2009 on

Otterness, Tom
bought much Fend work; corrects Times Square Show

Parnes, Laura
invited Fend to do what become "Fettecke" drawings

Polidori, Robert
ca. ten videotapes of Fend re ocean-basin idea, at Russian, Iranian embassies, in New York; 1978

Robinson, Walter
buys work, publishes essays by Fend

Rockenschaub, G.
has Fend write catalogue essay about Rockenschaub

Rolandi, Alessandro
invites Fend to be in Beijing Media Art Biennial

Rothbart, Daniel
invites Fend to White Box extravaganza, Anthony Haden-Guest picks up from there, for show Nov 2018

Rupp, Christy
offers to do logo for RAPID brand post-petroleum fuel stations; invites Fend to Urban Animals shows

Schachter, Kenny
buys work, sponsors Antarctica-centered world map; puts Fend in ROVE shows

Schneemann, Carolee
told Fend basic facts, gets project response (secret for now)

Scholte, Rob
proposed world atlas for Fend; all works now in Tenerife; in Dutch press, said he's collaborating with Fend on "Mission Impossible"; car-bombed next; had invited Fend to talk at Kasseler Kunstakademie

Sharits, Paul
invested more in Ocean Earth than anyone else, and did his painting efforts in OE's Bway loft

Sharp, Willoughby
layout for "Art of the State" show; biz links

Shanzhuan, Wu
asked Fend to respond to Three Gorges Dam question

Staehle, Wolfgang
founding shareholder, Ocean Earth; also, first initiator in Space Force and Falklands work, later in Chernobyl and acid-rain survey

Suzuki, Taro
asked for meeting re artists' air force; thus began "Space Force" and "Television Government"

Thorsdottir, Inga
asks Fend to "help her country," Iceland; builds dossier for OE; arranges talk(s) in Hamburg

Vidokle, Anton
asks Fend to do project on slope in Hudson Valley; it becomes a miniature waterwheel scheme; often re-meeting, encounters via Nieslukowski

Waltemath, Joan
joins Space Force 1979; finds very useful footage of cloud formation by Amazon/Orinoco, impact on Sahel Africa and North Africa; UN press conference

Weibel, Peter
puts Fend in twelve shows (two at ZKM), buys much work, publishes "Ocean Earth" with Graz retrospective

Weiss, David
bought Fend work; asked Monica Sprueth to take him into her gallery (but AFA overruled that)

WHY THIS LIST: artists must team up, in order to rise up and achieve change in the world.

This list does not include initiatives which Fend turned down.

In some cases, as with Shanzhuan, Fend made major commitments.

This list does not include hiring, e.g., by Juan Downey, Charlie Ahearn, Eric Mitchell, as that work was not related to the career.

This list does not include a teaching gig at the HGKZ in Zurich, even though the person inviting me to teach is an artist.

CHRONOLOGY
OF OCEAN EARTH

Because on many occasions, powerful institutions and governments have intervened, extralegally, in the mandated actions of Ocean Earth, this chronology—largely of abuses against the firm—is produced.

The chronology is an attempt at corporate practice of art, with architecture—or arrangement of inhabited space—as the outcome. We conduct architecture with the responsibilities listed by Leon Battista Alberti: to assure, for an inhabited area, clean air, living waters, circulatory space, and defense.

1968
A construction company is formed by Walter De Maria and Michael Heizer, meant to produce their designs around the world. With such a company, they turn down an invitation from Willoughby Sharp to take part in his show of Earth Art at Cornell. But the company becomes inoperable when the Dia Art Foundation (Schlumberger, one of the two biggest oil industry services companies in the world) takes over management of their careers. (In "Six Years," Lucy Lippard.)

"Ocean Project," by Dennis Oppenheim. In Puerto Rico: the assembling of waterplants, or macro-algae, into globules at sea, with subsequent combustion, as if of fuel. Sponsored by MoMA.

Much talk in the art world about avoiding the "museum-gallery system."

Political unrest: Paris riots, US Democratic Convention "the whole world is watching," assassination of Martin Luther King and RF Kennedy.

Start of Whitney Independent Study Program (WISP) by twenty-five-year-old-year-old Ron Clark, who remains there forever since. Vaccination of art-world people with "Marxism" so that they never do it? Violates antitrust law, and the US Constitution First Amendment, by restructuring the field of discourse within a US-centered art world.

1974–5
Fend turns down an offer, after one-week try-out, to work at World Bank in writing "Sector Reports" on debt-strapped "Third World" countries. Decides that Earth Art and film-work like that of Paul Sharits, and of Field Theory painting, can better model how to develop the planet. Hears Zbigniew Brzezinski at a diplomatic symposium propose a UN-backed Baltic Basin state, as opposed to the usual East–West divisions; he adopts this idea permanently.

1976
Dr. Wheeler North at Caltech is news-reported as pioneering the production of biogas from giant algae. Fend starts contacting him and other scientists (at US Navy, UCSB), adopting this idea permanently.

Fend writes "Agriculture Ends, Art Takes Over," befriends Dennis Oppenheim, and in years after many other artists… with letters.

1977–8
Founding of Collaborative Projects, a large collective producing art shows, films, cable-TV shows, most of the founders from Whitney ISP. "Space Window*," a show at Brown/RISD organized by Joan Waltemath and Eve Vaterlaus, in cooperation with NASA scientists. Fend conceives "Earth Net: An Economic System" after hearing Vincent Scully talk at Columbia University; is invited to exhibit, as an artist, at Caltech art museum.

1979
Jenny Holzer, a Whitney ISP alum, initiates The Offices of Fend, Fitzgibbon, Holzer, Nadin, Prince & Winters, including two other WISP alums (Fend turned down a recommendation to apply to the WISP, thinking he already studied Marx). This is meant to direct art practices to clients outside the art world, outside any community of collectors, museums, and galleries.

Taro Suzuki proposes to Fend that they form an "art air force." Given his boyhood in GE research city, and his Dad's experience in the US Army Air Force, he suggests "Space Force." Taro's Dad was in a Japanese-American detention camp… Taro and Fend proceed to speak of satellite monitoring and "Television Government."

1980–1
Harvard-trained lawyer Richard Cole sees The Offices and tells his boyhood friend, Fend, that a legal corporation is needed. Holzer proposes a non-profit successor, but Cole says that to reach clients outside the art world one needs a for-profit successor. Fend founds, with Cole's advice, Ocean Earth Construction and Development Corporation. Critic Jonathan Crary writes this up as a big step towards "Global Architecture." The Village Voice fires him for the article, meant for their annual arts special.

Paul Sharits becomes the biggest artist-shareholder in Ocean Earth after Fend. Others include all members of Space Force, including Bill Dolson, brought in by Taro, and Win Knowlton, a sculptor.

In aftermath of "Real Estate" show, with a plan for Jamaica Bay and Lower Eastside in New York City, Fend invited to Duisburg to propose plans for the Ruhrgebiet, in a city-planning project initiated by Joseph Beuys. But is mugged in NY, losing all flight money. Publishes only. The proposal gains critical notice in Germany, crucial in the 1990s.

Fend wins competition for a show at The Kitchen, to be conducted by Space Force, as an "operation" of Ocean Earth, in collaboration with Willoughby Sharp, called "Art of the State." Eve and Joan use their NASA contacts to give us excellent access to image-processing experts. Taro, Wolfgang, and Fend meet the image-processing company to produce work for the show, convincing them to deal with us "artists" due to the ideas, loudly voiced, of Paul Sharits. George Chaikin attends the end-symposium, and immediately joins.

Ingo Guenther attends too, at the encouragement of Wolfgang Staehle, but delays joining for almost two years. (His role is not discussable, due to an Oberlandesgericht Dusseldorf ruling in 1988.)

1982
Falklands satellite surveys for NBC News, and—at Staehle's suggestion—the BBC. Staehle and Fend meet and dine with BBC. But in the TV news production, with NBC, BBC, and OECD jockeying for camera position, TV-news veteran Coleen Fitzgibbon accompanies Fend, not Staehle. Just as well, since her Irishness makes her wary, and she sequesters video imagery being produced. British troops enter the computer lab waving guns in the air, declare everything in the room to belong to Her Majesty's Government. A US officer escorts the British. Fend goes to Argentinian Embassy to report what happened, as US is "neutral"; is stopped (but not arrested) by the FBI. Then he goes to US Navy for getting material back, and is turned down; in the lobby is a giant portrait of… Margaret Thatcher. Historical analysis since shows that the satellite data led to a very successful commando raid to destroy all Argentinian aircraft on the Falklands, and then to find a solid ground route of tanks landing on the eastern island, but first at Pebble Beach, western island, in order to attack the Argentines from the rear. In effect: the war ends quicker than expected due to "us," as forcibly seized.

Lebanon studies: soon after, US agents say that no laboratory in the US will be allowed to work with us; we simply relocate most video production for mass media to Europe. Earlier, immediately after the Falklands broadcasts, the US Defense Intelligence Agency asked us to work with them, especially on the Sharits's flicker practices of sifting through colors; they were told No.

Amazon Basin studies in response to request by UNEP North America office head, for a better atlas of the Caribbean. Ocean Earth-labeled map is of Amazon as part of a Caribbean Continuum, from Natal to Cape Hatteras. With Fitzgibbon, OE produces 3-D studies of the Amazon, concluding that the basin is unrelated to the bulk of Brazil. Several meetings with UNEP and other UN officials in NY, further to the ILO meeting arranged for The Offices by Holzer in 1980.

1983
Ronald Feldman proposes to head up "Space TV," with $5 million from him, for our operation, but we soon discover a US-government intervention to tell all labeled participants to do nothing of the sort. Feldman asked if had been approached; he answers, "I would not do such a thing." Meantime, projects for NBC, ABC, and Turner.

1984
Publish Television Government as "FERNSEHREGIE-RUNG" in Kunsthalle Berlin show and catalogue. Start acquisition of Persian Gulf satellite data (six month delay in arrival…) in disregard of US Navy admiral telling us by phone to not look at the Gulf. We reason, he had no legal or Constitutional authority for saying that. Result: a massive discovery; see "Source of Designs for the Iran–Iraq War."

1985
Algerian Ambassador to France, who had been negotiating between Iran and Iraq, reviews OE satellite imagery in three meetings, attended by Fend and Matta-Clark's sister Federica Matta, and concludes with the question: What can we propose to do with such massive earthworks to restore the savannah in what is now a Sahara Desert?

In Bonn, an Iranian Embassy official asks us, on seeing the satellite imagery, if we have an "Islamic Solution." Fend says: "Islamic Garden."

Publication and TV releases worldwide, extended to other areas, such as Russian missile and submarine bases, Libya's coast, and Nicaragua.

1986
Chernobyl data processed, in a superior way at GAF, Muenchen. But seized by German intelligence

people, who say we donated it to them. Much intervention by US and German government people, then confiscation by French authorities, and replacement of our genuine images at Sipa Press with fakes, under our OE name… by French agents. All reported on in December session at US Congress Office of Technology Assessment, with commissioned report for "Commercial Newsgathering from Space." Staehle and the unnameable in early video of Chernobyl data processing, in room with US and German government people, with what turn out to be entirely false interpretations of the "black streak."

1987
Documenta catalogue, with two pages for the unnameable, asserting that Ocean Earth is a paramilitary agency involved in the grey area between "Spionageverdacht und Journalismus." Only one artist is named. He's German. Fend complains by phone about violation of the company's intellectual property, invention, and name; documenta says, "It's only art." Fend goes to FBI to report; they tell him, though IT-2 international division, that he is the one who's in trouble, for not cooperating with government agents. Fend retreats to art world, but meantime discovers—with new colleague Sante Scardillo—that Iran has been benefiting from a steady stream of images and analyses provided to Iqbal Riza, a top UN official, since March 1985—for the same negotiation purposes as had been attempted with the Embassy of Algeria to France. Fend consults with experts at Council on Foreign Relations, then releases facts to International Herald Tribune: huge scandal. Dire warnings from various missions to the UN, saying this is the biggest scandal in UN history; Hans Janitschek, our longtime UN contact, has a scarier analysis. All relations with family siblings are stopped. We become "untouchable." Alan Jones shouts, "You've gone too far." A show is mounted at American Fine Arts, but all reviewers who attempt to cover it, e.g., Jutta Koether for Artforum, are told that it's unpublishable.

1988
Three trials against Fend, the Federal case dropped on "national security grounds" (my thirty-three-point brief revealed the contradictions), and the Dusseldorf case leading to news blackout. The trials prevent a plan to base in Holland, invited by Joep van Lieshout. Staying in NY is required.

1989
Back in Europe, funded by a prize, to participate with scientific credentials in "Global Monitoring and Assessments: Towards the twenty-first century," sponsored by UNEP, FAO, and an international forestry agency. Release findings about Chernobyl, published in London Times and US radio/TV, with Times reporter to become later the media director of UNEP. Patronage from David Weiss of Fischli & Weiss. Preparing to base, again, outside US. Monica Sprueth seeks to show, but Tanja Grunert and Esther Schipper get the deals, through American Fine Arts.

1990
Shows, and a book, in Cologne. "Kleine Fragen," an expose of a faked car-bomb event in relation to German currency unification, at Nagel. Controversy. Beginning of several-year patronage from Johannes and Louise Daxer, near Munich. Start of residency at Hospital Ephemere, Paris. "Dragonfly" years in Europe begin: Ocean Earth advertised in Paris, Cologne, Frankfurt… In response to the discoveries of news distortion (which prompted the overture to the UN): "NEWS ROOM"; in NY/Amsterdam, then Frankfurt (Weibel). Hans Ulrich Obrist asks for a "NEWS ROOM" manual: we say No; we want to make a business with it.

1991
Second UN press conference, attended by Dennis Oppenheim and Colin De Land, sponsored by Turkey, regarding "positive" program of Ocean Earth in Gulf using earthworks sold by Oppenheim to Iran; hostile reaction by Iran diplomats; debacle. Run-in with German authorities; told by US to stay away, but documenta invitation changes this.

Travels to Belgrade, with architect Kevin Gannon; negotiations with ecological-architecture firm CEP, for Tivat Bay, Montenegro.

"NEWS ROOM STOCKHOLM"—the most successful, with the smallest budget; brought in the Foreign Ministry. Included Daniel Birnbaum.

1992
Documenta. Retaliation for 1987 by insisting on Ocean Earth concept of how to organize what Germany was in, say, end 1942, in three ocean basin parts (as also published in the UNEP/FAO conference, 1989), and for an oceanographic approach to Europe. Publishing much in Amsterdam, Paris, always finding scandals, e.g., about Yugoslavia.

1993
Offshore rig designed for offshore macro-algae industry, with months of research sponsored by FRAC Poitou-Charentes under Olivier Chupin… later involved with Segolene Royal (worth pursuing?).

1994
Response to Wu Shanzhuan request, What shall be done with the Three Gorges Dam proposal? Further to request from his now-wife, Inga Svalan Thorsdottir, How can we help Iceland? These proposals, when shown in London, earn immediate heavy attack as megalomaniacal. An earlier show in Vienna, with same techniques of terrain models for earthworks, wins largest public-visitor rate in the gallery's history. Rob Scholte car-bombing; three meetings with Amsterdam police, etc.

1995
Fend initiates the exhibition "Mapping: A Response to MoMA," at American Fine Arts, which earns a more favorable NY Times review than the original MoMA show. Residencies in Sydney, Moscow, Genoa, San Sebastian, Bregenz. Aperto "On Board," curated by Jerome Sans: Venice Lagoon scheme.

1996
Chernobyl investigations in Russia and Belarus, backing up previous theories from satellite data. Shown in NY, but discouraged by agencies. Japanese funding for sharp upgrade of Giant Algae System.

Collaboration with naval architect known for pioneering current America Cup design formula: Marc Lombard, La Rochelle. To pursue.

1997
Giant Algae System brochure. Argues that building a marine biomass industry has a foundation in architectural logic. No ISBN, but released by Morses of NY, Conceptual art collectors.

1998
Sale of Montenegro footage (on ground and with satellite in 3-D flythrough) to NBC News, with broadcast leading, as Robert Windrem, the editor, says, to the US Navy deciding to not attack with helicopter gunships. This may have influenced later Montenegro decision to join NATO; there had been no bloody encounter.

1999
Ocean Earth package for Ukraine Mission to the UN, about coverup of Chernobyl data by various Western governments. The nuclear entourage from Germany was turned back at the Kyiv Airport, it appears (need verification). Soon after, German nuclear industry collapses, taken over by France. Ongoing questions about stability of Chernobyl site.

2000
RAPID: Post-Petroleum Fuel Stations, with designs by three architects and four artists, plus logo by Colab-member Christy Rupp. An example of collaborative art in action, prompted by the "Global Warming" sign at the Chelsea Exxon station. But… all collapsed due to a participant sending faxes to clients as if he were a professional architect, which he was and is not. Characteristic problem in art collaboration: inattention to legal rules. (We'd enforce the same rule

about “architecture” with “Bio Architecture Lab.” Ocean Earth has one licensed architect and two more academically-trained architects as stakeholders; plus a long record of publishing and speaking in an architecture context.)

“NEWS ROOM NEW YORK.” Near the UN. But we succeeded in reaching UN diplomats only eighteen years later, with “AFRICA THINKS.” Inviting (and receiving some) of the fifty-one African members of the UN, and the one China member of the UN.

2001
First production of biogas with waterplants, in Exe estuary, both fresh and saltwater. During 9/11, destruction of the Ocean Earth office, Americas project (for Venezuela) and many satellite photos, in the WTC. In Mute, during stay in The Hague, published plans for Afghanistan/Iran and for a US earthworks test site, at Lake Ivanpah/Roach/Jean in CA/NV border. Publish that to get beyond the present impasse, we must go “beyond petroleum.” The article is picked up by US Natural Resources Defense Council, which also publishes. But did a BP ad agency, or?, pick up on “beyond petroleum,” which they trademarked a few months later. Notice, too, that the $2.1 billion solar-thermal power plant, much promoted as THE best answer to climate change, is in Lake Ivanpah, and the Public Art Fund has massive projects in the same area, but none of what OE proposed has started.

Catherine Griffiths and I have visited and produced an update, 2018. An Exxon executive-suite veteran, just retired, explained to us, unaware of who we were, that each day she would find entities threatening Exxon’s business and organize sabotage, public discrediting, or other actions against them.

2002–4
Expelled from New Museum show for victims of WTC 9/11 disaster, for submitting a drawing showing parallel border practices under British Colonial Office in NY/NJ/CT/PA and Iraq/Kuwait/Iran/Saudi

Arabia. The same drawing wins exhibitions in key venues in Europe, complete with earthworks from Vienna 1993 show. Complete basin plan for Africa shown at Ars Electronica in Linz: debate with Paul Virilio, who had in 1985 said that we commit "la pornographie politique," although we met at La Coupole some dozen times in between. His was the typical attitude: interested, but wary. He warned that our practices could cause "le chaos." Really: just Physiocracy?

2005–7
Having moved with wife and child to Berlin, quickly asked to show in Nagel, Berlin. Gabriele Mackert, who curated the US–EU comparisons at Kunsthalle Wien, says to me, any exhibition by me in a German-government funded space, e.g., Haus der Kulturen der Welt, will be banned. Such turned out to be true.

2008
Move to New Zealand 2008, teaming up with early Ocean Earth pioneer, and stakeholder as of 2008, Heidi Mardon. Sites in mind, but market for methane gas, e.g., biogas, entirely wiped out by shift in NZ to 100% dependence on fossil fuel shipped from Singapore. All is occasioned by a show in Wellington, sponsored by the UNEP, the head of UNEP present, Ocean Earth winning a prize, Heidi Mardon receiving the prize while I have returned to Europe for more shows… and… soon after, the curating organization, called the Natural World Museum, based in Oakland, declares bankruptcy and turns all documents over to the law firm of Milbank, Tweed, Hadley & McCloy, the most famous Big Oil firm. Four months later starts a company spun out from Shell, with a Shell veteran in charge, involved in nearly exactly what we proposed in our G.A.S. brochure, including many Japanese scientists, our base for work as described, called "Bio Architecture Lab." It is based in Berkeley, CA. It has no architects, nor anyone thinking about architecture, on board. But it has our concept for anyone web-searching for "architecture" and "macro-algae."
How does one respond? By going to the court in

California saying that their name is "false advertising"?

In Berlin, I did a show of ocean-basin mapping for countries having an election that year or next: Sierra Leone, Romania, New Zealand, USA, Chile. Because Heidi Mardon had been invited to Chile in an official capacity, as part of the Southern Hemisphere discourse among nations, I had purchased 1:500,000 charts and mapped the country in what I thought could be its hydrometric areas, or bay basins. The array, in one big row, was impressive. It hung on a big wall of a gallery in Berlin. A Madrid art dealer wanted to show it in Madrid. She liked the ideas of Ocean Earth. She had already sponsored giant maps of the Persian Gulf Basin, and of the Iberian Current. We would meet to arrange for a show about Chile in Madrid. A phone call was received at 7 PM on the day of the meeting to say that she would be late; we must meet instead at 10:30 PM. The phone had a jolt; it went zap. Its keys could no longer be pressed. I went to the gallery at 10:30, and there she was, and the dealer, and a man from the art world known for speaking many languages and being everywhere. He said, "You may not do that show about Chile in Madrid." He explained the next day, in email, "because we don't want to help Banco Santander." He quoted words from Henry Kissinger.

In sum: the US had intercepted a phone call, and the US sent a man from among us in the art world, very popular and jovial, to tell me that the US forbids any show of this Chile in pieces being done in Madrid. After that event, his cover was blown. But that did not stop him from saying, at an opening in NY, that one should not be reading "China Daily," and so on. Now he is dead, and he has a generous obituary in Artforum...

For that Berlin show, I produced new basin-state flag versions of: China (announcement card, and flown in Shanghai (prior to arrest), Cuba, Spain, USA (the flag now is a map, of fifty states) (I made sixty basins, as a sixty-star flag, an update on

Jasper Johns?), Poland, South Africa, India (with a waterwheel instead of the spinning wheel).

2009
Invited to do 250,000 Euro scheme in Ruhr region, and do extensive testing of waterplant harvesting in NZ, with biogas as a result, but the link with the curators is taken over by Fraunhofer, which announces three months later that they alone will do what was already done, with me and others under Ocean Earth contract in New Zealand, and that I alone would be allowed to design and operate the pavilion, called Erneuerbar. Fraunhofer's director in the Ruhr, whom I never met, said that two PhD candidacies would be sponsored to do the "sehr gute Ideen." A Berlin lawyer said we could make a case against Fraunhofer. But the gallery Nagel, and then the curator, said I should have given up and let Fraunhofer take over the project, with me being the exhibitor of what would be THEIR intellectual property. I said No, with Heidi Mardon's assent. I was immediately expelled from the show, and from the Galerie Nagel.

2010
The NZ collaborator, seeing what happened, ran to his government for funding a PhD for him in this same "sehr, gute Ideen," received 120,000 NZD for the PhD, and had it reported in the news media as a continuation of "previous work with the American firm Ocean Earth." Heidi Mardon described it as a case of the powerful "knicking" (stealing) the ideas and work of the weak. The powerful, in this case, being the government's New Zealand Foundation for Research, Science and Technology, and the Waikato University. The weak, being a company of architects and artists with no academic credentials in science, but proven results, as the Ruhr Capital of Culture early on affirmed. In short: an artist or even architect is not regarded as scientifically qualified to do anything which scientists regard as their territory.
But we see, in the years since, that NOTHING has been done in the Ruhr by Fraunhofer with the "sehr gute Ideen," so that—in historical outcome—the academic entity simply sits on the idea, doing

nothing. We would have acted. A videotape of the action to take, made in September 2009, was taken by the video staffer for the Ruhr European Capital of Culture. He was promptly fired for his insubordination. Peter Weibel bought the video. The video staffer has yet to be paid, as we ended up being… in the best form of punishment, penniless. Sobering: our view is that even if the challengers to Big Oil are prominent scientists, e.g., at Caltech (as shown in correspondence to Ocean Earth in Vienna), they will be crushed anyway, as they are a threat to Big Oil.

2011
Invited to compete for the French ecology art prize, called "COAL" (why?), I submit a thorough application, and am declared one of ten finalists from a field of ten, but then comes in second, not first, and afterwards am told, in a cafe, that the past adventures with the Iran–Iraq war (which ones?) had tilted the vote against me. Does this mean that Ocean Earth should never have touched the subject? And that any blame for what the UN's Mr. Riza did should fall on them?

Merzbarn, UK Lake District, arranged by Littoral, Manchester. A terrifying experience. I was asked to produce tweets (140 characters) of all my thoughts. But such thoughts were very provocational, about Arab Spring (I blamed Churchill) and about Fukushima (I blamed Einstein). The hosts were furious with me for my thoughts. The next day, while traveling to Milan, I got mugged by five fit men losing many artworks and possessions… in Brussels. Survival at all became a top concern. The host in Milan has promised to publish my attack on Churchill, Einstein, and Freud, but has not done so yet after ten years. Too "hot"? Meantime, there were plenty of waterwheel investigations in the Lake District: one accomplishment.

"NEWS ROOM MILANO." Nowhere Gallery, Milan. Effort to publish what I wrote up as a condition of residence in the Merzbarn, English Lake District, as the first "international resident" of what had been a British gunpowder factory.

2012
“Uber die Grenze: MAY NOT BE SEEN OR READ OR DONE.” Essex Street. Numerous reviews, Contemporary Art Daily, follow-up show in Rome, White Columns Annual Review, US–Russia Submarine for Post-Petroleum Industry.

2013
White Columns Annual Review. Hawaii Energy Supply.

For a big ecology show at the Gemeente Museum, The Hague, with good budget, and assurances of up to 250,000 Euro, and with support from art dealer Fred Wagemans, efforts are made to realize the project earlier proposed for the Ruhr, but now conducted in Dutch canals, all being dammed with waters full of excess nutrients. Rowers were met and contacted. A budget and timetable were made. The Ministry of Economics expressed an interest. A public discussion was held. I prepared a list called “credibility,” of our scientific papers and articles in both scientific and mass-media journals. This attempt backfired. I was told next to meet an executive from Shell. We met at his home. He explained to me that anything like what I was proposing “would not be allowed.” So, Bye-Bye. It was explained that anything like what I propose, being harvest of plants to produce hydrocarbons, was already being funded by the Dutch Government and, through Holland, the EU, to nearly all Dutch universities, in direct communication with the established Big Oil companies. So, the future in biofuels is already decided. The total taxpayer outlay is ca. 33 million. So, the State works hand in hand with Big Oil. Any room for outsiders is forbidden… by the State.

2014
Tokyo. Permanent outdoor installation of Sea of Japan basin, at 1:500,000 scale NY. Essex Street. “Rebels are Reasonable.” Wordstacks on metal. Basinflags for Jamaica, Haiti, Algeria, Russia, UK, Belarus, Tigris–Euphrates in Syria/Iraq (wrongly colored; I intended Islamic garden colors), Libya,

Costa Rica. The general thesis: that alleged terrorist actions against colonial borders result from the borders, e.g., of Mali being absurd. Basis for current call for rescinding the Treaty of Berlin, fostering watershed organization of the "developing world" e.g., Africa and South Asia.

Aarhus, balloon bridge proposal with Eve Vaterlaus under OECD label, proposal commissioned by the Aarhus Museum, Denmark. Curator Tom Trevor. Berlin. Liszt. "LOMONOSOV FURTHERED." Scenario for Russia, extended into Ukraine and northern Black Sea Basin. Promote marine and aquatic biomass as LOCAL FUELS. Book produced by Andre Fuchs.

ZKM. Twenty meter display of algae-harvest submarine, adapted from Akula-class submarine but with LNG production on board. Further to eight meter color painting of ecological scenarios at Andrew Edlin, Chelsea.

2015
Formation of TVGOV in Miami, concluding a two month teaching residency with Agustina Woodgate (Argentina), Sofia Bastidas (Ecuador), Guillermo Leon Gomez (US, of Colombian background). Eco-tax proposals for Miami, Texas, Iowa, Puerto Rico, parts of the Great Basin (personally traveled).

TVGOV proposals for, with workshop, Israel. Exhibition of second version of "Decolonized Skies," as "Decolonized Lands," in Artport, Tel Aviv. All works disappear: confusion ensues in Basel and Milan.

Pinksummer, Genoa. "Forse." Which is Italian for "maybe." With "Chiesa del Africa." Also eco-tax scheme for Puerto Rico. Which was sold to Monaco.

Works from Artport in Tel Aviv were intended for the Genoa show, being seven panels about "Decolonized Countries." But such works "disappeared," and were replaced by other works allegedly confiscated by Tel Aviv Airport police (but not so). All very confusing. I had bits and pieces of objects, and at least could sell the

Puerto Rico eco-tax piece.

Dojima Biennial, Osaka. Work sold to chemical engineer; asked to base in Tokyo.

2016
Beijing Media Art Biennale. All works checked in for flight held at JFK, arriving too late to be shown. Chinese hosts, astonished, expand visa allowing thorough study of coastal macro-algae opportunities, with electricity as output. If the proposed Beijing vs New York ecorace were to occur, I know more what to do in Beijing and the Bohai Sea than what to do in NY and the Northeast Seaboard.

TVGOV sessions in Dallas. Visit reservoirs' development of local energy scenarios for Trinity Bay catchment (Lubbock–Dallas–Houston).

Residency in Pescara: address to the city government in Pescara fish market. Oracle, Berlin: two shows in sequence, a booklet published.

Unique cartographic production for ICI touring show, "Oceans After Nature."

Yerba Buena, California: ocean currents and gyres along latitude lines, planet-wide; hydrometric areas of California west of Colorado River Basin
Tufts University, Boston: energy autonomy in Massachusetts Bay (follow-through on commission by David Black from 2002).

Dublin City Gallery, Dublin: hydrometric areas for Ireland, with separation also into dam catchments, notably in River Shannon (follow-through on studies in Ireland 2003).

University of South Australia: hydrometric areas of Australia, notably Lake Eyre Basin (suited for tech-waste); follow-through on 1995 residency.

Parsons, New School: hydrometric areas of Northeast Seaboard, and—at lower-resolution, the entire Labrador Current in regional-sea segments;

production of array was censored, or physically blocked with empty shipments, four times; a Shell advance-man explained that it's "too political," causing ejection from a later-canceled show uptown.

Renaissance Society, Chicago. "Territories" show. They accept proposal for relating Great Lakes to the acute warming of the Gulf of Maine, but this is forbidden by third party. No one knows why. Different work is shown, but catalogue has text of Gulf of Maine proposal. Maybe showing a causal link is too "controversial"… and what if it's scientifically incorrect?

"AFRICA THINKS," presentation at MICA Foundation for the NY diplomats from China and all UN member-states from Africa. Some diplomats attend; lively discussion. Very pleased by this effort. All Missions to the UN have three invitation cards hand-delivered. A second "AFRICA THINKS" could be organized, especially since more than half the African member-states chose to not support a UN General Assembly condemnation of Russia war against Ukraine. One, Morocco, is normally a US ally. How come? What does Africa want? We mapped now how most of the important and bioproductive coastal waters are included. Can South Africa lead all of Africa to post-colonial territorial organization, at least in line with the hydrological thinking of French physiocratic diplomat Choiseul (1760s)?

2017
"Shadow Cabinet," in response to Trump Presidency. Fend is Shadow Secretary of Defense.
Wolfgang Staehle is Shadow Secretary of State, leaving NATO, but he backs out for art-world reasons? Drama. Gallery-artist Fred Lonidier is Shadow Secretary of Labor. In next version?, other gallery artist would be Shadow Cabinet members, e.g. Cameron Rowland at HUD or Agriculture (for reparations in National Forest land).

More work in Puerto Rico, especially with railroad and seaweed pileup from Amazon. Exhibition at leading non-profit space in San Juan, Embajada.

Second residency in Pescara. Meeting in Rome, sponsors ready to pay for base in Rome. Overruled by people from another Italian city.

Kunstraum Niederoesterreich, "Fluechtige Territorien." Interpret the tricolour of France to cover all of Europe, with Atlantic states having "liberte," since slavery is conducted in colonies, and inland sea states having "egalite" and neutrality, and far-eastern states (Caspian, Barents, and eastward) having traditions of communalism ("fraternite"). Peninsular strategies adopted throughout Europe under Napoleon's phrase, "L'armee des cotes de l'Ocean."

2018
Palermo, installations by Pinksummer (paid travel throughout Sicily). Mapping each hydrometric area. Revelations of China attempt to link Noto, in SE corner, with Misrata, in war-torn Libya. Galerie Barbara Weiss, display of works from Real Estate Show, 1980.

CLUI show on Southwest US, in comparison with Persian Gulf. University of Nevada, Las Vegas. As usual: alarms about drought get heard by too few, too powerless. A much bigger audience is needed. Frightening footage on wipeout of animals by the solar-thermal power station in Ivanpah basin, a birthplace of Earth Art. (Site was first singled out in Mute in 2001; by 2014, a solar-thermal alternative to our biomass scenario was set up, with huge losses in animal life and very modest energy supply, then a need for shutdown, all at $2.2 billion cost. Nature crime? (I attended a promotional event in Princeton of this $2.2 billion investment, and said on Twitter within two days that it would be a boondoggle. It was. Academic science blows it again, since it's never grounded in physical reality. It's grounded in theory, with gaps, of course.

2019
"Absence," in half-year delayed response to the collapse of the Ponte Morandi. Designs use foundations of original bridge, add bascule bridge sections supporting an ultra-light horizontal deck. Ideas based on Matta-Clark work. An Italian government "curator" compels cancellation of any challenge to Renzo Piano who had jumped on building a new bridge only days after collapse. A security interrogation is scheduled for Fend in JFK, for jeopardizing Italian–US relations. Under the NATO doctrine that an attack on one, or simply a design challenge, is an attack on all? Scandal discussed at Yale School of Architecture. Must any innovator defer to privilege of pre-established prestige? Meantime, no one knows what was another approach to the bridge-tunnel challenge. Art crime? Further sign of art-imprisonment:a major voice arises in Genoa for rethinking all urban infrastructure, and for extending rail plans into North Africa; this is suddenly canceled. No new thought allowed? Lennart Wolff and Elisa Linn are invited to "curate," but they're overruled by Italian state authorities.

Kirkenes, regarding Norway. What was scheduled to be an algae harvest became just a one-week show of plans for all of Norway and for the Arctic Ocean Basin. Objections from the Norwegian state oil company were cited; we can't allow for any initiatives in biofuel production without our control. Nature crime? Such a test has been okayed by Ursula Biemann to be in the cove in Lofoten where she lamented climate change, but amidst huge fields of Laminaria. This action with Biemann as subject for follow-through was canceled twice, apparently to prevent any "action" which would show how easily marine biomass can be collected, at a minimum industrial rate of ten tons wet per hour, or one hundred tons wet per day. Insistence on doing such a project in Atlantic Biennial leads to ouster: thou shalt not prove anything of scientific value.

Gig at Staedelschule, Frankfurt, leading to Korea proposal (first shown in Vienna), meant to be displayed in Basel on the day that Kim meets Trump. Gallery decides to not show Korea piece. It had already been shown in Vienna. Not allowed now? What must the artist do: be a thoughtless clown?

Museo Nivola, Orani. Sardinia curated by Lennart Wolff and Elisa R. Linn. First display of bicycle-fork waterwheel. Dammed reservoirs are modeled as deconstructed, with rubble becoming the rapids-filled riverbed. Each reservoir has muddy waters for growth of biomass to yield fuel. Each stretch of coastal waters, thus reinvigorated with soil runoff, can yield marine biomass, e.g. Gracilaria, for fuel. Local energy can be produced in the local saltwater bay basins. This could start in Alghero, meaning “algae.”

Embajada, San Juan, Puerto Rico. Attack on Elon Musk, and better ideas for energy production locally.

2020
Galerie Barbara Weiss, “BIRDS REIGN.”

“Urban Extrusion,” Manifesta, Marseille. Project largely collapsed due to COVID-19. Project published by Algae Biomass Organization, as scientific proposal, budgeted for forty thousand Euro, canceled due to pandemic. Alternative location: Thessaloniki, Greece.

2021
Bird-insect flyways via Austria: exact title in German Box, Georg Kargl Fine Arts, Vienna. Following through on what was proposed to documenta in 1995, for display in 1997, but shot down as an “attempt to take over documenta”; since that year, insect numbers decreased by 75%, migratory bird numbers by 40%. Institutional art takes priority over Nature? “RAM,” organized by Marie Angeletti, Marseille. Showing, at last, the proposal for Interxion, which could not occur with the COVID-19 shutdown. Now, to sell the proposal of surveys for each hydrometric area (under Irish law) of Africa and Southeast Asia as supplied by submarine-cable internet from

Marseille. $5 million for a complete service.

Mousse, article, but not describing the source of the main photo being a 1982 change-detection survey of military activity by Israeli forces near Lebanon.

Amazon "Crime" poster, edition of twenty-five, five AP, Essex Street. Published in Bookforum.

TVGOV in Liberated Latin America, installation in Buenos Aires Oceans, Bergen Kunsthall, Bergen, Norway. Macrocystis rig with entire Chile at 1:500,000 scale, where such rigs could be used for marine-biomass industry.

"NEWS ROOM WIEN," conducted by Valentinas Klimasauskas from Vilnius, Lithuania at Georg Kargl Fine Arts, using Arctic and Antarctic-centered chart.

2022
Kongo–Arktis flyways through Austria, with NATO in Svalbard, Russia in Franz-Josef-Land: competition on who produces eco-jet fuel first from Arctic Laminaria. Akademie der bildenden Kuenste Wien.

ICA Poster campaign. One hundred posters, plus five APs, of Antarctica-centered ocean-circulation, co-produced with Russian scientists, at their initiative, 1980–3 to 1998. Year 2000 version. One being given gratis to Russian Embassy, Vienna.

Peter Fend
AFRICA–ARCTIC FLYWAY: PHYSIOCRATIC STATES

Published by Sternberg Press
Co-published by Museo Nivola, Orani

This monograph is published on the occasion of the exhibition "Africa–Arctic Flyway," curated by Elisa R. Linn and Lennart Wolff at Museo Nivola, Orani, October 25, 2019–January 26, 2020.

Editors: Elisa R. Linn, Lennart Wolff
Copy editing and proofreading: Sofia Leiby
Graphic design: Dan Solbach
Printing: Brizzolis—Arte en gráficas, Madrid

ISBN 978-3-95679-632-6

Acknowledgments:
Giuliana Altea, Noah Barker, Antonella Camarda, Win Knowlton, Till Krause, Jason Loebs, Sarah Markgraf, Massimiliano Scuderi / Fondazione Zimei, Wolfgang Staehle, Eve Vaterlaus, Joan Waltemath, Peter Weibel, Universalmuseum Joanneum, Manifesta Foundation, Sharjah Art Foundation

The production of this monograph was accomplished through the generous support of: Barbara and Howard Morse / MICA Foundation, Cabinet Gallery, Fondazione Costantino Nivola, Galerie Barbara Weiss / Daniel Herleth & Bärbel Trautwein, Georg Kargl Fine Arts, Jurg Haller, Maxwell Graham / Essex Street, Migros Museum für Gegenwartskunst, Pinksummer Contemporary Art, Schulze-Fielitz Stiftung Berlin

MIGROSMUSEUM
für Gegenwartskunst

MUSEO
NIVOLA

Distributed by The MIT Press, Art Data, Les presses du Réel, and Idea Books

Sternberg Press
71–75 Shelton Street
London WC2H 9JQ
www.sternberg-press.com

Photo Credits:

p. 26: Wolfgang Staehle; p. 48: courtesy the artist and documenta, Kassel; p. 72: Lennart Wolff; pp. 73, 167: Valentino Congia / South Studio, courtesy the artist and Museo Nivola, Orani; p. 74: Adrienne Livingston; p. 78: Peter Fend; p. 146: Till Krause, courtesy the artist and Galerie für Landschaftskunst, Hamburg; pp. 150, 172: Jean-Christophe Lett, courtesy the artist and Manifesta 13, Marseille; p. 151: N. Lackner / UMJ; p. 156: Peter Fend, courtesy the artist and American Fine Arts, Co.; p. 157: Alessandro Falco, courtesy the artist and Fondazione Zimei, Pescara; p. 173: kunst-dokumentation.com, courtesy the artist and Georg Kargl Fine Arts, Vienna; pp. 184, 185: Ocean Earth / Earth Observation Satellite Company (EOSAT); p. 208: Peter Fend; pp. 210–211: Peter Riedlinger, commissioned by Sharjah Biennial, courtesy the artist and Sharjah Art Foundation, Sharjah; p. 212: Peter Fend, courtesy the artist and Nikolai Fine Art, New York; p. 214: Jens Ziehe, courtesy the artist, Galerie Barbara Weiss, and Sammlung Migros Museum für Gegenwartskunst